CAMBRIDGE ENGLISH PROSE TEXTS

Critics of the Bible, 1724–1873

Cambridge English Prose Texts consists of volumes devoted to substantial selections from non-fictional English prose. The series provides students with the opportunity of reading important essays and extracts from larger works which have generally been unavailable in suitable editions.

English critics were brilliant initiators and exploiters of biblical criticism. This momentous exercise, whereby the 'Holy Scriptures' became the object of human critique independent of church control, is illustrated by John Drury in the present volume with excerpts from such famous critics as Coleridge, Blake and Matthew Arnold, and lesser names such as Collins the Deist and Bishop Sherlock. Robert Lowth's famous lectures on the Psalms, which had an important influence on Blake and Christopher Smart, are well represented here, as is the famous contribution to *Essays and Reviews* by Benjamin Jowett.

This book provides the only available collection of biblical criticism from this important period of critical enquiry, the eighteenth and nineteenth centuries. The extracts are accompanied by a full editorial introduction, notes and a bibliography. They should be read by all students of literature and theology interested in the period.

CAMBRIDGE ENGLISH PROSE TEXTS

General editor: GRAHAM STOREY

Critics of the Bible
1724–1873

edited by

JOHN DRURY
Dean of King's College
Cambridge

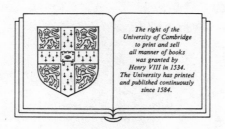

The right of the
University of Cambridge
to print and sell
all manner of books
was granted by
Henry VIII in 1534.
The University has printed
and published continuously
since 1584.

CAMBRIDGE UNIVERSITY PRESS

Cambridge
New York   Port Chester   Melbourne   Sydney

Published by the Press Syndicate of the University of Cambridge
The Pitt Building, Trumpington Street, Cambridge CB2 IRP
40 West 20th Street, New York, NY 10011, USA
10 Stamford Road, Oakleigh, Melbourne 3166, Australia

First published 1989

Printed in Great Britain at the University Press, Cambridge

British Library cataloguing in publication data

Critics of the Bible, 1724–1873
1. Bible – Critical studies
I. Drury, John, *1936 May 23–*
220.6

Library of Congress cataloguing in publication data

Critics of the Bible, 1724–1873/edited by John Drury.
p.   cm. – (Cambridge English prose texts)
Bibliography.
ISBN 0-521-32992-2 – ISBN 0-521-33870-0 (pbk)
1. Bible – Criticism, interpretation, etc. – Early works to 1800.
2. Bible – Criticism, interpretation, etc. – England – History.
I. Drury, John, 1936–   .   II. Series.
BS510.C75 1989
220.6'0942 – dc19

ISBN 0521 32992 2 hard covers
ISBN 0 521 33870 0 paperback

CE

Contents

Contents

Acknowledgements

I am particularly grateful to Ian Harris for putting me right on a number of points of fact and emphasis about Locke. Robin Jackson, who is preparing the Bollingen edition of Coleridge's *Confessions of an Inquiring Spirit*, generously gave me solutions, from his own researches, to obscurities of reference and chronology which had foxed me. The resourceful kindness of these two individuals has been matched by institutions. My time at the University of Sussex taught me the importance of the inter-disciplinary study of the Bible and its critics. It also set me up with the courage and skills to have a shot at it. In this regard I owe much to two Sussex colleagues, John Burrow and Stephen Medcalf. King's College, Cambridge has reinforced this enjoyable refusal to venerate conventional subject boundaries. I have been given help, information and encouragement on all hands at King's, and particularly by Frank Kermode, Tony Tanner and John Dunn. The staff of the Rare Books Room at the Cambridge University Library have been wonderfully patient and prompt. Graham Storey, as General Editor of this series, applied just the right doses of kindly reminder, with the barest touch of reproach, to keep me going when I had transgressed a dead-line. Lastly, I am grateful to my wife Clare for her interest in what I was doing. From her, and from her father Dennis Nineham, I have had the encouragement of the close company of people who believe in the critical enterprise as an important part of the enjoyment of life.

Editorial note

The presentation of texts, notes and other references has been designed to assist the modern
student and reader. The following points should be
noted. Original spellings have been retained, except
that the long s has been modernised throughout.
Authorial footnotes, where retained, are indicated
by letter; editorial notes are indicated by number
and are given as endnotes. In Robert Lowth's
lectures, the Bible references have been removed
from the original footnotes and placed in the text.
In order to help the reader, Bible references in
square brackets have been added to Benjamin
Jowett's text by the editor.

Introductory essay

Biblical criticism, as it is practised today, is a predominantly literary–historical business. The skills required are manifold and hard: knowledge of at least two ancient and two modern languages, of textual criticism and of testingly obscure episodes in history, of religion in its popular and its philosophical manifestations, of a vast and sometimes barely readable secondary literature. It is no wonder that, with all this on his hands, the biblical critic has little time or curiosity to spare for retrospect and the history of his subject. This fosters the illusion that biblical criticism is a very recent invention: a deception which is reinforced by the episodic protests of religious practitioners against the new-fangledness of criticism when it invades their piety. So it comes as a surprise to learn that biblical criticism as we know it is at least three hundred years old, and that even in its earlier phases it required skills and knowledge as diverse and difficult as it does now. Its pioneers, such as Spinoza and Locke, were, and needed to be, formidably learned and intelligent men. It comes as a surprise because these three centuries of effort have not officially been allowed to have an effect on the bastions of orthodox belief. They remain, apparently, what they were in the centuries of the foundation of Christianity. Criticism is optional and its official reception uncertain.

Once one has begun to trace modern biblical criticism backwards in time, one gets a disconcerting sense of regress. Twentieth-century Christians have been upset, as at the approach of an unprecedented threat, by Rudolf Bultmann's exposure of the determinative role of ancient mythology in the New Testament writings. But much the same terror was aroused by Strauss's *Life of Jesus Critically Examined* in 1835 which made clear that only absurdity could result from failure to realise the profound influence of Old Testament myth upon every page of the gospels. Strauss described the outcry which greeted his book as 'the cries of owls ... awakened much too inconsiderately by a harsh light' (preface to the first German edition, volume II) and 'on no higher a plane than those screams often heard from women upon the sudden report of a nearby shot' (preface to the second German edition). Strauss had made all too clear that incident after incident in the gospels had been generated, not by the disinterested recording of plain fact, but by the transformation of Old Testament texts into Christian occurrence. Creative exegesis in the interests of Christian belief was the crucible in which the gospels had been made. This insight had been brilliantly, even mischievously, explored a century before in Anthony Collins's *Discourse of the Grounds and Reasons of the Christian Religion* of 1724. His theme was that the exegetical method of the Christian evangelists was precisely the same as that used by Jewish rabbis, and it was greeted by a predictable furore. In each of these three instances, covering no less than three centuries, the fundamental cause of scandal was the same. The barriers which separated the biblical canon from all other literature were being dismantled by historical enquiry which moved freely back and forth over those boundaries as it explored the relation of canonical texts to their surrounding world. That is how modern biblical criticism works, its achievements in the realm of human history got at the expense of the holiness protected by ecclesiastical authority. The restoration of religious value once that was under way could best be hoped for at a point where a profound probing of humanity and history plumbed the depths of divinity. This was the task, prefigured in Sherlock's pessimism, which awaited romantic exegetes from Lowth to Arnold.

A small example of the regression which overtakes enquiry into modern biblical criticism is given by the genesis of this anthology. The original plan was that it should cover the nineteenth century in England. It was soon clear that this needed to be extended back into the eighteenth century when English scholars, most prominently Locke, clarified the methods which the more famous achievements of Germans exploited. Having decided that, and given Collins the first turn, the introduction clearly needed to introduce him by explaining something of what had happened to the reading of the Bible in seventeenth-century England and Holland, and how it had informed the biblical work of Collins's friend and master, Locke. What Thomas Mann found when he immersed himself in the Bible's earliest narratives to write his Joseph tetralogy is true of the story of biblical criticism too: the well of the past is very deep, even unfathomable.

In fact, the critical interpretation of the Bible, by one means or another, is as old as the Bible itself. A canon is a public thing, and the biblical canon, even in its prototypes, was constitutive of a national religion with universal aspirations, so it had to be publicly explained. Judaism became a focally bookish religion during its Babylonian exile

Introductory essay

in the sixth century BC because it was deprived of its centralised cult in the Jerusalem temple. The Jews who returned to Jerusalem in the next century were, according to a vividly circumstantial account in Nehemiah chapter 8, gathered together by Ezra the scribe at the Water Gate in Jerusalem for a collective, marathon reading of the proto-canon, 'the book of the law of Moses which the Lord had given to Israel' – the first five books of our Bible. This was simultaneously a great session of interpretation. While Ezra read from a specially constructed wooden pulpit 'above all the people' a corps of exegetes 'gave the sense, so that the people understood the reading'. The hermeneutical game had begun in a scene which corresponds very closely to the *mise-en-scène* of the Bible in English society two millennia later: the pulpit, the reading and exposition, and the attentive congregation whose mind and manners are to be shaped by it. The continuity is remarkable and testifies to the social depth and breadth within which the interpretation of the Bible went on in both the ancient and the modern world; and which has not evaporated in the post-modern world. Biblical criticism gathers and stimulates social and political currents. Just as Ezra the scribe re-formed the nation by one kind of biblical interpretation, so Jonathan Swift feared that another kind would promote social disintegration in eighteenth-century England if Collins's free-thinking were to catch on:

Why should not *William Penn* the Quaker, or any *Anabaptist, Papist, Muggletonian, Jew or Sweet Singer* have liberty to come into *St Paul's Church* in the midst of Divine Service, and endeavour to convert first the Aldermen, then the Preacher and Singing Men? Or pray, why should not poor Mr Whiston, who denies the Divinity of Christ, be allowed to come into the Lower House of Convocation and convert the clergy?

Prose Works of Jonathan Swift, ed. H. Davis, vol IV, p. 31.

Swift's fantasy of chaos in St Paul's Cathedral – the unorthodox and the unchristian at large in the national shrine – is the opposite of the order at Ezra's Water Gate gathering. It drew the plausibility necessary to make it frightening as well as funny from recent English history. Swift summoned up the sects which had had their heyday in the Commonwealth, interpreting the Bible by the inner light which dissolved intervening history and made all present to them and in them. Interestingly he then introduced 'poor Mr Whiston', a Cambridge don who had gone the other way and by careful examination of historical process had convinced himself, with some reason, that the most primitive form of Christian belief had not held the divinity of Christ. So Swift dramatised a double threat: the sectarians who

3

synchronically interpreted the scriptures as the key to the present, and Whiston who diachronically interpreted the scriptures as the product of a past which was by no means as like the present as orthodoxy required.

What had happened to make the Bible, the totem of cohesion, into a bone of contention? Before we reach for the factors in early modern history which brought this about, we need to go back to the Bible itself. It had formed and nourished the minds which criticised it, whatever new ideas had got into them as well. And while the critical tools which were now used were forged in the crucible of a new sense of the past and of new ways of describing it, it was the Bible itself which had taught them to think historically in the first place. That is the remarkable thing about the Bible. It begins with historical time and ends with it. From Genesis to St John's Revelation it traces a total history from creation, through patriarchs to Egyptian captivity and Exodus; then again through Judges and Kings to Babylonian captivity and exodus (notice the symmetry); finally to the Christian projection of the coming of Jesus as the Messiah who fulfilled all that had gone before in yet another version of the pattern of estrangement and restoration – this time ushering in the end of history. There was no book quite like it, with the possible exception of Virgil's *Aeneid* and its assimilation of the Homeric legacy into the Roman story as a rough parallel to the New Testament's relation to the Old. But the *Aeneid* was not the scripture of a universal religion with a long future. The Greeks had written history, but not with the biblical scope. The chronicles and genealogies of Mesopotamia claimed some of the scope but none of the rich historical realism which makes the Bible Blake's 'most entertaining of books' and a vast resource for human self-understanding. In the Bible religion's obvious concern to relate the present to the eternal, to achieve synchrony, is done within a constant preoccupation with the diachronic intricacies of the past.

The conjunction of these polarities gave the biblical writers their extraordinary energy. How did they do it? How did they get the one-thing-after-another of historical existence to combine with their theology of a single and eternal God? One way has edged in on us already: the repetition of the pattern of exile and return. Bible readers, like the Bible characters themselves and like Proust's narrating self going through ordeals so like those endured by his prototype Swann, get the meaning of a present moment by linking it to past ones. To be a Jew at hard labour in Egypt was to be like Adam toiling outside Eden. To be a Jew in exile by the waters of Babylon was to be like your fathers in Egypt, and so get hope of another Exodus. To be a Christian banned from the synagogues was to be the new holy people foreseen by exiled prophets. History was given significance by figures and types. A person at one moment understood himself as a representation of a hero of past time. Ezra on his pulpit reading the law with his aides expounding it was a Moses-come-again, resembling (in an unusually strict sense) Moses giving God's law from the mountain to Israel in the wilderness, with helpers to see to its practical application (Exodus 18). The Christian writers extended Moses' afterlife. Jesus on the mountain with his disciples gave the people a new law, the 'Sermon on the Mount' of Matthew 5–7 which is much occupied with criticism and interpretation of existing law. Jesus' very name recalls Moses' successor Joshua who fulfilled Moses' mission and led the people into the promised land. The Bible teems with such types and figures. Strauss had the keen, clinical nose for them of a man recently exiled from typology as an intellectual home. He was an archetypal modern critic with the acuity of the disinherited. Types and figures gave coherence to the Bible's long march through history. They correct the diachronic by synchronic pressure which bends the linearity of time into loops. Let that pressure dominate more strongly, so that it overwhelms time, and the result is the despair of Ecclesiastes in the face of eternal recurrence, or the Platonic faith of John the Evangelist in an eternal now into which history's becoming is collapsed. The overwhelming of history by significance results in ultimate ahistoricism. That is the danger for theology. The danger of criticism is the alienated suspicion, even disbelief, which it brings to the types and figures: a scepticism which unpicks the stitches which hold biblical history together.

But the Bible has another way of holding together. It binds history by a chain of prophecies and fulfilments. Its protagonists were the prophets: not only in the collections of their oracles which bear their various names, but also and very significantly in the historical narratives. Their God was the designer of both ethical laws and historical process. So by the application of divine moral critique to the events of their times they were able to predict the temporal rewards and punishments which were in store. The prophets knew God's historical will. It was intelligible because it was moral. As time went on, and particularly as times got much worse than they morally should have been and the just suffered punishments which should have fallen on the wicked, the predictions of the prophets became more important than their moral messages. They were an anchor for hope in otherwise hopeless times, such as the persecutions of Antiochus Epiphanes in the second century BC. Attention shifted from the present, with its human ambiguities and absurdities, to the future resolution of divine fulfilment. This change was helped by the increasingly literary, as opposed to previously oral, form of prophetic oracles. It meant that prophets of the past could be consulted for the elucidation of the tormented present. So the writer of the book of Daniel, trying to make sense of his bad times under Antiochus Epiphanes, went to prophecies made by Jeremiah four hundred years before in order to discover the divine time-scale (Daniel 9. 2, Jeremiah 25. 12; see also II Chronicles 36. 20). But the most industrious practitioners of this literary beachcombing were the early Christians. From St Paul onwards they regarded everything in the ancient scriptures as prophecy of their times and their Christ. So St Luke had the risen Jesus reassure the downcast disciples on the Emmaus road that all that had happened to him, including his shameful death, had been foretold. The entire corpus of Jewish scripture was its prediction. 'Beginning with Moses and all the prophets, he interpreted to them in all the scriptures the things concerning himself' (Luke 24. 27).

The prophetic articulation of history kept time as a line and so was clear of ahistoricism. But it made the line significant by making it divinely driven and determined – in perplexing times exclusively and very strongly so. More modest and regular notions of divine agency, such as were available in the seventeenth and eighteenth centuries with the filling in of the maps of causality by more and more natural factors at the expense of the supernatural, would be at issue with the very strength of prophetic history. Cooler and more realistic, above all more literal, views of history would also find such a strong survivor very hard to accommodate. For it drained the past, in which a prophecy was made, of real and independent meaning by channelling the prophecy so exhaustively into the present. If the prophets of the Old Testament were engaged in nothing but predicting Christianity, they had none of the vital connections with their own times which could make them intelligible to a disinterested historian.

At this point Anthony Collins entered, armed with both these objections. His belief in natural causalities discoverable by human reason on its own, took away from the need for divine determinism as an indispensable way of making sense. His appreciation of the rights of times and cultures other than Christian to their own significances was pitted against the nascent imperialism of early Christianity. By deploying both with irony he gave his urbanity the force of subversion. His particular targets are the links of prophecy and fulfilment which integrate the two parts of the Christian canon, Old Testament and New. To sever these lines of communication was to cut through the centre of the canon. Hence the strong reactions to his book. That reactions were just as strong, and perhaps rather less resourceful, to Strauss's book a hundred years later is a sign that, in the period covered by this anthology, the relations between the critics and the churches remained hostile in spite of the mediating efforts of minds as fine as Lowth's or Blake's or Coleridge's. It was not religious vitality which was threatened. In those three men the Bible found expositors as ardently admiring as it had ever had. The threat was to religious authority, and it was real and deep. For authority is concerned with public coherence and canon rather than vitality and experiment, or even relevance. And while criticism was to enhance wonderfully the variety and quality of ways of reading the scriptures, making them vivid and accessible in new ways, the very number and sharpness of its tools fractured the canonical monolith. While there were ways of putting it together again, none of them fulfilled the specifications of orthodoxy. Thus William Blake, in the extract printed here, exploited biblical synchrony up to the hilt by having Isaiah and Ezekiel to dinner, but transgressed orthodox bounds by making honest indignation and poetic genius the divine inspirations of the Bible: a lesson which he had learned from the Bishop of London, Robert Lowth. And though Thomas Arnold found the concentrated energy to keep biblical diachrony moving and plausible, strong theological determinism included, he did so at the cost of making parts of the Old Testament the legacy of a stage in moral development at which some barbarism had to be tolerated (as in the fourth form at Rugby) but which Christianity rendered anachronistic. Which was far from the Church's official view of the Old Testament, though it was Christian enough in intention and even had precedents in tradition such as the redundancy of the old Jewish cult declared by the writer of the Epistle to the Hebrews.

Although old ways of reading the Bible could still work, something new had come about which made a difference to them all. The biblical criticism with which we are concerned is strikingly a product of the early modern Western world and an important ingredient of its character. It did not have a single cause but was nourished by a complex of forces. It depended on such momentous developments as the rise of sovereign nation states (Hobbes's biblical criticism is a minor part of his essay on sovereignty, *Leviathan*); on the vast increase in the availability of ideas and knowledge brought about by the proliferation of printed books; on deep and subtle changes in how it felt to be a human being in relation to nature, time and God. The reformations of Christianity which took place in the sixteenth century were the necessary seedbeds of biblical criticism which, with brilliant catholic exceptions such as Richard Simon and Alexander Geddes, remained a protestant enterprise throughout its first two centuries. The best recent histories of it both start with the reformers: Hans Frei's *The Eclipse of Biblical Narrative* (Yale 1974) and Henning Graf Reventlow's *The Authority of the Bible and the Rise of the Modern World* (SCM 1984). It must be so, if only because the reformers increased the prominence and availability of the Bible to fill up the holes they had blown in previous authoritative and devotional structures. They promoted new and more historically literal ways of reading it as a way of clearing out the medieval typological clutter. They changed the political map of Europe so that, with Christendom dissolved, biblical critics whose views brought them under threat in one place could move to another and flourish there in congenial and stimulating company. We shall see all these things having their effects on the career of Collins's master, Locke.

The English reformer, Thomas Cranmer, was not an innovative man. So his manifesto 'Concerning the Service of the Church' which was first printed in the Anglican *Book of Common Prayer* in 1549 is a usefully conservative arrangement of some of the options available to him in the cause of reordering English Christianity. He asserted that in the early days of the Church, liturgy had served godliness by its concentration on the Bible, read and expounded. 'But these many years past, this godly and decent order of the Fathers hath been ... altered, broken and neglected by planting in uncertain stories, and legends.' The historical thinking here is not new or sophisticated. The invocation of a golden past, followed by a time of more recent decadence, is an old commonplace of general moralising. The Old Testament prophets had used it and, as one of the hardiest perennials of human thinking about history, it was to inspire countless restorers of the original and historical Jesus from Locke onwards through Reimarus to C. H. Dodd as they shovelled away layers of ecclesiastical accretion to reveal the pristine original and invented all sorts of critical tools for the task. But Cranmer indicated the ground of it all: the golden age could be brought into present life because it was in the Bible. Apparently, though, he did not notice that the success of this manoeuvre as a contribution to the political cohesion of public life depended on restricting consciousness of historical mutability to those apocryphal 'uncertain stories and legends'. The authority of the canonical scriptures remained intact by isolating them, no doubt with all the strength of unconsciousness, from the criticism meted

8

out to their uncanonical neighbours. A thin wall divided the Bible from the acids of criticism.

With Anthony Collins that wall was dramatically breached. He showed New Testament evangelists interpreting Old Testament prophecies with all the fantastic dexterity and disregard for literal truth of the Jewish rabbis – and founding their history on the results. The uncertain and the fabulous were in the gospels themselves. The ability to notice this startling phenomenon came from two features of Collins's world. First was the emphasis placed by the reformers two centuries before – and by his time explored in a large literature – on plain and literal interpretation as deliverance from the allegorical tropes of medieval Christendom. Second was the cultural pluralism of a world in which rabbis could be met or, more normally, their texts freely read. It was usually done in a much more pious mood than Collins's and was sustained by devout belief in the religious value of contemplation of the actual life of Christ which illuminated the inner man and informed moral action. These were features of the late medieval Devotio Moderna which nourished Erasmus. Holbein's famous picture of Erasmus working in his study comes to mind. It is worth keeping there. For alongside the public tableau of pulpit and congregation, which goes back to Ezra, another setting for biblical interpretation comes into prominence. It is the solitary individual scholar in his study or 'cabinet'. This might be traced back to early Christian pictures of evangelists writing at their desks. But whereas they are shown with one book only, the one which they are writing to divine dictation, the biblical scholars of the seventeenth and eighteenth centuries inhabited rooms which had become well-stocked libraries, like Collins's at his house at Great Baddow in Essex. It was a seclusion which was always in touch with a wide and plural literary world: the 'republic of letters' founded on the exchange of letters as well as the availability of books. As well as being the focus of a new intellectual richness it provided freedom to follow wherever truth might lead, unhampered by the immediate pressures of public order. The pluralism and the liberty sustained each other.

In the late 1640s Edward Hyde, the future Earl of Clarendon, found himself in enforced seclusion, a royalist in exile on the island of Jersey. He began his *Contemplations and Reflections upon the Psalms of David, Applying those Devotions to the Troubles of the Times*. The 'times' were David's, not Hyde's own. He believed 'that there were not many Psalms which may not be very naturally and literally applied to those very occasions and the particular state that David was then in, when he poured out those devotions' (p. 380 of the 1727 edition). The future historian of the Great Rebellion was learning his trade as a modern, historically literal, biblical critic. In an illuminating discussion of Hyde's work in *The Bible and Reason* (Philadelphia 1985) Gerard Reedy contrasts it with the kind of biblical exegesis favoured by Cromwell who believed his own career to be the fulfilment – the practical and even military exegesis – of Psalm 110 with its assembly for battle and smiting of kings. Typology remained a vivid option for *the* public man anxious for the authority of divine determinism. Hyde's natural and literal historicism was a counteraction by an involuntarily private man to the fanaticism latent in Cromwell's kind of exegesis. It got the biblical text under strong and verifiable control at a time when typology was proving a Pandora's box, as instantly useful to Cromwell's radical opponents as to himself. Nor was it without religious value of the coolly comfortable kind. The Psalms, with their frequent complaints of isolation and hopes for restoration, were a consolation to Hyde in his exile. He looked to them for general truths of human experience in which to frame his own. His combination of the literal and the general were to dominate the biblical exegesis of the Restoration divines of the Church of England as they hastened the demise of typology and the discrediting of its bumptious practitioners.

Thomas Hobbes, Hyde's contemporary, was monumentally on the side of literal–historical biblical criticism. In Chapter XXXIII of the third part of *Leviathan* (1651) he confronted 'The Number, Antiquity, Scope, Authority and Interpreters of the Books of Holy Scripture'. The list of topics was eloquent of the daunting multifariousness then visible in the biblical realm. Hobbes began by denying Moses' authorship of the entire Pentateuch on the unassailable ground that his death is described in one of its books, Deuteronomy. Already firmly established in the scepticism of modern biblical criticism by this observation, he went on to review the other Old Testament books historically. He assigned dates to each which were mostly later than orthodoxy supposed. He screened off their religious significance and treated them simply as historical documents to be chronologically ordered by means of their internal testimonies to their times of composition. At the end he came to the dramatically postponed topic of their authority. He divided it into private and public. 'If private, it obliges onely him, to whom in particular God hath been pleased to reveale it.' It should stay strictly within that limit if it is not to disrupt society in a welter of interpretative opinion. If it is public, then it belongs to the Christian commonwealth: Church and State collapsed into one society 'of men united in one person, their Soveraign'. So he brought biblical criticism within his great and single theme: 'the question of the Authority of the Scriptures, is reduced to this, *whether Christian Kings, and the Soveraigne Assemblies in Christian Commonwealths, be absolute in their own territories, immediately under God*'. Hobbes cooled biblical criticism by the application of his utterly detached chronological criticism, then clamped the lid of sovereignty onto the pot.

The trouble was that he had, by the authority of his own example, assigned the interpretation of the scriptures to historians. No doubt they would calm the ferment, particularly if their work was as religiously vacuous as his own. But they were private men, not necessarily religious officials confined by the pressing needs of public order. And if they were to imitate Spinoza, who combined historical criticism as radical as Hobbes's with fervent devotion, it was not likely that their thoughts could be confined within their studies. Historicism was biblical criticism's charter of freedom from ecclesiastical control. With history in charge, the preacher had a rival with whom he had to come to terms of some kind, the scholar in his study. The extracts from Sherlock in this anthology show that very Anglican animal, the bishop as biblical critic and not just ecclesiastical executive, seeking to combine historical literalism with religious significance for the faithful – to be both critic and preacher.

The dialogue between Church and study was fertilised by the entry of historical critics more sensitive than Hobbes to religious inwardness and inspiration. Such was the formidable French catholic, Richard Simon. His *Critical History of the Old Testament* appeared in English translation in 1682 and was widely read. He explained the inconsistencies and other historical shortcomings of the Old Testament records by a daring act of historical imagination. Our Old Testament is, according to him, the result of work done on more primitive records by a school of prophets whom he called 'publick writers'. They were 'not very polite writers ... they usually transposed or repeated the same thing ... sometimes they only begin one matter, and then on a sudden go to another, and afterwards reassume their former style of discourse' ('The Author's Preface'). So they left modern critics with problems: 'As then these Books are but the abridgement of much more large Records, one cannot establish upon the Scripture an exact and certain chronology' (I. i. 5). But Simon's 'publick writers' had the religious advantage of inspiration. 'The Authors of these additions or alterations were real Prophets directed by the Spirit of God' ('The Author's Preface'). Simon felt that this answered Spinoza's view that the writers of the Bible 'had been purely of humane authority'. Certainly he had achieved a mixture of close and suspicious historical reading with religious sensitivity in a remarkable thesis which is still plausible. His 'publick writers' were an early glimpse of the Deuteronomic editors of twentieth-century Old Testament criticism, or the scribes of Eric Heaton's *Solomon's New Men* (Thames and Hudson 1974).

Simon's belief in sources is as strong as Sanday's or Streeter's in the Oxford New Testament seminar early in this century. And his sense of the theological creativity of the men who edited them anticipates recent 'redaction criticism' of the gospels. As a catholic, Simon was more at home with a plural distribution of religious inspiration than his protestant counterparts who, even in his own time, preferred to ignore his school of editors and go straight to the texts for historical information. For a catholic there is more to Christianity than the Bible. There is tradition and there is the Church. So Simon's bets are already hedged: 'If the truth of religion remained not in the Church, it would be unsafe to search for it at present in Books which have been subject to so many alterations, and have in so many things depended on the pleasure of transcribers . . . If we join not tradition we can hardly affirm anything for certain in religion.' Like Loisy two centuries later, Simon was politically naive to suppose that his distinctively catholic biblical criticism would be welcome to the catholic authorities. Bossuet turned his guns on him and he ended his days in Dieppe, an emergency exit to Holland or England if needed. It was in these two protestant countries that the immediate future of biblical criticism lay. Which brings us to John Locke, whose achievement drew on residence in both countries and is the historical threshold of this anthology.

Locke was in Rotterdam by Friday 7 September 1683, a refugee from Charles II's increasing absolutism and the looming prospect of his succession by his Roman Catholic brother, James: a threat which Locke's patron Shaftesbury had failed to ward off. Shaftesbury had fled to Holland in the previous year and died there before Locke arrived. But intellectual dissidents from abroad had no need to be lonely for long in Holland. The asylum it provided for persecuted philosophers and critics made it seem that in the 1680s it virtually was the republic of letters. To the hostile eye of Marvell during England's Dutch Wars of the 1650s its religious tolerance and pluralism were great to the point of absurdity.

> Sure when religion did itself embark
> And from the East would Westward steer its ark,
> It struck, and splitting on this unknown ground,
> Each one thence pillaged the first piece he found:
> Hence Amsterdam, Turk–Christian–Pagan–Jew,

> Staple of sects and mint of schism grew,
> That bank of conscience, where not one so strange
> Opinion but finds credit, and exchange.
> In vain for Catholics ourselves we bear;
> The Universal Church is only there.
>
> *The Character of Holland*, 68–77

Locke's exile proved happy and creative: six years, as it turned out, of congenial company and opportunities to clarify ideas long meditated as well as to find new ones. His return to England with the Princess of Orange in 1689 was marked by the publication within a year of three major books, including his masterpiece *An Essay Concerning Human Understanding*.

But these publications by no means exhausted his mental store. As a devout Christian he had long pondered the foundations and rationality of his religion. Indeed, in the preface to the *Essay* he hinted that that magisterial enquiry was conceived by him as the prolegomenon to work on religion. He described the genesis of the *Essay* as a gathering of 'five or six Friends meeting at my Chamber, and discoursing on a subject very remote from this'. Without disclosing what that original topic was he recorded that 'it came into my thoughts, that we took a wrong course; and that before we set ourselves upon Enquiries of that Nature, it was necessary to examine our own Abilities, and see, what objects our Understandings were, or were not fitted to deal with'. When, a little later, he names 'Morality and Divinity as those parts of Knowledge, that Men are most concerned to be clear in' the reader is invited to see them as the topic for which the *Essay* is, as he called it, a 'clearing the ground a little.' Of what?

The world beyond the chamber where Locke and his friends discoursed was over-supplied by over-confident persons making life dangerous by claiming detailed and definite knowledge of God and his will. To withstand them by a cogent demonstration of the modest limits of the human mind would be a public service. In 1668 Benjamin Whichcote, ejected from the Provostship of King's College, Cambridge at the Restoration began to preach at St Lawrence Jewry. There is a tradition, believed by Maurice Cranston, that Locke attended his sermons, though it is possible that he assimilated Whichcote's ideas later via Tillotson. Whichcote's overall programme was a Christianity founded on a few vital and rational truths rather than a clutter of unverifiable dogma, and issuing in conduct marked by charity and tolerance. He formed an unshakeable faith in the rationality of a basic Christianity which could be found by, and not in resistance to, bold scepticism towards dogmatic claims. The 'short-ness of our knowledge' was a theme used by Whichcote to encourage modest views and practical charity. From his influence Locke's Christianity got its depth and austerity, its confidence and restraint, its public spirit.

A religious mind so set was ready to learn biblical criticism of the kind which would give sober, verifiable historical reality the whip hand over headier and more grandiose exegesis. His Dutch exile equipped him with it more richly than uninterrupted residence in England could have done. A few months after arriving in Holland he met Philip van Limborch, the Remonstrant theologian. Remonstrant Christianity was the Dutch double of Whichcote's: rational, doctrinally minimalist, ethical. It also fostered biblical criticism. There is parabolic serendipity in the fact that Locke and Limborch met at the dissection of a lioness which had died from the cold. For along with Locke's august rationalism went a more boyish interest in taking things apart and laying them out to see how they worked. Maurice Cranston, in his biography of Locke (Oxford University Press, 1957, p. 265) calls it 'the unformulated *ad hoc* empiricism of Newton and Boyle and the other Royal Society *virtuosi*'. Thanks to Hobbes, Spinoza and Simon, empirical study of scripture was already something more than *ad hoc*. It had rationale as well as techniques.

The year before Locke's flight from England, Simon's *Critical History of the Old Testament* had been published there. Locke's Westminster school-fellow Dryden had responded promptly to it in *Religio Laici*. His answer was Hobbesian.

> And, after hearing what our Church can say,
> If still our Reason runs another way,
> That private reason 'tis more just to curb
> Than by disputes the publick Peace disturb:
> For points obscure are of small use to learn:
> But *Common Quiet* is *Mankind's Concern*.

Locke shared Dryden's longing for common quiet, but had more faith in the social goodness of reason than to relegate its achievements to the private domain. He was already well practised in disciplining it by careful epistemological enquiry and political practicability, not by a repressive gesture like Dryden's. He remained an Anglican while Dryden turned to Roman Catholicism with the accession of James to the throne. Dryden had shown in *Absalom and Achitophel* (1681) that when still an Anglican he was at home with

14

scriptural typology, albeit with a touch of irony. It was a genre which never appealed to Locke. What Locke needed, as a sociable and friendly man, was a field of common and commonsensical discourse on the Bible. His appetite for empirical study of it had already been whetted by his friendship with Nicholas Toinard who was engaged on a 'harmony' of the gospels: in effect, an attempt to establish their chronology by laying them out in historical sequence so that the reader could compare and synthesise them into historical sequence. Though called *Harmonia Evangeliorum* it was more obviously a dissection of the gospels for purposes of historical reconstruction: a not very remote ancestor of the modern Synopsis, and something of a Trojan horse where harmony was concerned. Locke treasured the fascicles of it which Toinard gave him and admired its precision with the high praise of 'very useful'. He was always encouraging Toinard to complete it.

Toinard's work pointed in a direction very different from Simon's: not to the creativity of inspired editors but to the facts of history. This was Locke's orientation too, confirmed by the arrival in Amsterdam in 1684 of the Swiss biblical scholar Jean LeClerc to take up a chair in the Remonstrant University. The next year LeClerc published *Sentiments de Quelques Theologiens de Hollande sur l'Histoire Critique du Vieux Testament*, his bulky rejoinder to Simon. Locke read it straight away. He seems not to have enjoyed it very much. Perhaps its proto-Voltairean irreverence offended his piety. It was decidedly more polemical and point-scoring than genial, keeping the scriptures at a considerable emotional distance. But he agreed with its tendency, the discovery of facts by reason as opposed to Simon's resort to inspiration and church authority. And he learned from LeClerc the principle which was to guide his own later work on St Paul: that the critic would look for the author's design (like Clarendon) and the historical occasion which had evoked his work. This was a very powerful line of enquiry with a big future; not least with F. C. Baur and the Tubingen school of the nineteenth century. Incidentally, LeClerc also produced a gospel harmony which Locke possessed.

So when Locke returned to England he was well equipped in theory and technique for historical biblical criticism. First he had to see his epistemological and political works through the press, including the great *Essay*, and cope with reactions to it. In 1690 he retired, a famous and venerable man, to live with Sir Francis and Lady Masham at Oates in Essex. She was Damaris, the daughter of Ralph Cudworth the Cambridge Platonist and friend of Whichcote. It was at Oates that he wrote his two masterpieces of biblical criticism. *The Reasonableness of Christianity as Delivered in the Scriptures* was his quest for the historical Jesus, written with the Harmonies of Toinard and LeClerc at his elbow. It was published in 1695. His *Paraphrases and Notes on the Epistles of St Paul* were published posthumously between 1705 and 1707. Together they made a legacy to New Testament criticism as powerful as Albert Schweitzer's in our own century.

Locke's biblical work, overshadowed by his great *Essay* and political philosophy, is not as well known as it should be or once was. Like Coleridge, he gave it his later years, and for both men it was a fulfilment rather than a postscript or a remainder. Anyone who reads it now will find it surprisingly contemporary. Its lucid and sensitive historical method makes it equal to any of the works on Jesus and Paul which have proliferated since, often oblivious that they are saying ponderously what Locke had said before without obfuscation. Locke did not know as much as later exegetes, of course, and he is cool where romantic exegetes are warm. But his use of the basic strategies of criticism is pristine in its plain elegance.

At the beginning of *The Reasonableness of Christianity as Delivered in the Scriptures* Locke sets out his priorities: plainness and history. The literal and the diachronic mark his path when he describes the Bible as

a collection of writings designed by God for the instruction of the illiterate bulk of mankind in the way of salvation: and therefore in general and necessary points to be understood in the plain distinct meaning of the words and phrases, such as they may be supposed to have had in the mouths of the speakers, who used them according to the language of that time and country in which they lived, without such learned and forced senses of them, as are sought out, and put upon them in most systems of Divinity, according to the Notions that each one has been bred up in.

It is all there: the Bible as a public religious resource, rescued from dogmatic system and its forced (typological?) exegesis by the devout historian. It would have a single sense, creative of public order and quiet, rather than being a magazine for sectarian polemics. What Locke rescues above all is the historical reality of Jesus, belief in whom as God's Messiah is all that is intellectually required of Christians, whatever doctrines they might care to deduce from that. Locke goes through the gospels with a dogged patience which gets boring to modern readers more used to his line of enquiry than his contemporaries, pointing out that all that Jesus required of people doctrinally was faith in him. Here was unassailable authority for saving the attention that one might give to speculative dogma for something more beneficial – good works.

A remarkable feature of Locke's enquiry is the steadiness with which he faces a feature of the gospels which still perplexes critics: the strong element of deliberate secrecy whereby Jesus counteracts his public success. After all, Locke cherished plainness in public life, and it is disconcerting to a modern Christian believing in the elucidation of his faith that its founder should have sought to keep it secret. Locke clarifies the conundrum by two exertions of his historical sense. First, the sheer exigencies of time (and narrative, we might add nowadays) mean that not everything can, or even should, be understood straight away. Jesus presented 'such a manifestation of himself as every one at present could not understand, but yet carried such Evidence with it to those who were well disposed now, or would reflect on it when the whole course of his ministry was over' (p. 78) that they would understand who he was in the end. William Wrede came up with exactly that solution two hundred years later in *Das Messiasgeheimnis in den Evangelien* (1901) without noticing that Locke had preempted him. Locke's second answer to this problem is even more historically particular. He builds up a picture of first-century Judaism: bereft of prophetic leadership, under a foreign dominion and fervently expecting the Messiah. In so explosive a situation, unambiguous declaration by Jesus of his messiahship would have been so dangerous as probably to bring his ministry to a premature end:

If our Saviour had openly declared this of himself in his Life-time, with a train of Disciples and Followers everywhere owning and crying him up for their King, the *Roman* Governour of Judea could not have forborn to have taken notice of it, and have made use of their force against him. (p. 69)

This was a piece of historical analysis the moral force of which could be lost on no one in late seventeenth-century England. It is still a stock answer to the problem of Jesus' secrecy nowadays – even *the* stock answer – but never with reference to Locke, who presented it freshly as an historical solution of a problem insoluble by orthodox theology.

The Jesus who was thus restored to realistic history was a figure whom Locke could readily revere. There are, indeed, tones of Lockean self-portraiture in his praise of Jesus' 'wise and necessarily cautious management of himself' (p. 152) and 'the admirable wariness of his carriage'. This too is an early instance of a constant trait in the historical criticism of the gospels, enshrined in Schweitzer's famous metaphor of the liberal critic looking down the well of history for

Jesus, and seeing his own face reflected from below.

It is less of a hazard with St Paul. Withholding affection and total admiration from him is not a bar to orthodoxy. It is a possible advantage to disinterested study of him. The study of St Paul has been a less inhibited business than the study of the gospels throughout the modern period. Locke's *Paraphrases* of Paul's letters are preceded by a brilliant preface entitled *An Essay for the Understanding of St Paul's Epistles by Consulting St Paul Himself*. It begins with a series of historical observations. They include the importance of the historical context of each epistle, which has to be inferred from each with some difficulty; the language – 'Greek, but the Idiom or Turn of the Phrases may be truly said to be Hebrew'; Paul's own extreme intellectual fertility 'beset with a crowd of thoughts, all striving for utterance'. Locke then proposes repeated sequential readings of each epistle at a sitting as the best way he has found of understanding them. Only so can Paul's 'thread and coherence', his 'subject and tendency' become the governing criterion which it ought to be. This was a principle pioneered by Spinoza. Its practice can only be set in the study of the leisured and secluded reader. In church St Paul is read in extracts, and is thus barely if at all intelligible: 'chop'd and minc'd' as Locke says. The outstanding impression made by this little essay is of the sheer quality of reading which sustains it: in the last analysis, the best thing that criticism can do for a text. Good reading is ready to meet surprise and resistance. Locke's understanding of St Paul was open to both:

Nothing is more acceptable to Phansie than plyant Terms and Expressions that are not obstinate, in such it can find its account with Delight, and with them be illuminated, orthodox, infallible at pleasure and in its own way. But where the Sense of the Author goes visibly in its own Train, and the Words, receiving a determin'd sense from their Companions and Adjacents, will not consent to give Countenance and Colour to what is agreed to be right, and must be supported at any rate, there Men of established Orthodoxie do not so well find their satisfaction.

This is a passage to set the scene and the standards for subsequent biblical criticism. It makes clear that the biblical critic's independence of orthodoxy is not a pose or a tease, but a duty and a necessity. For only so can he achieve the sort of reading which Locke so eloquently describes. When he writes of the author's sense going its own way, every word finding its meaning from its 'Companions and Adjacents', he is pioneering the sort of attention to the text which Jowett and, above all, Matthew Arnold championed – and even foreshadowing something of Roland Barthes.

Locke's achievement, great and valuable in itself, is the sign that English biblical criticism is an established and going concern. It had drawn, and with Collins continued to draw, on the international facilities of Holland. It held the initiative until the end of the eighteenth century when the professionalism of the German universities first began to equal the professionalism of England's Herbert Marsh on the Gospels and Alexander Geddes, the London Scot, on the Old Testament. The Church of England allowed, more or less happily, the flourishing of biblical criticism. Its tolerant norms were hospitable towards it. There have been biblical critics on the bench of bishops from Marsh and Connop Thirlwall to Michael Ramsey who died in 1988. The alliance between Church and universities was strong – though not as strong as Jowett and his friends believed when they published *Essays and Reviews*. For at the same time, doing biblical criticism within any orthodox Christian communion, however easy-going, was to be at continual odds with norms of belief which have never been adapted to accommodate it. This was a brake on freewheeling speculation, always randomly applied, but it also ensured that biblical studies would not be secluded but take part in dramatic scenes on public stages. There was public responsibility in being a critic of the public writings round which Ezra reformed a nation and on which oaths were sworn in courts of law. Biblical criticism was a social calling and not necessarily a secure one, even in liberal England.

As well as taking its practitioners into the world of public debate and the politically viable, it took them on voyages of descent into the subterranean human world of raw feelings, myths, codes and dreams which press upon the daylight world from below. Lowth's astonishing lectures, preempting romanticism by a generation, affirm the passions of the human heart as the source of biblical religion. This sort of critique, though very different from Locke's, also needed and developed the growing apparatus of scholarship. In our own day it has attracted literary critics of the calibre of Frank Kermode, Gabriel Josipovici and Robert Alter to close biblical work. And it has had the result, astonishing to those accustomed to Lockean historical realism, of reviving serious interest in the typological and figural exegesis which the pioneers of modern biblical criticism up to C. H. Dodd had driven from the field.

The wheel has perhaps come full circle. But that is too simple a metaphor. We ought at least to allow the complication that more than one wheel turns in biblical criticism. The Bible is the public book which is read and expounded in church. Since the Reformation it has also been a private book studied in studies. It is the book of God. It is also, as Herder read it, a human book. So two wheels turn, at least. One is public and theocratic, the other private and humanist. The public-theocratic tradition can be found in this anthology in the extracts from Sherlock and Thomas Arnold. Both are concerned with the Bible as the record of God's actions on the grand public stage of world history. It is a tradition which has survived into the second half of the twentieth century, taking remnants of typology with it, and can be seen in books like *The Book of the Acts of God* (1957) by G. Ernest Wright and Reginald Fuller. But the horrors of twentieth-century history resist interpretation of this sort and have made 'biblical theology', as it is called, a battered and sickly survivor. So it is well for vital biblical criticism that it can draw on the modesty and profundity of the alternative, humanist, tradition. In terms of this anthology, it can be seen in Collins's work, beginning unpromisingly as something of a joke. To a radical Lockean like him, the imaginative tropes of rabbinic exegesis were fanciful absurdities. But with Lowth and Blake the flights of human imagination came to be seen as the primary subject matter of an urgent and vivid biblical Christianity, an exegetical duty rather than aberration. God was to be known in the depths from which such expressions emerged: in the radical subjectivity of which Kierkegaard is the great apostle; or the more urbane insistence of Matthew Arnold on an interiorised and ethical response, got through reading the Bible as poetry, to the 'eternal not-ourselves which makes for righteousness'. Theism does not so much disappear along this line of tradition as become apersonal and optional. In the late 1980s *The Literary Guide to the Bible* (1987) edited by Frank Kermode and Robert Alter gives Matthew Arnold's way the edge over his father's – which Matthew, with his sense of filial unworthiness, would have found some comfort.

1. Anthony Collins, 'Discourse of the Grounds and Reasons of the Christian Religion' (1724), Chapters I, IV, V, VIII (less paragraph 4), IX, X (extracted), XI

Anthony Collins's *Discourse of the Grounds and Reasons* sets sprightly and audacious prose over a clutter of footnotes. The material reason for the footnotes was Collins's large library 'in a very commodious room upstairs' in his house at Great Baddow in Essex (BM Addit. MSS 4282. f. 222). He was an avid and famous book collector and bought books for his friend John Locke. The library numbered 6906 items at his death and included nearly everything of importance in biblical criticism: Grotius, Hobbes, Spinoza, Simon, Le Clerc, Whiston – and of course, Locke. While the footnotes are a rhetorical device, parading his reading, the reading was wide and deep. He knew what the questions were and, with such a collection at his disposal, can claim to be a gathering point of biblical studies up to his time.

Yet he wrote with a tendentious energy which, in spite of the footnotes, was impatient of scholarly precision. Bentley had bitten him hard for this after the publication of his *Discourse of Free Thinking*, and a clear-eyed view of Collins's axe-grinding is necessary to the reader of the present text. His Christian theism was dominated, even overlaid, by an optimistic passion for free enquiry fed by Locke but outstripping his master; and a hatred of religious officialdom, particularly of priests, and Roman Catholics.

Collins's tendency is revealed by uncovering the route to the use of Surenhusius which makes the *tour de force* of his argument here. It went through three stages. Surenhusius's original book of 1713 was a compendious defence of the inaccurate quotations from the Old Testament made by the Christian writers of the New Testament.

Surenhusius was stung by rabbinic allegations of Christian corruption into demonstrating that the Christians, and Christ himself, used first-century techniques which were common to Jews and Christians. A friendly rabbi, who had been a temporary convert to catholic christianity, had helped him thread the mazes of these methods. The second stage was an abstract of Surenhusius's book which appeared in Michael de la Roche's *Memoirs of Literature* in 1717: one of the literary magazines which did so much to foster biblical criticism within the republic of letters at the time. De la Roche, a friend of Bayle and a French protestant refugee to England, concluded his review of Surenhusius with a prediction tinged by incitement.

If anyone undertakes to publish hereafter a new collection of *Criticks* upon the Holy Scripture, Mr Surenhusius will make a great figure among them. He has raised a dreadful Battery against the Jews: And because there is another Sort of Men, who are Apt to make use of their weapons, I would advise none of them to come near that Battery; for it will do mischief. (2nd edition of 1722, VI, p. 110)

Collins's book is, in effect, a gleeful exploitation of de la Roche's hint of mischief: the possibility of turning the 'Battery' of rabbinic exegesis on orthodox Christianity. Collins's glee is unmistakable at the end of Chapter IX (p. 34 below).

Thus by a most lucky accident of Mr Surenhusius's meeting and *conference* with a learned allegorical *Rabbin*, are the *rules* by which the apostles cited and apply'd the OT discover'd to the world; ... which *conference* seems not, in its nature and consequence, much unlike that between LUTHER and the *devil*. LUTHER reports himself to have had frequent conferences with the devil; in one of which he pretends he receiv'd from him the *arguments* for the *abolition of the sacrifice of the mass* ... The *Rabbin* establishes Christianity; and the *devil* protestantism.

For all its animus, Collins's exegesis of the texts he considers is sound. Recent New Testament criticism has vindicated his basic claim that a major part in the building of primitive Christianity was the adaptation, by means of allegory, of Old Testament texts, types and stories – not only prophecies – to its own use. It could not have been otherwise, since these Old Testament texts were the authoritative Bible of the first Christians and they, like Christ at Emmaus, 'interpreted ... in all the scriptures the things concerning himself' (Luke 24. 27). The reader need only consult modern commentaries such as J. M. Creed's on Luke or H. B. Green's on Matthew, referring to the infancy narratives which begin each gospel, and he will see Collins's theory settled in mainstream criticism. Collins can be seen as a precursor of Strauss, another contentious critic whose methods have survived time and obloquy. But Strauss was a romantic, enthusiastic for the truths of imagination – at least, when they could be transposed into Hegelian philosophy. Collins was a Lockean empiricist going by 'the common rules of grammar and logick' who viewed what he found as no better than 'very extraordinary' (IX). His critical success was only critical and lacked a frame of mind in which it could have positive religious value, as Strauss believed he had in Hegel.

As a critic, though, Collins is brilliant – hasty and slapdash, and so easy prey for Bentley, but intuitively very acute indeed. He was right about the use of the Old Testament in the New. He was also right in his apprehension of the symbolic nature of religious discourse. His discussion of the 'grafting on old stocks' by which religions change and develop in Chapter IV – explored sketchily but acutely in Chapter XI – is grounded in this conviction, which is endorsed by modern anthropologists and practitioners of Religious Studies. It is also informed by a vivid sense of history – 'the changeable state of all things'. Together, these insights make him a major modern critic of religion. Here again the stimulus of his intuition was negative. He was taking against Jenkin's *The Reasonableness and Certainty of the Christian Religion* of 1700 to which he often refers in the footnotes. Jenkin defended the authenticity of the fulfilment of Old Testament prophecies in the New by walling off 'the divine revelation contained in the Holy Scriptures' from the 'uncertain and ambiguous' oracles of other faiths. He was abusive of the 'novelty' of Islam and considered 'the theology of the elders absurd': Collins's putting Christianity on a plane with religions in general is a symmetrical contradiction of Jenkin. It is a negative movement, though it results in perspicuous critique.

The text which follows here consists of the central part of Collins's book, abbreviated by the omission of Chapters II, III, VI, VII, and the last paragraph of VIII. Chapter X appears here without Collins's synoptic comparison of Isaiah 7 and Surenhusius's commentary on it (pp. 64–70 of the first edition), and without Collins's remarks on Matthew 11. 14 and 13. 54 (pp. 75–6 of the first edition). Chapter XI here stops with its section 2 (p. 91 of the first edition). This leaves intact Collins's basic argument: that New Testament Christianity is founded on the Old Testament by way of allegorical interpretation.

Part I
Of the Grounds and Reasons of Christianity

I
That *Christianity is founded on Judaism, or the New Testament on the Old*

CHRISTIANITY is founded on Judaism, and the New Testament on the Old; and JESUS is the person said in the New Testament to be promis'd in the Old, under the character of the MESSIAS of the Jews, who, as such only, claims the obedience and submission of the world.[1] Accordingly, it is the design of the authors of the *New*, to prove all the parts of christianity from the Old Testament, which is said to contain *the words of eternal life;[a]* and to represent JESUS and his apostles, as *fulfilling*, by their mission, doctrines, and works, the predictions of the *prophets*, the historical parts of the Old Testament, and the *Jewish law;[b]* which last is expressly said to *prophecy[c]* of, or tipify, christianity.

---

[a] John 5. 39.   [b] Matt. 5. 17.   [c] Matt. 11. 13.

Anthony Collins

IV
That it is a common and necessary method for new revelations to be built and grounded on precedent revelations

THIS method of introducing christianity into the world by building and grounding it on the Old Testament, is agreeable to the common method of introducing *new revelations* (whether real or pretended) or any *changes* in religion, and also to the *nature of things.*[a] For if we consider the various *revelations*, and *changes* in religion, whereof we have any tolerable history, in their beginning, we shall find them for the most part to be grafted on some old stock, or founded on some preceding *revelations*, which they were either to supply, or fulfil, or retrieve from corrupt glosses, innovations, and traditions, with which by time they were incumber'd: and this, which may seem matter of surprize to those, who do not reflect on the changeable state of all things, has happen'd; tho' the old *revelations*, far from intending any change, engraftment, or new dispensation, did for the most part declare they were to last *for ever*, and did forbid all alterations and innovations, they being the *last dispensations* intended.

This *grafting on old stocks*, we see by experience to be the case of all the *sects*, which alike and according to the natural course of things, rise up in the several great and domineering religions of the world. Nor is it less true of the domineering religions themselves; some of which we know to have been originally, but such *sects* themselves.

Thus the mission of MOSES to the *Israelites* suppos'd a former revelation of God (who from the beginning seems to have been constantly giving a succession of dispensations and revelations) to their ancestors:[b] and many of the religious precepts of MOSES were borrowed,[c] or had an agreement with the religious rites of the heathens, with whom the *Israelites* had correspondence, and particularly with the religious rites of the *Egyptians*, (who upon that account seem confounded with the *Israelites* by some pagans,[d] as both their religious rites were equally, and at the same time prohibited by others;[e]) to whose religious rites the *Israelites* seem to have been *conformists* during their abode in *Egypt;*[f] not excepting JOSEPH himself, who by his post in the administration of the government,[g] his match with the prince or *priest* of *On*'s daughter, made up by

[a] Stanhope's *Charron of Wisdom*, l. 2, c. 5, p. 103, etc.   [b] Exod. 3.
[c] Simon. Hist. Crit. du Vieux Test. p. 50. *Spencer* de Legibus, etc. *Stanhope*'s Dissert. in Charron *of Wisdom*, vol. 2. pp. 93, 97. *Marsham* Canon Chronicus, etc. p. 181.
[d] *Strabo*, ll. 16 and 17.   [e] *Taciti* Annales, l. 2. *Sueton.* in Tiber.
[f] Jos. 24. 14. Amos 5. 26. Acts 7. 43.
[g] Gen. 41. 40, 45. Ibid. 42. 15, 32. Ibid. 44. 5.

PHARAOH himself, his manner of *swearing*, his *eating* with the *Egypt-ians*, his practise of heathen *divination*, and, above all, by his political conduct, seems to have been a most true member of, and convert to, the establish'd church of *Egypt*.[2]

The mission of ZOROASTER to the *Persians*, suppos'd the *religion of the* Magians; which *had been for many ages past, the antient national religion of the* Medes *as well as* Persians.[a]

The mission of MAHOMET suppos'd *christianity*, as that did *judaism*.

And the *Siamese*[b] and *Brachmans,*[c] both pretend, that they have had a *succession of incarnate Deities* among them, who, at due distances of time, have brought new revelations from heaven, each succeeding one depending on the former; and that religion is to be carry'd on in that way for ever.

And if we consider the *nature of things*, we shall find, that it must be difficult, if not impossible, to introduce among men (who in all civiliz'd countries are bred up in the belief of some reveal'd religion) a reveal'd religion wholly new, or such as has no reference to a preceding one:[d] for that would be to combat all men in too many respects, and not to proceed on a sufficient number of principles necessary to be assented to by those, on whom the first impressions of a new religion are proposed to be made.

Perfect novelty is a great and just exception to a religious institu-tion;[e] whereof religious sects of all kinds have been so sensible, that they have ever endeavour'd to give themselves, in some manner or other, the greatest antiquity they well could, and generally the utmost antiquity. Thus St LUKE says, that *God* spake of the Red-eemer *by the mouth of all his prophets, which have been since the world began.*[f] St PAUL defends himself and the christian religion from the charge of novelty, when he says, *after the way, which ye call heresy, so worship I the God of my fathers, believing all things that are written in the law and the prophets;*[g] declaring hereby, that christianity was so far from being *heresy*, or a new opinion, that it was the doctrine of the Old Testament. And christian divines date the *antiquity* of chris-tianity from the time of *the fall* of ADAM,[h] asserting; that CHRIST was then *promis'd* in these words, *the seed of the woman shall break the*

---

[a] *Prideaux's Connect.* vol. I. p. 214. *Pocock, Spec. Hist.* Arab. pp. 147–149.
[b] *Gervaise*, Hist. de Siam, 3*d.* pt. c. 1. *Tachard*, Voyage de Siam, vol. 1. p. 396, etc.
[c] *Delon* Des Dieux Orient, pp. 10–30. Philos, Transac. Ann. 1700. p. 734, etc.
[d] *Charron of Wisdom*, l. 2, c. 5.
[e] Defenso S. *Augustini* contra. *J. Phereponum.* pp. 185, 187.   [f] Luke I. 70.
[g] Acts 24. 14.
[h] Taylor's *Preservat. against Deism*, p. 213, etc. Whiston's *Sermons and Essays*, pp. 59–78. Stillingfleet's *Sermons*, fol. p. 187.

---

serpent's head,[a] which they say contain *the gospel in miniature;*[b] and that, from that time, men have been sav'd by faith in the said *promise* of CHRIST to come, who was *the Lamb slain from the foundation of the world;*[c] CHRIST's death *looking backward as well as forwards.*[d]

And an eminent divine thinks he can with great probability settle the precise time, when the christian *covenant* began. He says, that ADAM was created on the sixth day at nine in the morning;[e] that he *fell* about *noon,* that *being the time of eating;* and that CHRIST was *promis'd about three a-clock in the afternoon.*

So that the truth of christianity depends, as it ought, on antient revelations, which are contain'd in the Old Testament, and more particularly and immediately on the *revelations* made to the *Jews* therein.

V
That the chief proofs of christianity from the Old Testament, are urged by the apostles in the New Testament

HOW christianity depends on those *revelations,* or what *proofs* are therein to be met withal in behalf of christianity, are the subjects of almost all the numerous books written by divines and other apologists for christianity; but the chief and principal of those *proofs* may be justly supposed to be urged in the New Testament by the authors thereof; who relate the history of the first preaching of the gospel, and were themselves, either apostles of JESUS, or companions of the apostles.

VIII
That those proofs are typical or allegorical proofs

OF the *strength* or *weakness* of the proofs for christianity out of the Old Testament we seem well qualify'd to judge, by having the Old and New Testament in our hands; the first containing the proofs of christianity, and the latter the application of those proofs. And we should seem to have nothing more to do, but to compare the Old and New Testament together.

But these *proofs* taken out of the *Old,* and urg'd in the *New* Testament, being, sometimes, either not to be found in the *Old,* or not urg'd in the *New,* according to the literal and obvious sense,

[a] Gen. 3. 15.   [b] Taylor, Ibid. *and* Beveridge *on the Articles of the Church of* England, p. 138.
[c] Heb. 9. 24, 25, 26. Ibid. 11. 7, 13.   [d] Tillotson's *Sermons,* vol. 5. pp. 66, 67.
[e] Lightfoot's *Works,* vol. 2. p. 1324.

which they seem to bear in their suppos'd places in the *Old*, and therefore not proofs according to scholastick rules; almost all christian *commentators* on the bible,[a] and *advocates* for the christian religion, both antient and modern, have judg'd them to be apply'd in a secondary, or typical, or mystical, or allegorical, or enigmatical sense, that is, in a sense different from the obvious and literal sense, which they bear in the Old Testament.

1 Thus for example, St MATTHEW after having given an account of the conception of the virgin MARY, and of the birth of JESUS, says, *all this was done that it might be fulfill'd, which was spoken by the prophet, saying,* 'Behold a virgin shall be with child, and shall bring forth a Son, and they shall call his name IMMANUEL.'[b] But the words, as they stand in ISAIAH, from whom they are suppos'd to be taken, do, in their obvious and literal sense, relate to a *young woman* in the days of AHAZ, king of *Judah*, as will appear by considering the context.[c]

When REZIN, king of *Syria*, and PEKAH, king of *Israel*, were confederates in arms together, against *Ahaz*, king of *Judah*; ISAIAH the prophet was sent by God first to comfort AHAZ and his nation, and afterwards to assure them by a *sign* or miracle, that his enemies should in a little time be confounded.[d] But AHAZ refusing a *sign* at the prophet's hands, the prophet said, *The Lord shall give you a sign: Behold a virgin*[e] (or *young woman*[f]) *shall conceive and bear a son, and shall call his name* IMMANUEL. *Butter and Honey shall he eat; that he may know to refuse the evil, and chuse the good. For before the child shall know to refuse the evil and chuse the good, the land shall be forsaken of both her kings.*[g] And this sign is accordingly given AHAZ by the prophet, who *took two witnesses,*[h] and in their presence *went unto* the said virgin or young woman, call'd the *prophetess,*[i] who in due time *conceiv'd and bare a son,* who was nam'd IMMANUEL;[j] after whose birth, the projects of REZIN and PEKAH were soon confounded, according to the *prophesy* and *sign* given by the prophet.[k]

---

[a] Origen, Eusebius, Jerom, (*who says directly to* Pammachius, *that the Passages alledg'd by* Paul, *out of the old Testament,* aliter in Suis locis, aliter in Epistolis Paulinis sonant) Cyril, Chrysostom, Austin *among the Antients. And among the Moderns,* Sextus Senensis *in* Bibl. Sancta; Glassius *in* Philologia Sacra; Grotius *in* Vetus *and* Nov. Test. and sicut at *in* Isa. 53. 1. *in* Psal. 22. 1. *and in* Matt. 1. 22; *Cuneus* dans sa Republique des Hebreux, l. 3. c. 8. vol. 1 p. 376; *Simon* Hist. Crit. du V. T. pp. 97, 98. Hist. Crit. du Nov. Test. c. 21. and 22. Suppl. aux Ceremonies des Juiss. p. 7; Jenkins's *Reasonab. of the Christian Religion;* Nichols *Conference with a Theist.* vol. 3d. White *on* Isaiah; *Dupin* Dissert. Prelim. sur la Bib. Choisie, vol. 27. pp. 388–399. *See* WHISTON's *Confession of this Matter in* Essay, etc. p. 92.
[b] Matt. 1. 22, 23.   [c] Isa. 7. 14.   [d] c. 7.   [e] v. 14–16.
[f] *Vide* Erasmum *in* Matt. c. 1. v. 30.
[g] *See* Isaiah 8. 4.   [h] Ibid. v. 2. 18.   [i] v. 3.   [j] *See* Grotius *in* Matt. 1. 22.
[k] Isa. 8. 8, 10. Ibid. 7. 14. and 8. 4.

And the prophet himself puts it past dispute, by express words, as well as by his whole narration, that his own child was the *sign* mention'd, when he says, *Behold I and the children, whom the Lord hath given me, are for signs and for wonders in Israel; from the Lord of hosts, that dwelleth in mount Sion.*[a]

This is the plain drift and design of the prophet, literally, obviously, and primarily understood; and thus is he understood by one of the most judicious of interpreters, the great GROTIUS. Indeed, to understand the prophet as having the conception of the virgin MARY and birth of her son JESUS literally and primarily in view, is a very great *absurdity*, and contrary to the very intent and design of the *sign* given by the prophet.[b] For the *sign* being given by the prophet to convince AHAZ, that he brought a message from the Lord to him to assure him that the two kings should not succeed against him;[c] how could a virgin's conception and bearing a son seven hundred years afterwards, be a *sign* to AHAZ, that the prophet came to him with the said message from the Lord? And how useless was it to AHAZ, as well as absurd in itself, for the prophet to say, *Before the child*, born seven hundred years hence, shall distinguish between *good* and *evil, the land shall be forsaken of both her kings?*[d] which should seem a banter[3] instead of a sign. But a prophesy of the certain birth of a male child, to be born within a year or two, seems a proper *sign*; as being not only what could not with certainty be foretold, except by a person inspir'd by God; but as immediately or soon coming to pass, and consequently evidencing itself to be *a divine sign*, and answering all the purposes of *a sign*. And such a *sign* is agreeable to the divine conduct on the like occasions. God gave GIDEON[e] and HEZEKIAH[f] immediate *signs* to prove, that he spoke to them; and that the things promis'd to them should come to pass. Had he given them remote *signs*, how could they have known, that the *signs* themselves would ever have come to pass? And how could those *signs* evidence any thing? Those *signs* would have stood in need of other *signs* to manifest, that God would perform them in time.

This prophesy therefore not being fulfill'd in JESUS according to the literal, obvious, and primary sense of the words, as they stand in ISAIAH; it is suppos'd, that this, like all the other prophesies cited by the apostles, is fulfill'd in a secondary, or typical, or mystical, or allegorical sense;[g] that is, the said prophesy, which was then literally fulfill'd by the birth of the prophet's son, was again fulfill'd by the

---

[a] Ibid. v. 19. [b] *White* in hunc locum, and Pref. p. 20. [c] Isa. 7. 14. and 8. 4.
[d] Isa. 8. v. 15, 16.
[e] Judg. 6. [f] 2 King. 20. [g] *Le Clerc* Bib. Univ. Tom. 20. p. 54.

birth of JESUS, as being an event of the same kind, and intended to be signify'd, either by the prophet, or by God who directed the prophet's speech. I say, *like all other prophesies cited by the apostles*, not only upon having myself particularly consider'd all those prophesies, but upon what I find asserted by an eminent divine, who says, *'Tis possible in the consideration of single prophesies to find out some other person or event*, (besides JESUS and the matters relating to him) *to which these might be adapted without great violence to the text.*[a] And this suppos'd *allegory* or *obscurity* (which indeed reigns in all prophesies that ever were, whether Pagan, Jewish, Christian, or Mahometan, that have existed before the events to which they have been referr'd) is so far from being made matter of objection, that the necessity thereof is contended for, in order to make the prophesies of the Old Testament reach the *end* for which they were design'd.[b] The great clearness of prophesies has ever been deem'd a mark among intelligent people, whether believers or unbelievers in prophesy, that they have been made after the event; and thus from their great clearness, as well as from other topicks, almost all criticks now condemn the present collection of *Sybiline oracles* as forg'd.[4]

* * *

2 Again, St MATTHEW gives us another prophesy, which he says was *fulfill'd*. He tells us, that JESUS was carry'd into *Egypt*, from whence he return'd after the death of HEROD, *that it might be fulfill'd which was spoken of the Lord by the prophet, saying*, 'Out of *Egypt* have I call'd my son.'[c] Which words being word for word in HOSEAH, and no where else to be found in the Old Testament, are suppos'd to be taken from thence;[d] where, according to their obvious sense, they are no prophesy, but relate to a past action, and that to the calling the children of *Israel* out of *Egypt*; as, I think, is denied by few. This passage therefore, or, as it is stil'd, *prophesy* of HOSEAH is said by learned men to be mystically or allegorically apply'd in order to render MATTHEW's application of it just; and they say, all other *methods* of some *learned men to solve the difficulties* arising from the citation of this prophesy, *have prov'd unsuccessful.*[e]

3 MATTHEW says, JESUS *came and dwelt at* Nazareth, *that it might be fulfill'd, which was spoken by the prophets, saying*, 'He shall be call'd a

---

[a] Stanhope's *Boyl. Lect. Serm.* 7. 1701. p. 27.
[b] Montagu's *Acts and Monuments*, etc. c. 2. Sect. 2. etc. *Augustin* De Doctr. Christian. l. 2. c. 5. Stanhope, Ibid. pp. 11–32. Jenkins's *Reason. of Christ.* vol. 2. pp. 159–170.
[c] Matt. 2. 15.   [d] Hos. 11. 1.
[e] *See* Whiston's *Lect.* p. 12. Ibid. *Essay*, etc. p. 88, etc. *Simon* Hist. Crit. du N. Test. c. 21. p. 260. *Cunaeus* Rep. des Heb. vol. 1. p. 376. *Huetii* Dem. Evang. p. 730.

Nazarene.'[a] Which citation does not *expressly* occur in any place of the Old Testament, and therefore the Old Testament cannot be literally fulfill'd therein.

IX
The nature of typical or allegorical proofs and reasoning

IN order to understand the full force of the *proofs* for christianity, it is necessary to understand the nature and rules of typical, mystical, and allegorical reasoning. Which is what I shall now endeavour to explain to the reader.

To suppose that an author has but one meaning at a time to a proposition (which is to be found out by a critical examination of his words) and to cite that proposition from him, and argue from it in that one meaning, is to proceed by the common rules of grammar and logick; which, being human rules, are not very difficult to be set forth and explain'd. But to suppose passages cited, explain'd, and argu'd from in any other method, seems very extraordinary and difficult to understand, and to reduce to *rules*. Accordingly, notwithstanding it is suppos'd by the learned interpreters of the New Testament and the several christian apologists, that the apostles apply'd the passages they cite out of the Old Testament to their purposes after a typical, or mystical, or allegorical manner; and notwithstanding, both ancients and moderns do almost universally make application of passages of the Old Testament (to say nothing of their manner of interpreting the New Testament, and the *revelation* of St JOHN in particular) in some such manner, not only as to matters, that relate to the gospel of JESUS, but to the matters and events of all times: yet the *rules* of thus applying passages of scripture seem not understood by many of those persons, who contend, that the apostles us'd that method, or who use it themselves. For I find it lamented by a *Boylean Lecturer*, that *the* Jewish *Traditions or* RULES *for interpreting scripture, which had been received among the ancient* Jewish *Rabbins,*[b] and were followed by the apostles in their interpretations of the Old Testament, were *lost*. And so lately as 1708, I find in the reverend Dr JENKIN the following passage:[c] He, on occasion of St STEPHEN's giving an historical account of several matters contrary to what we read in the Old Testament, and arguing before the *Sanedrin* from thence, says, that St STEPHEN *would never have produced any thing out of the Old Testament before the Sanedrin, nor would St* LUKE *have*

---

[a] Matt. 2. 23.   [b] Stanhope's *Boyle's Lect. Serm.* 8. 1701. p. 23.
[c] Jenkin's *Reasonab. of the Christ. Relig.* vol. 2. p. 320.

recorded it soon after, if it had been capable of any disproof or confutation, whatever difficulties at this distance of time there may appear to us to be in it. And so in all other cases we may depend upon it, that the apostles, and other disciples, who had such demonstrative evidence for the conviction of unbelievers, by a constant power of miracles, would never make use of any arguments to the Jews from the Old Testament, but such as they well knew, their adversaries could never be able to disprove or deny. For there were then certain methods of interpretation, as we may learn from JOSEPHUS, which are now lost; and they disputed from acknowledg'd maxims and rules: the only difference and matter of dispute, was in the application of them to the particular case; however our ignorance of things, then generally known, may now make it difficult to reconcile some texts of the New Testament with those of the Old from whence they are cited.[a]

But since that time, the learned SURENHUSIUS, professor of the *Hebrew* tongue in the *illustrious school* of *Amsterdam*, has made an ample discovery to the world of the *rules* by which the apostles cited the Old Testament, and argued from thence, in a *treatise*;[b] wherein the whole mystery of the apostles applying scripture in a secondary or typical, or mystical, or allegorical sense seems unfolded. I shall therefore state this matter from SURENHUSIUS; who himself gives the *substance*, as well as the *occasion* of his work, in his *preface*.[5] He says,[c] 'That when he considered the various opinions of the learned about the passages of the Old Testament quoted in the New, he was *filled with grief*, not knowing where to set his foot, and being much concerned, that what had been done with good success upon profane authors, could not be so happily perform'd upon the sacred.'

He tells us, 'That having had frequent occasions to converse with the *Jews*, (on account of his application to *Hebrew* literature from his youth) who insolently reflected on the New Testament; affirming it to be plainly corrupted, because it seldom or never agreed with the Old Testament, some of whom were so confident in this opinion, as to say, they would profess the christian religion, if any one could reconcile the New Testament with the Old; he was the more *griev'd*, because he knew not how to apply a remedy to this evil. But the matter being of great importance, he discours'd with several learned men about it, and read the books of others, being perswaded, that the authors of the books of the New Testament had writ nothing, but what was suited to the time, wherein they liv'd, and that CHRIST and

[a] *Joseph.* de Bello, Jud. l. 3. c. 14.
[b] Tractatus in quo secundum Veterum Theologorum Hebræorum formulas allegandi, et modos interpretandi, conciliantur loca ex V. in Nov. Test. allegata. Amstel. 1713. p. 712.
[c] *For this Extract out of* SURENHUSIUS, *I am for the most part obliged to the learned and ingenious Mons.* De la Roche; *from whose* Memoirs of Literature *I have in great measure taken it.*

his apostles had constantly follow'd the method of their ancestors. After he had long revolv'd this *hypothesis* in his mind, at last he met with a Rabbin well skill'd in the *Talmud*, the *Cabala*, and the *allegorical books* of the Jews.[6] That Rabbin had once embrac'd the christian religion, but was again relaps'd to Judaism, on account of the idolatry of the papists, yet not perfectly disbelieving the *integrity* of the New Testament. Mr SURENHUSIUS ask'd him, what he thought of the passages of the Old Testament, quoted in the New, whether they were rightly quoted or not? and whether the Jews had any just reason to cavil at them? And at the same time he propos'd to him two or three passages, which had very much exercis'd the most learned christian commentators. The Rabbin having admirably explain'd those passages, to the great surprize of our author, and confirm'd his explications by several places of the *Talmud*,[a] and by the writings of the Jewish commentators and allegorical writers; Mr SURENHUSIUS ask'd him, what would be the best method to write a treatise, in order to vindicate the passages of the Old Testament which have been quoted in the New? The Rabbin answer'd, that he thought the best way of succeeding in such an undertaking, would be to peruse a great part of the *Talmud*, and the allegorical and literal commentaries of the most ancient Jewish writers; to observe their several ways of quoting and interpreting scripture; and to collect as many materials of that kind, as would be sufficient for that purpose. Mr *S.* took the hint immediately: he read several parts of the *Talmud*; he perus'd the jewish books above-mention'd, and observ'd every thing that might be subservient to his design. And having made a large collection of those materials, he put all his *Theses* into order, and digested them into four books: The first whereof treats *of the forms of quoting, illustrating, and reconciling the scriptures*, in 59 *Theses:* The second treats *of the manner of quoting*, in 20 *Theses:* The third treats *of the manner of interpreting*, in 25 *Theses:* And the fourth treats *of the manner of expounding and reconciling the genealogies*, in 35 *Theses*.'[7] Then he proceeds in a fifth book to explain and justify all the quotations made from the Old Testament in the New, by his foregoing *Theses*.

As to the *forms of quoting*, which is the subject of his first book, he says, 'that in order to vindicate and reconcile any passage of the Old Testament quoted in the New, one must in the first place observe, what *form of quoting* the apostles made use of; because from thence one may immediately know, why they alledge the following words in a certain manner, rather than in another, and why they depart more

[a] *See* Scaligerana, p. 265.

or less from the *Hebrew* text. Thus a different sense is imply'd in each of the following *forms of quoting* used by the sacred writers of the New Testament: *it has been said: it is written: that it might be fulfill'd which was spoken: the scripture says: see what is said: the scripture foreseeing: is it not written: wherefore he says: have you never read: what says the scripture; as he spoke*, etc. Besides, he says, it ought to be consider'd, why in those quotations God is introduc'd under the name of *Lord* or *God*, or *Holy Ghost*, and sometimes the writer himself, or the scripture; and likewise, why the persons or things in question are introduc'd speaking. Lastly, it ought to be observ'd, when and why a passage of the New Testament is alledg'd in the New without any previous form of quoting; and why some traditions, and history almost forgotten, are sometimes occasionally brought in, as if they made a part of scripture?' In the second book, which treats *of the manner of quoting*, he shows, 'that the books of the Old Testament have been dispos'd in a different order at different times, and have had different names, which is the reason, why a writer or a book, is sometimes confounded with another in the New Testament.' Besides, he produces several reasons, 'why the sacred writers of the New Testament might, and even were oblig'd to alledge the passages of the Old Testament otherwise than they are express'd in the original, *viz.* because the ancient *Hebrew* doctors affirm'd, that in the time of the MESSIAS some obscure and difficult passages of scripture should be clear'd, and the impropriety of words mended, the intricacy of the stile remov'd, words dispos'd in a better order, and a mystical sense drawn out of the literal, that the vail being taken away, truth might plainly appear to every body. The author infers from thence, that the Jews cannot reasonably find fault with the apostles for putting a spiritual sense upon several passages of the Old Testament.' In the next place he shows, that the jewish doctors take a prodigious liberty in quoting the scripture, and gives us several instances of it. The last is very remarkable, and made Mr SURENHUSIUS very angry with the seeming absurdity of the Rabbins. But, says he, 'when I saw St PAUL do so too, my anger was appeas'd.'

In the third book, which treats *of the manner* of interpreting the scriptures, he shows, 'how the authors of the *Gemara*,[8] and the ancient allegorical writers, and others, interpreted the scripture in such a manner, as to change the mean literal sense of the words into a noble and spiritual sense. To that end the jewish doctors used *ten ways* of citing and explaining the Old Testament;' which for their curiosity and importance, I shall here recite at large after my author.[9]

1 The first is, 'reading the words, not according to the points plac'd

under them, but according to other points substituted in their stead; as we see done by PETER, *Acts* 3. 3; by STEPHEN, *Acts* 7. 43; and by PAUL, I *Cor.* 15. 54; II *Cor.* 8. 15; and *Heb.* 3. 10; and 9. 21; and 12. 6.'

2 The second is, 'changing the letters, whether those letters be of the same organ (as the jewish grammarians speak) or no;[10] as we see done by PAUL, *Rom.* 9.33; I *Cor.* 11.9; *Heb.* 8.9; and 10.5; and by STEPHEN, *Acts* 7. 43.'

3 The third is, 'changing both letters and points; as we see done by PAUL, *Acts* 13. 41; and II *Cor.* 8. 15.'

4 The fourth is, 'adding some letters and taking away others.'

5 The fifth is, 'transposing words and letters.'

6 The sixth is, 'dividing one word into two.'

7 The seventh is, 'adding other words to those that are there, in order to make the sense more clear, and to accommodate it to the subject they are upon; as, is manifest, is done by the apostles throughout the New Testament.'

8 The eighth is, 'changing the order of words; which he shews to be done in many places of the New Testament.'

9 The ninth is, 'changing the order of words, and adding other words; which are both done by the apostles in citing passages out of the Old Testament.'

10 The tenth is, 'changing the order of words, adding words, and retrenching words; which is a method often us'd by PAUL.'

Thus by a most lucky accident of Mr SURENHUSIUS's meeting and *conference* with a learned allegorical *Rabbin*, are the *rules*, by which the apostles cited and apply'd the Old Testament, discover'd to the world; to which they had been for several ages lost, as has been observ'd from the rev. doctors STANHOPE and JENKIN, above-mention'd. Which *conference* seems not, in its nature and consequence, much unlike that between LUTHER and the *devil*. LUTHER reports himself to have had frequent conferences with the devil;[11] in one of which he pretends he receiv'd from him the *arguments* for the *abolition of the sacrifice of the mass*, which he urges in his book, *De Abrog. Miss. Privat*. The *Rabbin* establishes christianity; and the *devil* protestantism!

X

The nature of allegorical reasoning further shewn by application of it to several particular instances cited from the Old Testament and urg'd in the New Testament

To compleat this account of the nature of mystical or allegorical reasoning, I shall conclude with showing, how my author applies some of the *Theses* laid down by him in his three first books to the prophesies cited above by me as not *literally*, but *mystically* fulfill'd.

I The first prophesy is contain'd in these words of MATTHEW, *all this was done, that it might be fulfill'd, which was spoken by the prophet, saying*, 'behold a virgin shall be with child, and shall bring forth a son, and they shall call his name IMMANUEL.'[a]

Mr SURENHUSIUS observes, that MATTHEW urges the quotation from the prophet, as *a confirmation of what is said*,[b] just before by the angel to JOSEPH.[c] *As if the angel had said*, 'what I have said to you concerning your wife MARY being with child by the Holy Ghost, ought not to appear so wonderful and unheard of a thing to you; for it was foretold of the Lord, by the prophet ISAIAH, that a virgin should be with child without the concurrence of a man, whose off-spring should be call'd IMMANUEL. This passage ought not to have been unknown to you, but since you did not know it, I refer you to it, and bid you carefully consider it, that you may more easily apprehend the unusual conception of your wife MARY, and take her home to you.' And he proves this to be the sense from *the form of quoting*. For he observes, that *the form of words* 'that it might be fulfill'd which was spoken,' *often signifies, according to the gemarick doctors*, 'that it might be confirm'd which is said.'[d] So that *the sense of the place is as if the evangelist had said*, 'By this means, by what has now happen'd in MARY, is confirm'd this place of ISAIAH, where it is foretold, that a virgin shall conceive without the concurrence of a man.' And he adds, that *the design of the evangelist was not to oppose the Jews, and prove to them, that JESUS was the true MESSIAS; but to shew to those, who did believe JESUS to be true MESSIAS, how the whole divine oeconomy of former times, having always the CHRIST, as it were, in view, had form'd all things to resemble him.*[e] Which *notion* my author supposes to have prevail'd always among the Jews, and makes to be the general key, whereby to understand all the Old Testament, and

[a] Matt. 1. 22, 23.   [b] *Surenhusius*, pp. 150, 151.   [c] Matt. 1. 20.
[d] Thesis 2 da de formulis allegandi.
[e] I Pet. 1. 20. II Cor. 10. 11. Gal. 4. Eph. 1.

especially this prophesy before us, which he explains at large by this key, as we shall see by and by.[a] So that the reader may observe how the *virgin's conception* in *Isaiah*, as apply'd by MATTHEW, relates to the virgin MARY in an allegorical sense, *viz.* as a *type*, like all the ceremonies of the *law*, and the passages of *history* in the Old Testament, which are all deem'd *types* of JESUS, as representing beforehand what he was to go through and ordain; and, in particular, like SARAH's *conception* in her old age of ISAAC, which by the ancients and moderns is made a type of the virgin MARY's conception of JESUS; like ABRAHAM offering up ISAAC, which was a type of CHRIST's being offer'd up on the cross; like ISAAC's carrying the wood on his shoulders, which was a *type* of CHRIST's carrying his cross; and like the lifting up of the brazen serpent in the wilderness, which was a *type of* CHRIST's being lifted up on the cross.[b] 12

* * *

II The second prophesy mentioned by me was, *Out of Egypt have I called my son; which* MATTHEW applies to JESUS's coming out of *Egypt*, and introduces with the same *form of quoting* used in the preceeding prophesy, *that it might be fulfilled which was spoken of the Lord by the prophet, saying.*[c]

1 First, Mr S says, that it appears by the form of quoting used, that the words of HOSEAH, which relate primarily to the children of *Israel's* being called out of *Egypt*, are *confirm'd* by JESUS's coming out of *Egypt*, that is, the coming of the children of *Israel* out of *Egypt* was a type or figure of JESUS's coming out of *Egypt*; and so the latter confirm'd the former.[d]

2 Secondly, he says, the jewish doctors are used to detach passages from their connection, and put a sense upon them, which has no relation to what goes before or follows after, as he shows in *Thesis 9. l. 1.*

3 Thirdly, the words of the prophet are, *when Israel was a child, then I loved him, and called my son out of Egypt.* By which my author thinks, that the prophet marks out the time of the coming of CHRIST, and may be thus understood. 'When the people of *Israel* were in their infancy as to light (which happen'd in the time of our Lord, when religion was wholly corrupted by false traditions) God called his son out of *Egypt* to preach the gospel in *Judea.*'[e] And *this answer*, he *thinks ought to satisfy the Jews, being suited to the manner of explaining scripture*

---

[a] *Surenhusius*, pp. 159, 160.
[b] Lesley's *Truth of Christ. demonst.* pp. 132, 133. Jenkin's *Remarks on* Whiston's *Sermons*, p. 54. Ibid. *Reasonableness of Christ. Rel.* vol. 1. p. 235.
[c] *Surenhusius*, pp. 182, 183.   [d] Ibid. and l. 1. Thes. 2.   [e] Ibid. 183, 184.

used by the old jewish doctors, whom MATTHEW *followed*. But if this last be not deem'd satisfactory, Mr *S* has another way of drawing out the *allegorical sense*, which he wants for his purpose, or would find out: and thus he interprets MATTHEW citing the prophet. 'You Jews know, that the prophet HOSEA says, *when Israel was a child, then I loved him, and called my son out of Egypt*; which words seem, according to their letter, to relate to the children of *Israel:* but I will explain them to you in a more useful manner, which is by you call'd *allegory*. I grant indeed, that the children of *Israel* may in a sense be call'd the son of God or of the Lord:[a] but if you can believe it, that very JESUS CHRIST, who was born among you at *Bethlehem*, he, I say, is properly the son of God, who almost in the same manner as the children of *Israel* were oblig'd to go into *Egypt* on account of the famine, was oblig'd to go thither to avoid the tyranny of HEROD. So that you may see, for the confirmation of your faith, that this did not befal the MESSIAS by chance, but by divine appointment, as it happen'd formerly to your fathers. Wherefore the prophet said, that the Lord *call'd his son out of Egypt*, and that at a time when you in respect of true religion were in a state of infancy. Besides the *form of quoting* used on this occasion, *that it might be fulfill'd which was spoken of the Lord by the prophet*, always refers to a mystical sense hid under the literal one.[b] But to say all in a word, the people of *Israel* were the first born adopted son of God, and JESUS was the natural son of God.'

III The third prophesy mentioned by me, as not literally fulfill'd, is contain'd in these words, *And he came and dwelt in a city call'd* Nazareth, *that it might be fulfill'd which was spoken by the prophet*, 'He shall be call'd a *Nazarene*.'[c] Which prophesy is found by SURENHU-SIUS in three places of the Old Testament, and very ingeniously explain'd by him; tho' it seems not to occur any where.[13]

[1] First, he observes, that the prophets not only foretold things by *types* and *allegories*, but by *enigmas*.[d] They foretold things by the former, when the things themselves were imply'd without any change of words; and they foretold by *enigmas* when the things were to be found out by a change of words: and when a prophesy of one or the other sort was accomplish'd, the jewish doctors used to say, *that it might be fulfill'd which was spoken*. This being so; ISAIAH having foretold, that the MESSIAS should dwell in *Galilee*,[e] it was almost the same thing as if he had said, the MESSIAS should dwell at *Nazareth*, which was a city of *Galilee*. It being thus foretold that the MESSIAS

[a] Exod. 4. 22. Jer. 31. 9.   [b] L. 3. Thes. 14.   [c] Matt. 2. 23.
[d] *Surenhusius*, p. 195–204.
[e] Isaiah, c. 9.

was to dwell at *Nazareth*, it is thereby imply'd that he should be intituled to, or call'd by the name *Nazarene:* for, tho' he was never call'd a *Nazarene*, yet being intituled to that name by dwelling at *Nazareth*, it was prophesy'd, *He shall be call'd a Nazarene;* to be call'd by a name being all one as to be intituled to a name. This enigmatical prophesy therefore of the MESSIAS's being to dwell in *Galilee*, rightly understood, was as much as to say, *He shall be call'd* (or be intituled to the name) *Nazarene;* which was fulfill'd by JESUS's dwelling at *Nazareth*.

[2] Secondly, he conceives MATTHEW alluded also to this passage of ISAIAH, *And there shall come forth a rod out of the stem of* JESSE, *and a branch* (Netser) *shall grow out of his roots.*[a] Where the argument lies in the word *Netser*; which is by the *hebrew* doctors call'd, *An argument drawn from the similitude of words, without regard had to the sense of the place*; the term *Netser*, approaching to, and therefore *enigmatically* signifying *Nazarene*. So that JESUS's dwelling at *Nazareth*, which intituled him to the name *Nazarene*, fulfill'd the prophesy, *He shall be called a Nazarene*, or Netser.

[3] Thirdly, he cites another text, wherein the MESSIAS is called *Tsemah*, that is to say, *a branch.*[b] Now the word TSEMAH having the same signification with *Netser*; *Netser* may be put in the room of *Tsemah*, whereby the prophet may be said to call the MESSIAS *Netser*, which is to call him *Nazarene*.

These texts of the Old Testament are some of those, which my author, after the jewish doctors, supposes reserv'd for explanation till the times of the MESSIAS; when the *engimas* contain'd in them were to be unridled, or the prophesies contain'd in them were to be shown to be fulfill'd.

*   *   *

Thus I hope, I have given such a state of the case from SURENHU-SIUS,[c] as may qualify the readers to judge of that *scheme* and its *rules*, which the apostles follow'd in arguing from the Old Testament, and to understand the force of the apostles arguments, which were grounded thereon. But if not; I refer them to the *Treatise* itself of SURENHUSIUS; wherein the most ingenious and learned author has set in the justest light the *rules* of reasoning used by the Jews, and follow'd by the apostles, and shown the pertinency of all the quotations made by the apostles from the Old Testament, according to those *rules*; and consequently has truly defended christianity, by showing how the apostles grounded it on the Old Testament,

---

[a] Isaiah 11. 1. See *Lightfoot's* works, vol. 1. p. 498.   [b] Zach. 6. 12.
[c] *See* Ockley's *Letter at the end of* Wotton's *Preface to Miscellaneous Discourses, etc.*

beyond what any author ever did before him. It is indeed possible, that in the application of the jewish *rules* of interpretation and reasoning, to the passages cited and urg'd by the apostles out of the Old Testament, he may not always have hit upon those peculiar *rules*, which the apostle had, in every citation, more particularly in view: for many of those *rules* will equally serve the same purpose; and therefore those, which he does not on some occasions make use of, may have been the *rules*, which the apostles had in view, as also those, which he does make use of, may not sometimes be the *rules*, which the apostles had immediately in view. But yet nothing can be plainer, from the reasonings of the apostles, and from the common way of reasoning used among the Jews, known both by their *practice* and *rules*, as they are both explain'd with the greatest clearness by SUREN-HUSIUS; than that, the apostles, who manifestly argu'd, not by scholastick rules, and interpreted not the passages they cited out of the Old Testament according to the obvious and literal sense they bore therein, did proceed by such *rules* as are set forth by him.[a]

The learned Mr *Ockley* in a letter written to and publish'd by Dr *Wotton*, says, *If* he *had an opportunity,* he *would certainly have gone thro' the books of the New Testament under a Jew. Whatsoever some of our gentlemen may think, this* he *is well assured of, that they understand it better then we do. They are thoroughly acquainted with all the forms of speech, and all the allusions, which (because they occur but rarely) are obscure to us, tho' in common and very familiar use among them; as has been admirably demonstrated by the learned* SURENHUSIUS,[b] *in his* Reconciliator.[14]

XI

An answer to an objection, *that the allegorical reasonings of the apostles were not design'd for absolute proofs of christianity, but for proofs* ad hominem, *to the Jews, who were accustomed to that way of reasoning*

IT may be objected, from divers learned authors, to what I have advanc'd, 'that christianity is not grounded on the prophetical or other quotations made from the Old in the New Testament; but that those quotations being allegorically apply'd by the authors of the New Testament, are only arguments *ad hominem*, to convince the Jews of the truth of christianity, who allowed such a method of arguing to be valid; and are not arguments to the rest of mankind.'

To which I answer;

[a] *Le Clerc.* Bibl. Chois. tom. 25. p. 413.
[b] Wotton's *Miscell. Discourses of the Scribes and Pharisees, etc. at the end of the preface.*

1 First, that this distinction is the pure invention of those who make the objection, and has not only no foundation in the New Testament, from whence only it should be taken; but is utterly subverted by it. For the authors of the books of the New Testament always argue absolutely from the quotations they make out of the books of the Old Testament. MOSES and the *prophets* are every where represented to be a just foundation for christianity. And PAUL expresly says, that *the gospel which was kept secret since the world began, was now made manifest by the scriptures of the prophets* (wherein that gospel was secretly contain'd) *to all nations,*[a] by the means of the preachers of the gospel, who gave the secret or spiritual sense of those *scriptures*. Besides, the authors of those books, being convinc'd long before the publication of them, that the gospel was to be preach'd to the Gentiles as well as Jews, must be suppos'd to design their books for the use of all men, for Gentiles as well as Jews. To both whom therefore they reason'd allegorically in those books; as particular apostles also did in their *sermons,*[b] therein recorded, with greater success on Gentiles than on Jews; and as PAUL did before FELIX, when he said, he took his christianity from *the law and the prophets*, as well as before AGRIPPA.[c] It should therefore seem strange, that *books* written to all the world by men equally concern'd to convert Gentiles as well as Jews, and *discourses* made expressly to *Gentiles* as well as to *Jews*, should be design'd to be pertinent only to Jews: much less to a very few Jews. For from the time the Jews began to allegorize their sacred books (which was long after the captivity) there was an opposition made to that method; and the *Sadducees* in particular, who were a numerous sect, oppos'd for a considerable time before and in our Saviour's time, the new explications, and profess'd to follow the pure text of scripture, or to interpret it according to the literal sense.[d] And tho' the *Pharisees*, who made up the body of the Jews, (as well as the *Essenes*)[15] used the allegorical method in the times of JESUS and the Apostles; yet they in great measure quitted that method, when christianity prevail'd, which was built on that method; and argu'd, as is well known, against the New Testament for allegorizing the *law and the prophets.*[e] And there has been for a long time, and is at this time as little use of allegory in those respects among them, as there seems to have been during the time the books

[a] Rom. 16. 25, 26,   [b] Acts 13. 15–48, and 26. 22, 23, and 10. 37–43.
[c] Ibid. 24. 14. Ibid. 26. v. 6. and 7. 22, 23.
[d] *Simon*. Hist. Crit. du Vieux Test. pp. 92, 97.
[e] Allix's *Judgement of the Church against the Unitarians*, c. 23. Simon. Ibid. p. 371. Ibid. Hist. Crit. du Nov. Test. p. 245. Mangey's *Remarks on* Toland's *Nazarenus*, p. 37. *Spencer* de Leg. Hebr. p. 185.

of the Old Testament were written, which *seem the most plain of all antient writings*; and wherein there appears not the least trace of a typical or allegorical intention in the authors, or in any other Jews of their times.[a] All the books written by Jews against the christian religion,[b] (some whereof are printed; and others go about *Europe* in manuscript) chiefly attack the N Testament for the allegorical interpretations of the Old Testament therein,[c] and that with the greatest insolence and contempt imaginable on that account, and oppose to them a literal and single interpretation as the true sense of the Old Testament. And accordingly the *allegorical interpretations* given by *christian expositors* of the prophecies, are now the *grand obstacle and stumbling-block in the way of the conversion of the Jews to christianity.*[d]

2 Secondly, there will be no ground for this distinction, if we consider how much *allegory* was in use among the pagans; being cultivated by many of the philosophers themselves as well as by theologers; by some as the method of delivering doctrines; but by most as the method of explaining away what, according to the letter, appear'd absurd in the antient fables or histories of their gods.[e]

Religion itself was deem'd a mysterious thing among the Pagans,[f] and not to be publickly and plainly declar'd. Wherefore it was never simply represented to the people, but was most obscurely deliver'd and vail'd under *allegories*, or *parables*, or *Hierogliphicks*; and especially among the *Egyptians, Chaldeans*, and the oriental nations.[g] *Si quis noverit perplexè loqui, loquatur: Sin minus taceat;*[16] was a maxim of the

---

[a] Jenkin's *Reas.* vol. 2. p. 153. *Le Clerc.* Bib. Univ. tom. 10. 234. Ibid. Bib. Cho. tom. 27. pp. 391, 392. *Cuneus* Rep. des Hebr. vol. 1. p. 377, 378, 395.

[b] *Scripta* Judæi in *Limborchii* Amica Collatione; and WAGENSELII *Tela Ignea Satanae, which is a collection of Jewish Books against Christianity, wherein* Rabbi Isaac's Munimen fidei *makes the chief figure.*

    Some of these are cited and answer'd by KIDDER *in his* Second *and* Third *Volumes of his* Demonstration of the Messias; *and others are cited by* BASNAGE *in his* Histoire de Juif. *But the most important seem to me to be three* Spanish *Manuscripts.* 1. Fortification de la fe; *which is a translation of the aforesaid* Munimen fidei, *publish'd by* WAGENSEIL. 2. Providentia Divina de Dios con Israel, *by* SAUL LEVI MORTERA. *This* MORTERA *was the Master of the famous* SPINOZA; *and this Work of his is esteem'd by the Jews to be the forewdest book they have against Christianity. They are forbid, under pain of excommunication, to lend it to any christian, for fear of drawing a storm upon themselves for producing such strong objections against the christian religion. Wherefore no Copies are to be procur'd of it but by the greatest accidents.* 3. Prevenciones Divinas contra la vana Ydolatria de las gentes, *by* ISAAC OROBIO, *who was that learned Jew, that had the famous Controversy with* LIMBORCH, *concerning the truth of the christian religion mentioned above. He had been Professor of Philosophy and Physick in the Universities of Alcala and Sevil, and was a great Master in School-Divinity after the mode of the Spanish Universities. The history he gave of himself, and especially of his sufferings in the Inquisition to Mr* LIMBORCH *and* LE CLERC, *is extremely curious.* LIMBORCH *Hist. Inquis.* pp. 158, 159, 223. LE CLERC, Bib. Univ. tom. 7. p. 289, etc.

[c] Allix's *Judgement of the Jewish Church against the Unitarians*, p. 423.

[d] Whiston's *Lectures*, p. 13. Mangey's *Remarks on* Toland's *Nazarenus*, p. 123.

[e] *Cicero* De Nat. Deor. ll. 2 and 3.

    Le Clerc Bibl. Chois. tom. 7. p. 80, etc. *Spencer* de legibus Hebr. p. 9.

[f] *Spencer* de legibus, p. 182, etc.   [g] *Simon* Hist. Crit. des Commentateurs, p. 4.

Jews, but equally thought right and true by the Pagans.[a] They allegoriz'd many things of nature, and particularly the heavenly bodies; whence came the saying, *tota est fabula cælum*.[17] They allegoriz'd all their antient fables and stories,[b] and pretended to discover in them the secrets of natural philosophy, medicine, politicks, and, in a word, all arts and sciences. The works of HOMER in particular have furnish'd infinite materials for all sorts of allegorical commentators to work upon; and there is an ancient book yet extant treating expressly of the *allegories of* HOMER,[c] written by the famous HERA-CLIDES of *Pontus*.[18]

The *antient greek poets were reputed to involve divine, and natural, and historical notions of their gods under mystical and parabolical expressions;*[d] and are accordingly so interpreted by the *greek scholiasts*.

The *Sybilline verses*, the *answers* given at *Oracles*, *sayings* deliver'd under *agitation*, and *dreams* (all which the antients call'd *divinations by fury*[e]) were seldom or ever plain, and usually receiv'd some allegorical interpretation by the skilful in divination; as did also the numerous *signs* and *prodigies*, which, in the course of things often happen'd.

The pythagorean philosophy was wholly deliver'd in mystical language; the signification whereof was intirely unknown to the world abroad, and but gradually explain'd to those of the sect, as they grew into years, or were proper to be inform'd. And in this PYTHAGORAS came up to SOLOMON's character of *wise men*, who dealt in *dark sayings*,[f] and acted not much unlike the most divine teacher that ever was. Our Saviour *spake with many parables the word unto the multitude, as they were able to hear it: but without a parable spake he not unto them: and when they were alone, he expounded all things to his disciples.*[g]

The *stoick* philosophers are particularly famous for *allegorizing* the whole heathen theology, and all the fables of the poets. And CICERO, in the person of BALBUS, the *stoick*,[h] gives us a curious specimen of their method in his *books* of the *nature of the gods*.

We have several treatises of heathen philosophers on the subject of allegorical interpretation;[i] from one of which, written by CORNUTUS the stoick, and from some other philosophers, *Platonists* and *Stoicks*, the famous ORIGEN is said to have deriv'd a great deal of his skill in

[a] Robinson's *Natural History of* Cumberland, etc. pt. 2 *Introd.* p. 9.
[b] *Clerici* Hist. Eccles. pp. 23, 24.
[c] Apud *Gale* Opuscula Mythologica.   [d] Dodwell's *Letters of Advice*, etc. p. 172.
[e] *Cicero* de Divinatione.
[f] Prov. 1. 6.   [g] Mark 4. 33, 34.   [h] *Cicero* De Nat. Deorum, l. 2.
[i] *Gale* Opuscula Mythologica, etc.

allegorizing the books of the Old Testament.*a* And ORIGEN thought the allegorical method not only just and true in itself, but *proper* to give *the Pagans a more exalted notion of the holy scriptures, which seem'd too low and mean to them,* and *useful to convert the learned of his time to the christian religion.*b* Nor was the great St AUSTIN less allegorical than ORIGEN in his interpretations of scripture;*c* in which method he greatly improv'd himself by studying platonick authors.

Many of the primitive fathers, and apologists for christianity, who for the most part wholly address themselves to Pagans, reason allegorically, not only from natural and artificial things (proving; that CHRIST was to suffer on the *cross,* from things made after the *fashion of a cross;*d* that there must be *four gospels*e* and no more, from the *four winds* and *four corners of the earth*; and that CHRIST was to have *twelve apostles,*f* because the *gospel* was to be preach'd in the *four* parts of the world, in the name of the *Trinity, three* times *four* making *twelve*; and because there were *twelve bells*g* which hung at the bottom of the jewish high priest's garment) but from the Old Testament exactly in the same manner with the apostles; which implies, that they look'd on *allegories* to be proper topicks for Pagans: and some of them had particular reason to do so from their own experience, who while they were philosophers themselves, and before they *became christians,*h* were accustom'd to it. It is also well known, that THEOPHILUS ANTIOCHENUS, CLEMENS of *Alexandria,*i* (who was the disciple of PANTÆNUS) and ORIGEN, as well as the *Gnosticks,* allegoriz'd in their explications and commentaries, the books of the New Testament; which commentaries may be justly suppos'd written for the use of Pagans as well as Jews and Christians, in order to give them all a more exalted notion of christianity, and of the New Testament.

In a word, *this method of writing in* matters of religion, (practis'd by *apostles, companions of the apostles,* and *most primitive fathers) was generally used, not only among the Jews, but among the wiser and more philosophical part of the Gentiles too: and from both came to be almost universally receiv'd among the primitive christians:* as says our most learned and judicious archbishop WAKE.*j* And our learned DODWELL says,*k* that *Oneirocriticks and Hieroglyphicks, and other*

---

a *Porphyrius* apud *Euseb.* Hist. Eccl. l. 6. c. 19.   *b* *Simon* Hist. Crit. du V. Test. p. 391.
c Ibid. p. 399.
d *Justin Martyr* and *Min. Felix.*   *e* *Irenæus.*   *f* St. *Austin.*
g *Justin Martyris* Opera, p. 260. *See also* MONTAGU Origines Ecclesiastica, *wherein there is a learned Dissertation upon the* Type TWELVE, p. 121. etc. pars posterior.
h Wake's *Prelim. to Genuine Epistles of St. Clement,* etc. p. 75.
i *Simon* Hist. des Comment. pp. 3, 4, 5, c. 1.
j *Wake,* Ibid. pp. 71–75. *See also* Lenfant. Preface Gen. sur son Nov. Test. p. 3.
k Dodwell's *Letters of Advice,* etc. p. 208.

Anthony Collins

Pagan mystical arts of concealment, are of *use* towards understanding the *prophetical books of the Old Testament* (the *whole indulgence of God in granting the spirit of prophesy[a]* to the Jews *being plainly accommodated to the heathen practise of divination*); and that *the revelations of the gospel[b]* being *made for the sake of all mankind,* its *reasonings* (which for the most part are allegorical) *were suited to the understanding of the generality of the people of that age* (and by consequence *to the people of future ages*) and in particular to that *of the philosophers,* who were the *leaders among the Gentiles.* Wherefore the arguments of the apostles were so far from being arguments *ad hominem* to the Jews, that they were then equally conclusive to great numbers among the Gentiles: and the *prophecies* cited from the Old in the New Testament; tho' *shining in a dark place,[c]* were a *light* both to Jews and Gentiles.

And I add, that almost all modern Religionists, whether Christians, Pagans, or Mahometans, are as fond of allegories, as the antients were. Which seems to make *allegorizing* the most suitable method of applying to the understanding of men. And therefore the allegorical arguments of the apostles were proper for all sorts of religious men, as well as Jews, and at present are more proper for others than Jews, (among whom there has been for a long time a direct anti-allegorical sect call'd *Caraites*) who, as they knew nothing of the allegorical method till long after the captivity, and when they became *Hellenis'd,[d]* so they rejected that method, as to all *prophesies* and other quotations taken from the Old Testament by the apostles, soon after the rise of christianity, and now contend for one single sense against any allegorical meaning of them, and argue against allegorical interpretations as absurd in themselves, no less than *atheists* and *deists,* and *Sadducees* (who, as is before observ'd, never receiv'd the allegorical interpretations of their Brethren-Jews[e]) or such (rational) Christians as Mr WHISTON: tho' herein the Jews seem to act a most inconsistent part; for unless they use the allegorical method, *they will not be able to establish their own belief of a MESSIAS to come, which yet is one of the fundamental articles of their religion.[f]* That article, in the judgment of the famous Rabbi ALBO,[g] has no other foundation than the authority of tradition. *For,* says he, *there is not any prophesy, either in the law, or the prophets, that foretels his coming by any necessary exposition of it, with respect to him, or which may not from the circumstances of the text be well explain'd otherwise.* In a word, a

---

[a] Ibid. p. 113. [b] Dodwelli Prolegomena ad Stearn de Obstinatione. [c] II Pet. 1. 19.
[d] *Clerici* Hist. Eccles. p. 24. [e]*Simon* Bib. Crit. vol. 4. p. 508.
[f] *Simon* Hist. Crit. du Nov. Test. pp. 246, 247.
[g] *Albo* Oratio 1. c. 1. apud *Allix*'s Judgment of the Jewish Church against the Unitarians, p. 411.

44

learned author maintains, 'that the books of the Old Testament are of little use for the conversion of the Jews. For almost all which is said to be spoken in the Old Testament of the MESSIAS must be interpreted mystically, before it can appear to be spoken of him, and by consequence very remotely from what the words do naturally signify'.[a]

[a] *Smalcius* apud Ibid. p. 414.

2. Thomas Sherlock, 'Discourses on the Use and Intent of Prophecy' (1726), Discourses II and III

Within a month or two of the publication of Collins's book about prophecy, Thomas Sherlock was replying to it in a series of sermons in the Temple Church, of which he was Master. He was famous as a preacher, cogent rather than eloquent, and a man well seasoned in the management of rows and debates. He had helped the authorities of the University of Cambridge in their efforts to control Bentley. He had led the Lower House of the Church's Convocation in withstanding an attack on the Test and Corporation Acts by Bishop Hoadley of Bangor, carrying on with pamphlets when Convocation was prorogued by the nervous Whig Ministry. This exchange came to be known as 'The Bangorian Controversy'. As an Orthodox and Tory Churchman, Sherlock had Collins in his sights for some time. In 1714, as Vice Chancellor of Cambridge and momentarily on good terms with Bentley (as much as anyone could expect there) he had stage-managed the University's vote of thanks to him for his *Remarks Upon a Late Discourse of Free Thinking*: Bentley's rejoinder to a previous, and as notorious, book by Collins. Bentley went for Collins's scholarship and soon had it in shreds. Sherlock, himself embattled against Collins eleven years later and on the question of prophecy, thought strategically rather than accumulating tactical successes like Bentley. He went for the general issues and explored their human interest.

The result is a minor masterpiece of Tory theology. It succeeds as a reply to Collins, not by taking direct issue with him, but by restoring dramatic religious value to prophecy as a major feature of the Bible which Collins had been happy to leave looking silly. It is Tory in its motivation; defending the normative against clever subversion, the privileged against profanation. It is Tory also in its emphasis on the fallenness of mankind, the doctrine by which conservative Christians both plumb tragic depths and evade sharp issues. The theological corollary of this limitation of human claims is 'the belief of God's supreme dominion, which is the foundation of all religion'. Sherlock's thought is strung between these two poles of strong theism and flawed humanity. They are connected to one another, not by philosophy but by prophecy. Prophecy is not meant to satisfy or employ the curiosity of the inquisitive. God has intended it for a serious and practical use: it gives fallen humanity just enough insight into divine purpose to forestall despair. It is a matter of hope. Sherlock's fundamental mode is not theoretical system but narrative. The two sermons printed here are the first stages in his grand tour of the biblical history. He sees the world in the old frame of providential ordering of history. Just as the Bible makes prophecy and fulfilment the

46

shaping rhythm of history, so does he. He is of one mind with the Old Testament's Deuteronomic historians and with the New Testament writers on the question of how history works. He is not alienated from it like Collins.

Yet this ancient scheme had to be made convincing to the eighteenth century: to the lawyers to whom Sherlock preached and to a wider public. This meant that theism and theology were not enough. There had to be humanism, or at least humanity in a qualitative sense, and there had to be empirical reason. Sherlock's humanity is most evident in his sense of the calamity and failure endemic to humanity and the cold comfort which reason and natural religion bring to it – 'their hopes must flow from another spring'. The old providential scheme of history is given contemporary religious value by virtue of its encounter with the sad depths which Deists skated over. Sherlock dwells on the fall of Adam. He handles it with the sense of drama which St Paul brought to it, and with the same forensic metaphors (apt to his legal congregation):

suppose a man, after all equitable allowances made, to be condemned under and by the law of nature, and living in daily expectation of execution. I ask, what sort of religion would you advise him to in the mean time. – Natural religion? To what purpose? – He has had his trial and condemnation by that law already, and has nothing to learn from it but the misery of his condition.
(p. 58 following)

But if the fall brings out the best in Sherlock – court-room drama, sense of the tragic and practical humanity – it also gets him into difficulty as an empirical reasoner. Collins's levity at this point had been inept, but he made it difficult to take the story literally. While Sherlock does not want to take it entirely literally, because he recognises the practical and historical necessity of its parabolic dress, he does insist that it happened because rational hope (his implicit theme) must be grounded in history. He is not happy in the borderlands of myth. His argument creaks and wobbles. He is too practical and compassionate to be amused like Collins. And too modern to be at ease. He is more successful in the next stage of his argument, showing that from the human point of view (God himself knew better) the Christian character and fulfilment of ancient Jewish prophecies is retrospectively apprehended. Only when and after Christ had come was it possible. This bars the way to apocalyptic know-alls and indicates Sherlock's continual summons to the reader to look at the long view and the whole sweep. And once again it shows his fundamentally historical mentality, operating on the threshold between old theistic and modern atheistic historiography.

Discourse II

LET us proceed to consider the character which St Peter gives of prophecy, and the degree of evidence which we may reasonably expect from it. 'Prophecy is a light shining in a dark place, and we do well to give heed to it until the day dawn.'[1] St Peter's meaning is this: 'the time will come when the things ye hope for shall be placed in a clear light, when you shall see all your expectations fully justified in the accomplishment; in the meanwhile ye do well to attend to prophecy, though but a small glimmering light, and shining at a distance in a dark place, yet the best you have, or can have at present.' Metaphorical expressions and similitudes ought not to be rigidly and strictly canvassed; it is sufficient to see the general import and meaning of them; which in the present case is very clear, and amounts to this, that the knowledge God gives us of things future by the means of prophecy is but an imperfect obscure knowledge, nothing to be compared to the clear knowledge that will attend on the manifestation of the things themselves.[2]

I shall endeavor to confirm this proposition by the authority of Scripture, and to suggest some observations which may be of use when we are called on to judge of the nature of prophecy, and the evidence arising from it.

Whether prophecy be a clear evidence before the completion or no, is no matter of controversy; so far from it, that they who tell us prophecy is the best argument even for Christianity, do not yet think it a clear one.[3] But without regard to any man's opinion, it will be proper to see what notion the inspired writers themselves had of the word of prophecy.

If we look into the first Epistle of St Peter, we shall find that the ancient prophecies, of which he speaks in the text,[4] and which he styles the 'more sure word of prophecy,' were not apprehended or clearly understood by those inspired persons who delivered them; for there he represents them 'searching what or what manner of time the Spirit of Christ which was in them did signify, when it testified beforehand the sufferings of Christ, and the glory that should follow:' I. II. To the same purpose our Saviour speaks, Matt. 13. 17. 'Many prophets and righteous men have desired to see those things which ye see, and have not seen them; and to hear those things which ye hear, and have not heard them.' St Paul gives the like account of the gift of prophecy under the gospel dispensation: 'We know in part, and we prophecy in part; but when that which is perfect is come, then that which is in part shall be done away. Now we see through a glass darkly; but then face to face: now I know in part, but then shall I know even as also I am known:' I Cor. 13. 9, 10, 12. Now if the prophets and righteous men of old, to whom the word of God came, did not clearly understand the things which they foretold, but employed themselves in searching and examining the prophetical testimonies of the Spirit which was in them; if the prophets of the New Testament knew only in part, and prophesied only in part, seeing but darkly as through a glass; it is most evident that others, in all appearance less qualified than they to understand the determinate sense of the prophecies, could have but a confused and indistinct notion of the things foretold.

The prophet Daniel, after a very extraordinary vision, which he reports in his last chapter, immediately adds, 'I heard, but I understood not: then said I, O my Lord, what shall be the end of these things? And he said, Go thy way, Daniel; for the words are closed up and sealed till the time of the end.' The answer here given to Daniel is very like the answer which our Saviour gave the Apostles, on a like inquiry made by them: they ask, 'Lord, wilt thou at this time restore again the kingdom to Israel? And he said unto them, It is not for you to know the times or seasons which the Father hath put in his own power:' Acts 1. 6, 7. It did belong to them undoubtedly and to every believing Jew, 'to give heed to the word of prophecy' according to St Peter's exhortation in the text; and since it did not belong to them to know the times and seasons, it is evident the word of prophecy was not intended to give a clear and distinct light in this case.

These last passages relate to such prophecies especially as seem to design the times and seasons of God's working; and these predictions being oftentimes delayed in the accomplishment much beyond the expectation of those to whom they were delivered, it brought the prophets and their predictions frequently into contempt, and gave the people occasion to harden themselves against the fears and apprehensions of the evils threatened. Hence came the reproach on the prophets taken notice of by Ezekiel: 'The vision that he seeth is for many days to come; and he prophesieth of the times that are far off:' 12. 27. which speech grew up into a proverb: 'What is that proverb that ye have in the land of Israel, saying, The days are prolonged, and every vision faileth?' ver. 22. The case is very much the same in regard to other prophecies. Whoever looks into the prophetical writings will find that they are generally penned in a very exalted style, full of bold figures describing the judgment or the mercies of God; representing spiritual blessings under the images of temporal prosperity, and oftentimes such images as cannot possibly admit of a literal interpretation. In which case, though we may see the general intent and meaning, and find sufficient ground for hope and fear from the scope of the prophecy, yet we can with no certainty fix the precise and determinate manner in which the words are to be fulfilled.

Prophecy is, by the author of prophecy, thus described: 'I have multiplied visions, and used similitudes, by the ministry of the prophets:' Hosea 12. 10. Which similitudes are elsewhere spoken of as 'dark speeches' delivered to the prophets in visions and in dreams: Numb. 12. 6, 8. For this reason the Jews, when they spoke with contempt of their prophets, were used to say, 'Doth he not speak parables?' Ezek. 20. 49. Our Saviour seems to speak of the ancient prophecies under the same character: 'Know ye not,' says he to his disciples, 'this parable? and how then will ye know all parables?' Mark 4. 13. That is, if ye understand not this plain parable, of the sower, how will ye understand all the ancient prophecies[5] relating to the gospel, which are much harder parables?

These passages are sufficient to prove that prophecy was never intended to be a very distinct evidence; and to show St Peter's meaning in comparing the word of prophecy to a light shining in a dark place, and in making this evidence so much inferior to the evidence we are to receive, when the fulness of time comes for the manifestation of God's promises.

But allowing this to be the case of prophecy at the time of delivery, are we not however to expect to find the prophecy clear and distinct, and exactly corresponding to the event, whenever the event comes into existence? and consequently, is it not absurd, after an event is come to pass, to apply any ancient prophecies to it, that do not manifestly, to the eyes of common sense, appear to belong to it? These questions being admitted, another will be asked: how comes it to pass that many of the prophecies, applied by the writers of the gospel to our Saviour and his actions, are still dark and obscure; and so far from belonging evidently to him and him only, that it requires much learning and sagacity to show even now the connexion between some prophecies and the events?

In answer to these questions, we must observe that the obscurity of prophecy does not arise from hence, that it is a relation or description of something future; for it is as easy to speak of things future plainly and intelligibly, as it is of things past or present. The same language serves in both cases with little variation. He who says the river will overflow its banks next year, speaks as plainly as he who says it did overflow its banks last year. It is not therefore of the nature of prophecy to be obscure, for it may easily be made, when he who gives it thinks fit, as plain as history.

On the other side, a figurative and dark description of a future event will be figurative and dark still when the event happens, and consequently will have all the obscurity of a figurative dark description as well after as before the event. The prophet Isaiah describes the peace of Christ's kingdom in the following manner: 'The wolf shall dwell with the lamb, and the leopard shall lie down with the kid, and the calf, and the young lion, and the fatling together, and a little child shall lead them:' II. 6. Nobody, I suppose, (some modern Jews excepted,) ever understood this literally; nor can it now be literally applied to the state of the gospel. It was and is capable of different interpretations: it may mean temporal peace, and that either public of kingdoms and nations, or private among the professors of the gospel: it may prefigure an internal and spiritual peace, the tranquillity of mind which sets a man at peace with God, himself, and the world. But whatever the true meaning is, this prophecy, expounded by the rules of language only, does no more obtrude one determinate sense on the mind since the coming of Christ, than it did before. But then we say, the state of the gospel was very properly prefigured in this description, and is as properly prefigured by an hundred more of the like kind; and since they all agree in a fair application to the state of the gospel, we strongly conclude that the gospel state was the thing foretold under these and many other like expressions. So that the argument from prophecy for the truth of the gospel does not rest on this, that the event has necessarily limited and ascertained the particular sense and meaning of every prophecy; but in this, that every prophecy has in a proper sense been completed by the coming of Christ. It is absurd therefore to expect clear and evident conviction from every single prophecy applied to Christ; the evidence must arise from a view and comparison of all together.

Prophecies are not all of one kind, or of equal clearness: the most literal prophecies relating to Christ were not always at the time of the delivery the plainest; for many of these relating to the most surprising and wonderful events under the gospel, wanted not the veil or cover of figurative language; for being plainly foretold, they could hardly, for the seeming incredibility of the things themselves, be received and admitted in their true literal meaning. 'A virgin shall conceive a son' was a proposition which seemed to want some other interpretation than a literal one, which was inconsistent with all experience of the world; and therefore probably this prophecy was not understood by the ancient Jews, as importing a miraculous conception. The event has not made this prophecy clearer than it was before; the language of it was as well understood in the prophet's time as now; but common sense led every man to understand it in a

Thomas Sherlock

sense agreeable to nature and experience: but the event has showed us that the plain literal sense, however inconsistent with the experience of nature, is the true sense. In like manner the prophecies from which the resurrection of Christ is inferred, were obscure and dark, from a seeming inconsistency between the several parts of them. It is foretold that Christ should be 'despised and rejected of men,' a man of sorrow and affliction; that his affliction should pursue him even to the grave; and it is also foretold that, notwithstanding these sufferings and a wretched death, he should 'prolong his days,' and have an everlasting kingdom, and see the work of the Lord prosper in his hands. These prophecies are not at all plainer now than they were in the beginning; but the plain sense appeared at that time loaded with contradictions: here was one born to misery and affliction, and yet he was the heir of an everlasting kingdom: he was condemned, executed, laid in the grave, and after all this he was to prolong his days, and see the work of the Lord prosper in his hands. The resurrection of Christ reconciled all these difficulties and seeming inconsistencies; and we now readily admit these prophecies in their plain literal sense; which was a very plain sense before, though a very hard one to be imagined or believed.

You may observe then, that the most literal prophecies have received the greatest confirmation and the most light from the event. For the difficulty in this case not lying in the darkness or obscurity of the expression, but in the seeming impossibility of the thing foretold, such seeming impossibility the event fully cleared; but no event can make a figurative or metaphorical expression to be a plain or a literal one, or restrain the language of any prophecy to one determinate sense only, which was originally capable of many.

I have said thus much to show what sort of clearness and evidence we ought to expect from prophecies after their accomplishment. It is a great prejudice against this argument when men come to it expecting more from it than it will yield. This they are led to by hearing it often said that prophecy, however dark and obscure at first, grows wonderfully plain on the accomplishment; which in some cases, as I have shown, is in fact true, but is not, cannot be so in all cases.

You may think it perhaps strange that I should be here pleading, as it were, for the obscurity of ancient prophecies; whereas you may very well conceive it would be more to the purpose of a Christian divine to maintain their clearness. Now as Moses in another case said, 'I would to God all the Lord's people were prophets;' so say I in this case, I would to God all the prophecies of the Lord were manifest to all his people. But it matters little what we wish for or think best; we must be content with such light and direction as God has thought proper to bestow on us; and to inquire why the ancient prophecies are not clearer, is like inquiring why God has not given us more reason, or made us as wise as angels: he has given us in both cases so much light as he thought proper, and enough to serve the ends he intended.

It is doubtless a mistake to conceive prophecy to be intended solely or chiefly for their sakes in whose time the events predicted are to happen. What great occasion is there to lay in so long beforehand the evidences of prophecy to convince men of things that are to happen in their own times; the truth of which they may if they please learn from their own senses? How low an idea does it give of the administration of Providence, in sending prophets one after another in every age from Adam to Christ, to imagine that all this apparatus was for their sakes who lived in and after the times of Christ, with little regard to the ages to whom the prophecies were delivered? As I think the prophecies of the New Testament are chiefly for our sake, 'who live by faith and not by sight;' so I imagine the ancient prophecies had the like use, and were chiefly intended to support the faith and religion of the old world. Had it been otherwise, a set of prophecies given some few years before the birth of Christ, would have served our purpose as well as a series of prophecies given from the very beginning, and running through every age.

Let us then consider the use of prophecy, and this will help us to conceive the degree of clearness which ought to attend it. Some people are apt to talk as if they thought the truth of some facts recorded in the gospel depended on the clearness of the prophecies relating to them. They speak, for instance, as if they imagined the certainty and reality of our Saviour's resurrection were much concerned in the clearness of the prophecies relating to that great and wonderful event; and seem to think that they are confuting the belief of his resurrection, when they are trying to confound the prophecies relating to it. But can any thing be more absurd? For what ground or pretence is there to inquire whether the prophecies, foreshowing that the Messiah should die and rise again, do truly belong to Jesus, unless we are first satisfied that Jesus died and rose again? We must be in possession of the fact before we can form any argument from prophecy; and therefore the truth of the resurrection, considered as a fact, is quite independent of the evidence or authority of prophecy.

The part which unbelievers ought to take in this question, should be to show from the prophets that Jesus was necessarily to rise from the dead, and then to prove that in fact Jesus never did rise: here would be a plain consequence. But if they do not like this method, they ought to let the prophecies alone; for if Jesus did not rise, there is no harm done if the prophets have not foretold it; and if they allow the resurrection of Jesus, what do they gain by discrediting the prophecies? The event will be what it is, let the prophecies be what they will.

There are many prophecies in the Old Testament relating to the Babylonish captivity, and very distinct they are, describing the ruin of the holy city, the destruction of the Temple, the carrying the tribes into a distant country, and the continuance of the captivity for seventy years. Can you suppose these prophecies intended to convince the people of the reality of these events when they should happen? Was there any danger they should imagine themselves safe in their own country, when they were captives at Babylon, unless they had the evidence of prophecy for their captivity? or, that they should think their temple standing in all its glory, when it was ruined before their eyes? If the supposition be absurd in this case, it is so in every case; for the argument from prophecy is in all instances the same. It is plain then that matters related in the gospel do not depend for their reality on the evidence of prophecy; they may be true though never foretold, or very obscurely foretold; nay, they must be admitted as true before we can so much as inquire whether any prophecy belongs to them.

But if this be the case, that we must admit all the facts of the gospel to be true before we can come at the evidence of prophecy, what occasion have we, you will say, to inquire after prophecy at all? Are not the many miracles of Christ, his resurrection from the dead, his ascension to heaven, the pouring forth the gifts of the Spirit on the Apostles, their speaking with tongues, and doing many wonders in the name of Christ, sufficient evidence to us of the truth of the gospel, without troubling ourselves to know whether these things were foretold, or in what manner they were foretold? To answer this question plainly, I think such facts, once admitted to be true, are a complete evidence of the divine authority of a revelation; and had we known no more of Christ than that he claimed to be attended to as a person sent and commissioned by God, he needed no other credentials than these already mentioned; and it would have been impertinent to demand what prophet foretold his coming. For in a like case, who foretold the coming of Moses to be a lawgiver to Israel? God had promised Abraham to give his posterity the land of Canaan; but that he would give it by Moses he had not promised; that he would talk with him 'face to face,' and deliver his law to him, and by him to the people, he had not foretold: the authority therefore of Moses as a divine lawgiver stands on the miraculous works performed by him, and the wonderful attestations given to him by the presence of God in the mount in the eyes of all the people; but on prophecy it does not stand, for of him there were no prophecies. This shows that prophecy is not an evidence essential to the proof of a divine revelation; for it may be spared in one as well as another.

But the case of the gospel differs from that of the law; for though the law was not prophesied of, the gospel was: he who delivered the law was one of the first who prophesied of the gospel, and told the people so long beforehand, 'that God would raise a prophet like unto him, whom they must hear in all things:' by which prediction he guarded the people against the prejudice which his own authority was like to create against a new lawgiver; telling them beforehand that when the great prophet came, their obedience ought to be transferred to him. The succeeding prophets speak more fully of the office, character, sufferings, and glory of the Saviour of Israel, and the desire of all nations. Now one of the characters which our Saviour constantly assumes and claims in the gospel is this, that he is the person spoken of by Moses and the prophets. Whether he is this person or no must be tried by the words of prophecy; and this makes the argument from prophecy so far necessary to establish the claim of the gospel; and it has been very justly as well as acutely observed, that the proof of this point must rely intirely on the evidence of prophecy. Miracles in this case can afford no help; if the prophets have not spoken of Christ, all the miracles in the world will not prove that they have spoken of him.[6]

These considerations show how far the gospel is necessarily concerned in prophetical evidence. Christ has done the works which no man ever did, and given the fullest evidence of a divine commission; but he claims to be the person foretold in the law and the prophets; and as truth must ever be consistent with itself, this claim must be true, or it destroys all others. This is the point then to be tried on the evidence of prophecy: is Christ that person described and foretold under the Old Testament or no? Whether all the prophecies relating to him be plain or not plain; whether all the ways used by the Jews of arguing from the Old Testament, be convincing to us or no, it matters little: the single question is, is there enough plain to show us that Christ is the person foretold under the Old Testament? If there is, we are at an end of our inquiry, and want no farther help from prophecy; especially since we, to use St Peter's expression, have, in this case, 'seen the day dawn, and enjoyed the marvellous light of the gospel of God.'

I am not now speaking of the great advantage that may be made of prophetical evidence for convincing unbelievers of the truth of the gospel, but am considering how far the truth of the gospel necessarily depends on this kind of evidence. These are two very different inquiries. It is necessary for us to show that Christ is the person promised to be a Saviour to Israel; and when we have shown this, no opposer of the gospel has more to demand. But we may carry our inquiries much farther; we may contemplate all the steps of Providence relating to the salvation and redemption of mankind in the several ages of the world, and by a comparison of all the parts, may discern that Christ was indeed the end of the law, and of all promises made to the fathers: that all the deliverances given by God to his people were but shadows, and as it were an earnest of the great deliverance he intended to give by his Son: that all the ceremonials of the law were representations of the substance of the gospel: that the Aaronical sacrifices and priesthood were figures of better things to come. But these inquiries do not stand in the rank of things to be necessarily proved to every believer; they do not enter into the 'principles of the doctrine of Christ,' as the Apostle to the Hebrews expressly tells us; but belong to those 'who go on to perfection;' which distinction given by the Apostle in the fifth and sixth chapters to the Hebrews,[7] is well worth considering, as being a key to open the true use of all typical and allegorical applications of Scripture.

Discourse III

IT is necessary to take this matter higher, to look back to the rise and progress of divine prophecy, and to observe what ends the wisdom of God intended to serve by means of it. It is no commendation of prophecy to say that it is very dark and obscure; nor yet can it be a reproach, provided it answers all the ends designed by Providence. To enable ourselves therefore to judge of prophecy, we must inquire to what end prophecy was given; and this is the subject I now propose to your consideration.

It will not be said, because it cannot be maintained, that we have any right to the knowledge of things future. God is not obliged either in wisdom or goodness, and much less in justice, to declare to us the things which shall be hereafter. In regard therefore to the knowledge of futurity, whether it be little or much, or nothing, that God thinks fit to communicate to us, we can have no reason to complain; for having no right, we can pretend no injury. Since therefore we have no demand on God for this sort of knowledge in any degree whatever, it is evident that, whenever we have it, we must ascribe our having it to some special reasons of Providence; which reasons alone can limit the degree of light and knowledge which ought to attend on the word of prophecy. For if we have from prophecy so much light as fully answers the end of giving the prophecy, I would fain know on what reason we can form a complaint for want of more? I mean this, to show how absurd it is for men to take counsel of their curiosity, when they consider the use and weight of prophecy; in this view they will find nothing to satisfy them: they may go on for ever asking why are we not told more, or more distinctly? Which questions we may promise to answer whenever they inform us on what right they demand to be told any thing; which if they cannot do, all such complaints must be laid aside; and we must come to the only proper and material consideration, what end did the wisdom of God propose to serve by the ancient prophecies, and how has this end been served by them?

'By prophecy I understand all the declarations which God has made concerning the future state of mankind in this world or in the next; consequently all the hopes and expectations which are grounded on God's promises, and do not result from reason and natural knowledge, I refer to prophecy as their original.' If there be any other kind of prophecy not comprehended in this description, there may be, perhaps, before we take leave of this subject, a proper place to consider it; but at present I shall confine myself within the limits of this description.

It cannot be supposed that God has delivered prophecies only to satisfy or employ the curiosity of the inquisitive; or that he gave his Spirit to men merely to enable them to give forth predictions for the amusement and entertainment of the world; there must be some end intended worthy of the Author.[8] What end can you conceive worthy of God but the promotion of virtue and religion, and the general peace and happiness of mankind? These things belong to him, as creator and governor of the world; these things are his province.

It is true, you will say, these things do belong indeed to God; but what has prophecy to do with these things? God can govern the world without letting us into his secrets; and as for virtue and religion and our own happiness, he has given us a plain law to walk by, the result of that reason and knowledge with which he has endowed us. Prophecy can never contradict or overrule the light of reason and nature; nor can we suppose that we came so imperfect and unfinished out of the hands of our Creator, as not to have light enough to see our own duty, and to pursue our natural happiness, but to want at every turn an admonisher at our elbow.

Let us allow the original state of nature to be as perfect and complete as you desire.

But what if the case should be altered? how will matters stand then? It is no unreasonable supposition this; for since man was created a moral agent, with freedom of will, it was possible for him to fall; and consequently, possibly he may have fallen. Let us suppose for the present this to be the case; and tell us now, from natural religion, what must such sinners do? Repent, you will say; for it is agreeable to the goodness of God to accept repentance, and to restore offenders to his favor. Very well; but how often will this remedy serve? May sin and repentance go on for ever in a perpetual round? To allow this differs nothing from allowing a liberty and impunity to sin without repentance. If God is governor and judge of the world, there must be a time for judgment; and men may, after all reasonable and equitable allowances made, be ripe for judgment. Let this be the case then: suppose a man, after all equitable allowances made, to be condemned under and by the law of nature, and living in daily expectation of execution: I ask, what sort of religion you would advise him to in the mean time. – Natural religion? – To what purpose? – He has had his trial and condemnation by that law already, and has nothing to learn from it but the misery of his condition. I do not mean that the sense of natural religion will be lost in such a man. He may see, perhaps more clearly than ever he did, the difference between good and evil, the beauty of moral virtue, and feel the obligations which a rational creature is under to his Maker; but what fruit will all this knowledge yield? what certain hope or comfort will it administer? A man with a rope about his neck may see the equity and excellency of the law by which he dies; and if he does, he must see that the excellency of it is to protect the virtuous and innocent: but what is this excellency to him, who has forfeited the protection of all law? If you would recommend natural religion, exclusive of all other assistance, it is not enough to show from principles of reason the excellency and reasonableness of moral virtue, or to prove from the nature of God that he must delight in and reward virtue: you must go one step farther, and prove from the nature of man too, that he is excellently qualified to obey this law, and cannot well fail of attaining all the happiness under it that ever nature designed for him. If you stop short at this consideration, what do you gain? What imports it that the law is good, if the subjects are so bad, that either they will not or cannot obey it? When you prove to sinners the excellency of natural religion, you only show them how justly they may expect to be punished for their iniquity: a sad truth, which wants no confirmation! All the possible hope left in such a case is, that God may freely pardon and restore them; but whether he will or no the offenders can never certainly learn from natural religion.[9]

Should God think fit to be reconciled to sinners, natural religion would again become the rule of their future trial and obedience: but their hopes must flow from another spring; their confidence in God must and can arise only from the promise of God; that is, from the word of prophecy; for which reason prophecy must for ever be an essential part of such a sinner's religion.

This reasoning agrees exactly with the ancientest and most authentic account we have of the beginning of prophecy in the world. When God had finished all his works, and man, the chief of them, he viewed them all, and behold they were very good. How long this goodness lasted we know not; that it did not last very long is certain. During the time of man's innocence there were frequent communications between God and him,[10] but not the least hint of any word of prophecy delivered to him. The hopes of nature were then alive and vigorous, and man had before him the prospect of all that happiness to which he was created, to encourage and support his obedience. In this state natural religion wanted no other assistance, and therefore it had no other.

But when the case was altered by the transgression of our first parents; when natural religion had no longer any sure hopes or comforts in reserve, but left them to the fearful expectation of judgment near at hand; when God came down to judge the offenders, and yet with intention finally to rescue and preserve them from the ruin brought on themselves; then came in the word of prophecy, not in opposition to natural religion, but in support of it, and to convey new hopes to man, since his own were irrecoverably lost and extinguished in the fall.

The prophecy then given being the first, and indeed (as I conceive) the groundwork and foundation of all that have been since, it well deserves our particular consideration.

It may be expected perhaps that the way should be cleared to this inquiry, by removing first the difficulties which arise from the historical narration of the fall; and could any thing material be added in support of what is commonly said on this subject, the time and pains would be well placed: but the more and the oftener this case is considered in all its circumstances, the more will the commonly received interpretation prevail; which is evidently the true ancient interpretation of the Jewish church, as appears by the allusions to the history of the fall, to be met with in the books of the Old Testament.

To some unbelievers, if I mistake not their principles, the history of the fall would have been altogether as incredible, though perhaps not quite so diverting, had it been told in the simplest and plainest language.[11]

It is to little purpose therefore to trouble them with an account of the genius of the eastern people and their language; for you may as soon persuade them that a serpent tempted Eve as that any evil spirit did. If you ask why the Devil might not as well speak to Eve under the form of a serpent, as give out oracles to the old heathen world under that and many other forms, you gain nothing by the question: for oracles, whether heathen or Jewish, are to them alike; they dispute not their authority, but their reality. This is a degree of unbelief which has no right to be admitted to debate the question now under consideration.

As to others who are not infidels with regard to religion in general, yet are shocked with the circumstances of this history; I desire them to consider that the speculations arising from the history of the fall, and the introduction of natural and moral evil into the world, are of all others the most abstruse and farthest removed out of our reach; that this difficulty led men in the earliest time to imagine two independent principles of good and evil;[12] a notion destructive of the sovereignty of God, the maintenance of which is the principal end and design of the Mosaic history. Had the history of man's fall plainly introduced an invisible evil being to confound the works of God, and to be the author of iniquity, it might have given great countenance to this error of two principles; or, to prevent it, Moses must have written a history of the angels' fall likewise; a point, I suppose, to which his commission did not extend, and of which perhaps we are not capable judges: and since this difficulty might in a great measure be avoided, by having recourse to the common usage of the eastern countries, which was, to clothe history in parables and similitudes, it seems not improbable that for this reason the history of the fall was put into the dress in which we now find it.

The serpent was remarkable for an insidious cunning, and therefore stood as a proper emblem of a deceiver; and yet, being one of the lowest of the creatures, the emblem gave no suspicion of any power concerned that might pretend to rival the Creator.

This method has not so obscured this history, but that we may with great certainty come to the knowledge of all that is necessary for us to know. Let us consider the history of Moses, as we should do any other ancient eastern history of like antiquity: suppose, for instance, that this account of the fall had been preserved to us out of Sanchoniatho's Phœnician history,[13] we should in that case be at a loss perhaps to account for every manner of representation, for every figure and expression in the story; but we should soon agree that all these difficulties were imputable to the manner and customs of his age and country, and should show more respect to so venerable a piece of antiquity than to charge it with want of sense, because we did not understand every minute circumstance. We should likewise agree that there were evidently four persons concerned in the story; the man, the woman, the person represented by the serpent, and God. Disagree we could not about their several parts. The serpent is evidently the tempter; the man and woman the offenders; God the judge of all three. The punishments inflicted on the man and woman have no obscurity in them; and as to the serpent's sentence, we should think it reasonable to give it such a sense as the whole series of the story requires.

It is no unreasonable thing surely to demand the same equity of you in interpreting the sense of Moses, as you would certainly use towards any other ancient writer. And if the same equity be allowed, this plain fact undeniably arises from the history – that man was tempted to disobedience and did disobey, and forfeited all title to happiness and to life itself; that God judged him, and the deceiver likewise under the form of a serpent. We require no more, and will proceed on this fact to consider the prophecy before us.

The prophecy is part of the sentence passed on the deceiver; the words are these: 'I will put enmity between thee and the woman, and between thy seed and her seed: it shall bruise thy head, and thou shalt bruise his heel:' Gen. 3. 15. Christian writers apply this to our blessed Saviour, emphatically styled here 'the seed of the woman,' and who came in the fulness of time to 'bruise the serpent's head,' by destroying the works of the Devil, and restoring those to the liberty of the sons of God who were held under the bondage and captivity of sin. You will say, what unreasonable liberty of interpretation is this? Tell us by what rules of language the seed of the woman is made to denote one particular person, and by what art you discover the mystery of Christ's miraculous conception and birth in this common expression? Tell us, likewise, how bruising the serpent's head comes to signify the destroying the power of sin, and the redemption of mankind by Christ? It is no wonder to hear such questions from those who look no farther than to the third chapter of Genesis, to see the ground of the Christian application. As the prophecy stands there, nothing appears to point out this particular meaning; much less to confine the prophecy to it. But of this hereafter. Let us for the present lay aside all our own notions, and go back to that state and condition of things, which was at the time of the delivery of this prophecy; and see (if haply we may discover it) what God intended to discover at that time by this prophecy, and what we may reasonably suppose our first parents understood it to mean.

They were now in a state of sin, standing before God to receive sentence for their disobedience, and had reason to expect a full execution of the penalty threatened: 'in the day thou eatest thereof, thou shall surely die.' But God came in mercy as well as judgment, purposing not only to punish, but to restore man. The judgment is awful and severe; the woman is doomed to sorrow in conception; the man to sorrow and travel all the days of his life; the ground is cursed for his sake; and the end of the judgment is, 'dust thou art, and unto dust thou shalt return.' Had they been left thus, they might have continued in their labor and sorrow for their appointed time, and at last returned to dust without any well-grounded hope or confidence in God: they must have looked on themselves as rejected by their Maker, delivered up to trouble and sorrow in this world, and as having no hope in any other. On this foot, I conceive, there could have been no religion left in the world; for a sense of religion without hope is a state of frenzy and distraction, void of all inducements to love and obedience, or anything else that is praiseworthy. If therefore God intended to preserve them as objects of mercy, it was absolutely necessary to communicate so much hope to them as might be a rational foundation for their future endeavors to reconcile themselves to him by a better obedience. This seems to be the primary intention of this first divine prophecy; and it was necessary to the state of the world, and the condition of religion, which could not possibly have been supported without the communication of such hopes. The prophecy is excellently adapted to this purpose, and manifestly conveyed such hopes to our first parents. For let us consider in what sense we may suppose them to understand this prophecy. Now they must necessarily understand the prophecy, either according to the literal meaning of the words, or according to such meaning as the whole circumstance of the transaction, of which they are a part, does require. If we suppose them to understand the words literally, and that God meant them so to be understood, this passage must appear ridiculous. Do but imagine that you see God coming to judge the offenders; Adam and Eve before him in the utmost distress; that you hear God inflicting pains and sorrows and misery and death on the first of human race; and that in the midst of all this scene of woe and great calamity, you hear God foretelling, with great solemnity, a very trivial accident that should sometimes happen in the world: that serpents would be apt to bite men by the heels, and that men would be apt to revenge themselves by striking them on the head. What has this trifle to do with the loss of mankind, with the corruption of the natural and moral world, and the ruin of all the glory and happiness of the creation? Great comfort it was to Adam, doubtless, after telling him that his days should be short and full of misery, and his end without hope, to let him know that he should now and then knock a snake on the head, but not even that without paying dear for his poor victory, for the snake should often bite him by the heel. Adam surely could not understand the prophecy in this sense, though some of his sons have so understood it; a plain indication how much more some men are concerned to maintain a literal interpretation of Scripture than they are to make it speak common sense. Leaving this therefore as absolutely absurd and ridiculous, let us consider what meaning the circumstances of the transaction do necessarily fix to the words of this prophecy. Adam tempted by his wife, and she by the serpent, had fallen from their obedience, and were now in the presence of God expecting judgment. They knew full well at this juncture that their fall was the victory of the serpent, whom by experience they found to be an enemy to God and to man; to man, whom he had ruined by seducing him to sin; to God, the noblest work of whose creation he had defaced. It could not therefore but be some comfort to them to hear the serpent first condemned, and to see that, however he had prevailed against them, he had gained no victory over their Maker, who was able to assert his own honor and to punish this great author of iniquity. By this method of God's proceeding they were secured from thinking that there was any evil being equal to the Creator in power and dominion; an opinion which gained ground in aftertimes through prevalence of evil, and is, where it does prevail, destructive of all true religion. The condemnation therefore of the serpent was the maintenance of God's supremacy; and that it was so understood, we have, if I mistake not, a very ancient testimony in the book of Job: 'With God is strength and wisdom; the deceived and the deceiver are his;' that is, equally subjected to his command: Job 12. 16. The belief of God's supreme dominion, which is the foundation of all religion, being thus preserved, it was still necessary to give them such hopes as might make them capable of religion toward God. These hopes they could not but conceive, when they heard from the mouth of God that the serpent's victory was not a complete victory over even themselves; that they and their posterity should be enabled to contest his empire; and though they were to suffer much in the struggle, yet finally they should prevail and bruise the serpent's head, and deliver themselves from his power and dominion over them. What now could they conceive this conquest over the serpent to mean? Is it not natural to expect that we shall recover that by victory, which we lost by being defeated? They knew that the enemy had subdued them by sin; could they then conceive hopes of victory otherwise than by righteousness? They lost through sin the happiness of their creation; could they expect less from the return of righteousness than the recovery of the blessings forfeited? What else but this could they expect? For the certain knowledge they had of their loss when the serpent prevailed, could not but lead them to a clear knowledge of what they should regain by prevailing against the serpent. The language of this prophecy is indeed in part metaphorical, but it is a great mistake to think that all metaphors are of uncertain signification; for the design and scope of the speaker, with the circumstances attending, create a fixed and determinate sense. Were it otherwise, there would be no certainty in any language; all languages, the eastern more especially, abounding in metaphors.

Let us now look back to our subject, and see what application we are to make of this instance.

This prophecy was to our first parents but very obscure; it was, in the phrase of St Peter, but a light shining in a dark place: all that they could certainly conclude from it was, that their case was not desperate; that some remedy, that some deliverance from the evil they were under, would in time appear; but when, or where, or by what means, they could not understand: their own sentence, which returned them back again to the dust of the earth, made it difficult to apprehend what this victory over the serpent should signify, or how they who were shortly to be dust and ashes, should be the better for it. But after all that can be urged on this head to set out the obscurity of this promise, I would ask one question: was not this promise or prophecy, though surrounded with all this obscurity, a foundation for religion, and trust and confidence towards God after the fall, in hopes of deliverance from the evils introduced by disobedience? If it was, it fully answered the necessity of their case to whom it was given, and manifested to them all that God intended to make manifest. They could have had towards God no religion without some hopes of mercy: it was necessary therefore to convey such hopes; but to tell them how these hopes should be accomplished, at what time and manner precisely, was not necessary to their religion. And what now is to be objected against this prophecy? It is very obscure you say; so it is: but it is obscure in the points which God did not intend to explain at that time, and which were not necessary to be known. You see a plain reason for giving this prophecy, and as far as the reason for giving the prophecy extends, so far the prophecy is very plain: it is obscure only where there is no reason why it should be plain; which surely is a fault easily to be forgiven, and very far from being a proper subject for complaint.

But if this prophecy conveyed to our first parents only a general hope and expectation of pardon and restoration, and was intended by God to convey no more to them; how come we, their posterity, to find so much more in this promise than we suppose them to find? How is it that we pretend to discover Christ in this prophecy, to see in it the mystery of his birth, his sufferings, and his final triumph over all the powers of darkness? By what new light do we discern all these secrets? by what art do we unfold them?

It is no wonder to me that such as come to the examination of the prophecies applied to Christ expecting to find in each of them some express character and mark of Christ, plainly to be understood as such antecedently to his coming, should ask these or many other the like questions, or that the argument from ancient prophecy should appear so slight and trivial to those who know no better use of it.

'Known unto God are all his works from the beginning;' and whatever degree of light he thought fit to communicate to our first parents or to their children in after times, there is no doubt but that he had a perfect knowledge at all times of all the methods by which he intended to rescue and restore mankind: and therefore all the notices given by him to mankind of his intended salvation must correspond to the great event, whenever the fulness of time shall make it manifest. No reason can be given why God should at all times, or at any time, clearly open the secrets of his providence to men; it depends merely on his good pleasure to do it in what time and in what manner he thinks proper. But there is a necessary reason to be given why all such notices as God thinks fit to give should answer exactly in due time to the completion of the great design. It is absurd therefore to complain of the ancient prophecies for being obscure, for it is challenging God for not telling us more of his secrets. But if we pretend that God has at length manifested to us by the revelation of the gospel the method of his salvation, it is necessary for us to show that all the notices of his salvation given to the old world, do correspond to the things which we have heard and seen with our eyes. The argument from prophecy therefore is not to be formed in this manner: All the ancient prophecies have expressly pointed out and characterised Christ Jesus; but it must be formed in this manner: All the notices which God gave to the fathers of his intended salvation are perfectly answered by the coming of Christ. He never promised or engaged his word in any particular relating to the common salvation, but what he has fully made good by sending his Son to our redemption. Let us try these methods on the prophecy before us. If you demand that we should show you, *a priori*, Christ Jesus set forth in this prophecy, and that God had limited himself by this promise to convey the blessing intended by sending his own Son in the flesh, and by no other means whatever; you demand what I cannot show, nor do I know who can. But if you inquire whether this prophecy, in the obvious and most natural meaning of it, in that sense in which our first parents and their children after might easily understand it, has been verified by the coming of Christ; I conceive it may be made as clear as the sun at noon-day, that all the expectations raised by this prophecy have been completely answered by the redemption wrought by Christ Jesus. And what have you to desire more than to see a prophecy fulfilled exactly? If you insist that the prophecy should have been more express, you must demand of God why he gave you no more light; but you ought at least to suspend this demand till you have a reason to show for it.

I know that this prophecy is urged farther, and that Christian writers argue from the expression of it, to show that Christ is therein particularly foretold: he properly is the 'seed of a woman' in a sense in which no other ever was; his sufferings were well prefigured by 'the bruising of the heel;' his complete victory over sin and death by 'bruising the serpent's head.' When unbelievers hear such reasonings, they think themselves intitled to laugh; but their scorn be to themselves. We readily allow that the expressions do not imply necessarily this sense; we allow farther that there is no appearance that our first parents understood them in this sense, or that God intended they should so understand them: but since this prophecy has been plainly fulfilled in Christ, and by the event appropriated to him only, I would fain know how it comes to be conceived to be so ridiculous a thing in us to suppose that God, to whom the whole event was known from the beginning,[a] should make choice of such expressions as naturally

---

[a] 'Remember the former things of old, for I am God, and there is none else; I am God, and there is none like me: declaring the end from the beginning, and from ancient times the things that are

conveyed so much knowledge as he intended to convey to our first parents, and yet should appear in the fulness of time to have been peculiarly adapted to the event which he from the beginning saw, and which he intended the world should one day see; and which when they should see, they might the more easily acknowledge to be the work of his hand, by the secret evidence which he had inclosed from the days of old in the words of prophecy. However the wit of man may despise this method, yet is there nothing in it unbecoming the wisdom of God. And when we see this to be the case not only in this instance, but in many other prophecies of the Old Testament, it is not without reason we conclude that under the obscurity of ancient prophecy there was an evidence of God's truth kept in reserve, to be made manifest in due time.

As this prophecy is the first, so it is the only considerable one in which we have any concern from the creation to the days of Noah. What has been discoursed therefore on this occasion may be understood as an account of the first period of prophecy. Under this period the light of prophecy was proportioned to the wants and necessities of the world, and sufficient to maintain religion after the fall of man, by affording sufficient grounds for trust and confidence in God; without which grounds, which could then no otherways be had but by promise from God, religion could not have been supported in the world. This prophecy was the grand charter of God's mercy after the fall. Nature had no certain help for sinners liable to condemnation; her right was lost with her innocence. It was necessary therefore either to destroy the offenders, or to save them by raising them to a capacity of salvation, by giving them such hopes as might enable them to exercise a reasonable religion. So far the light of prophecy extended. By what means God intended to work his salvation he did not expressly declare; and who has a right to complain that he did not, or to prescribe to him rules in dispensing his mercy to the children of men? This prophecy we, on whom the latter days are come, have seen fully verified; more fully than those to whom it was delivered could perhaps conceive. View this prophecy then with respect to those to whom it was given, it answered their want and the immediate end proposed by God; view it with respect to ourselves, and it answers ours; and shall we still complain of its obscurity?

The bringing in of prophecy was not the only change in the state of religion occasioned by the fall. Sacrifice came in at the same time, as

not yet done; saying, My counsel shall stand, and I will do all my pleasure:' Isa. 46. 9, 10.
'The works of the Lord are done in judgment from the beginning: and from the time he made them, he disposed the parts thereof:' Ecclus 16. 26.

appears by the course of the history;[14] and it is hardly possible it should come in, especially at the time it did, any otherwise than on the authority of divine institution. It is the first act of religion mentioned in the sacred story to be accepted by God, which implies strongly that it was of his own appointment; for we can hardly suppose that such a mark of distinction would have been set on a mere human invention. In later times, when the account of things grows clearer, sacrifice appears to be appointed by God as an expiation for sin; and we have no reason to imagine that it was turned aside from its original use. There is indeed no express declaration of the use of sacrifice in religion at its first appearance, and yet something there seems to be in the account that may give light in this matter. We read that 'Cain brought an offering of the fruit of the ground, and Abel of the firstlings of his flock, and the fat thereof: the Lord had respect unto Abel and to his offering; but unto Cain and to his offering he had not respect.' Allowing the maxim of the Jewish church to have been good from the first institution of sacrifice, 'that without blood there is no remission,'[15] the case may possibly be this: Abel came a petitioner for grace and pardon, and brought the atonement appointed for sin; Cain appears before God as a just person wanting no repentance; he brings an offering in acknowledgement of God's goodness and bounty, but no atonement in acknowledgement of his own wretchedness. The expostulation of God with Cain favors this account: 'If thou dost well, shalt thou not be accepted? And if thou dost not well, sin lieth at thy door:' that is, if thou art righteous, thy righteousness shall save thee: if thou art not, by what expiation is thy sin purged? It lieth still at thy door. Add to this, that the Apostle to the Hebrews says, 'that Abel's sacrifice was rendered excellent by faith:'[16] what could this faith be, but a reliance on the promises and appointments of God? which faith Cain wanted, relying on his well-doing.

If you admit this interpretation, it plainly shows that the true religion instituted by God has been one and the same from the fall of Adam, subsisting ever on the same principles of faith; at first on only general and obscure hopes, which were gradually opened and unfolded in every age till the better days came, when God thought good to call us into the 'marvellous light of his gospel.'[17]

This piece of history is all the account we have of the religion of the antediluvian world. It was proper to be considered for the relation there is between prophecy and the state of religion in the world; and for this reason also, because sacrifice may perhaps be found to be one kind of prophecy or representation of the one great sacrifice once offered for the sins of the world.

3. Robert Lowth, 'Lectures on the Sacred Poetry of the Hebrews' (1753, translated from Latin into English by Richard Gregory in 1787), Lectures IV (extracted), V (less first and last paragraphs), XIV, XVII (less the first two paragraphs and the second half of the lecture, viz. pp. 377–387 of the 1787 edition), XIX

Hoadley, Sherlock's sparring partner in the Bangorian controversy, became Bishop of Winchester and patron of the young Robert Lowth. He set him up in the living of Overton before he was made Professor of Poetry at Oxford, and when he resigned his chair after ten years he made him Archdeacon of Winchester. Lowth had made his poetic debut while a scholar at Winchester College. Both men were Whigs, Lowth further enjoying the patronage of the great Whig family of Cavendish, accompanying the young Marquis of Hartington on the Grand Tour. His Christianity was appropriately enlightened and allied to the cause of liberty. In a sermon of 1758 he gave his version of Church history. Christianity 'was published to the world in the most enlightened age', and had emerged from centuries of repressive superstition

when letters revived, and reason regained her liberty; when a spirit of inquiry began to prevail ... Christianity immediately emerged out of darkness, and was in a manner republished to the world in its native simplicity. It has always flourished or decayed together with learning and liberty: it will ever stand or fall with them. It is therefore of the utmost importance to the cause of true religion, that it be submitted to an open and impartial examination; that every disquisition concerning it be allowed its full course.

Robert Lowth (jr) *Memoirs of the Life and Writings of the Late Right Reverend Robert Lowth*, London, 1787, p. 14 (n.)

'Native simplicity' in religion, brought to light by learned and free literary criticism, is the theme of these famous and splendid lectures. Given in

Oxford between 1741 and 1750, they were published in the Latin in which they were delivered in 1753. Michaelis brought out a German edition at Göttingen. In 1787 they were translated into English by George Gregory, a literary autodidact and former theatrical director. Gregory's translation is used here, shorn of the accumulation of footnotes by Michaelis, Kennicott and others which Gregory added. Those notes are rich evidence of the interest aroused by the lectures in England and Germany. Michaelis and Herder's enthusiasm for them got them into the mainstream of developing Old Testament criticism, and into German literary culture at large: *via* Herder they even influenced Goethe. But without those notes the reader is nearer to the original lecture form.

In the preface of his translation Gregory announced that the lectures 'are more calculated for persons of taste and general reading, than for what is commonly termed the learned world' because they contained few 'nice philological disquisitions and no abstruse metaphysical speculations' (p. vii). Gregory was right about Lowth's accessibility and his sustained preference for historical actuality rather than dogmatic speculation – which is spectacularly absent. Its place is taken by a deep and searching interest in the expression of human passion (his son says that Lowth was moody and short-tempered). But there was, in fact, plenty here for 'the learned world', as we have noticed already: above all Lecture XIX 'The Prophetic Poetry is Sententious', in which Lowth's discoveries of Hebrew versification, made tentatively and gradually in the course of the preceding lectures, are set out in detail and in their historical matrix. As well as having been taken into the structure of succeeding Old Testament criticism, they have altered the appearance of bibles. Lowth broke up the previously continuous text of psalms and prophetic oracles into the short lines of parallelism. Modern bibles (Revised Standard Version, Jerusalem, New English etc.) have followed his lead.

This form of poetry appealed to Christopher Smart and William Blake. Smart admired Lowth's work for 'its elegance, novelty, variety, spirit and (I had almost said) divinity' (*Universal Visiter*, Jan./Feb. 1756). Blake, in his introduction to *Jerusalem*, abandoned the 'monotonous cadence' of English blank verse for 'a variety in every line, both of cadence and of number of syllables'. And the debt went deeper than form. Lowth's vivid sense of history gave the poets the possibility of being biblical psalmists and prophets themselves, by setting Hebrew poetry on an emotional base which romantics could share. In his first lecture he had proclaimed poetry as the primal literature of humanity, more energetic than philosophy's 'cold precepts' or history's 'dull and spiritless examples'. Historical and religious/moral primacy coincide. In Lecture V he promises a return to Hebrew antiquity's 'inmost sentiments, the manner and connection of their thoughts'. And in an eloquent passage on Plato's mirror he celebrates, in Berkeleyan vein, the mind's creative powers. When he deals with the sublime in Lectures XIV and XVII he emphasises the expression of passion 'bursting from the glowing bosom with matchless force and impetuosity' in poetry which 'reveals the vivid irregularities' of the heart. We have got, by history, to the crucible of romanticism. When we hear this clerical academic saying that 'the passions and affections are the elements and principles of action; they are all in themselves good, useful and virtuous' we realise that in one generation enlightened Christianity has come a long way from Collins and is nearer to Blake. Hannah More's praise of 'illustrious Lowth' as a modern Elisha in *Sensibility, a Poetical Epistle* (1772) is apt:

> He seized his mantle as the prophet flew
> And caught some portion of his Spirit too.

The elegant, but slightly pedantic, translations of biblical texts are Lowth's own and not from the King James Bible.

Lecture IV
The Origin, Use, and Characteristics of the Parabolic, and also of the Sententious Style

The poetic style of the Hebrews bears the general title of *Parabolic* – Its constituent principles are the sententious, the figurative, and the sublime – The source of the Parabolic style and its original use: among other nations; among the Hebrews – Certain examples of it preserved from the first ages in the writings of Moses – *1* The sententious kind; its nature and effects.

*   *   *

The origin and first use of poetical language are undoubtedly to be traced into the vehement affections of the mind. For what is meant by that singular frenzy of poets, which the Greeks, ascribing to divine inspiration, distinguished by the appellation of *enthusiasm*, but a style and expression directly prompted by nature itself, and exhibiting the true and express image of a mind violently agitated? When, as it were, the secret avenues, the interior recesses of the soul are thrown open; when the inmost conceptions are displayed, rushing together in one turbid stream, without order or connexion. Hence sudden exclamations, frequent interrogations, apostrophes even to inanimate objects: for to those, who are violently agitated themselves, the universal nature of things seems under a necessity of being affected with similar emotions. Every impulse of the mind, however, has not only a peculiar style and expression, but a certain tone of voice, and a certain gesture of the body adapted to it. Some, indeed, not satisfied with that expression which language affords, have added to it dancing and song; and as we know there existed in the first ages a very strict connexion between these arts and that of poetry, we may possibly be indebted to them for the accurately admeasured verses and feet, to the end that the modulation of the language might accord with the music of the voice, and the motion of the body.

Poetry, in this its rude origin and commencement, being derived from nature, was in time improved by art, and applied to the purposes of utility and delight. For as it owed its birth to the affections of the mind, and had availed itself of the assistance of harmony, it was found, on account of the exact and vivid delineation of the objects which it described, to be excellently adapted to the exciting of every internal emotion, and making a more forcible impression upon the mind than abstract reasoning could possibly effect; it was found capable of interesting and affecting the senses and passions, of captivating the ear, of directing the perception to the minutest circumstances, and of assisting the memory in the retention of them. Whatever therefore deserved to be generally known and accurately remembered, was (by those men, who on this very account were denominated *wise* (Ecclesiasticus 44. 4)) adorned with a jocund and captivating style, illuminated with the varied and splendid colouring of language, and moulded into sentences comprehensive, pointed, and harmonious. It became the peculiar province of poetry to depict the great, the beautiful, the becoming, the virtuous; to embellish and recommend the precepts of religion and virtue, to transmit to posterity excellent and sublime actions and sayings; to celebrate the works of the Deity, his beneficence, his wisdom; to record the memorials of the past, and the predictions of the future. In each of these departments Poetry was of singular utility, since before any characters expressive of sounds were invented, at least before they were commonly received, and applied to general use, it seems to have afforded the only means of preserving the rude science of the early times; and in this respect, to have rendered the want of letters more tolerable: it seems also to have acted the part of a public herald, by whose voice each memorable transaction of antiquity was proclaimed and transmitted through different ages and nations.

*   *   *

[Omission of a heavily annotated paragraph on the primacy of poetry 'among heathen nations'. Ed.]

Thus all science human and divine was deposited in the treasury of the Muses, and thither it was necessary on every occasion to resort. The only mode of instruction, indeed, adapted to human nature in an uncivilized state, when the knowledge of letters was very little, if at all diffused, must be that which is calculated to captivate the ear and the passions, which assists the memory, which is not to be delivered into the hand, but infused into the mind and heart.

That the case was the same among the Hebrews; that poetry was both anciently and generally known and practised by them, appears highly probable, as well from the analogy of things, as from some vestiges of poetic language extant in the writings of Moses. The first instance occurs in one of the most remote periods of the Mosaic history, I mean the address of Lamech to his wives, which is indeed but ill understood in general, because the occasion of it is very obscurely intimated: nevertheless, if we consider the apt construction of the words, the exact distribution of the period into three distichs,[1] and the two parallel, and as it were corresponding, sentiments in each distich; I apprehend it will easily be acknowledged an indubitable specimen of the poetry of the first ages:

> Hadah and Sillah hear my voice;
> Ye wives of Lamech hearken to my speech;
> For I have slain a man, because of my wounding;
> A young man, because of my hurt.
> If Cain shall be avenged seven times,
> Certainly Lamech seventy and seven.   (Genesis 4. 23, 24)

Another example, which I shall point out to you, appears no less to bear the genuine marks of poetry than the former, and that is the execration of Noah upon Ham; with the magnificent predictions of prosperity to his two brothers, to Shem in particular, and the ardent breathings of his soul for their future happiness: these are expressed in three equal divisions of verses, concluding with an indignant repetition of one of the preceding lines:

> Cursed be Canaan!
> A servant of servants to his brothers let him be!
> Blessed be Jehovah the God of Shem!
> And let Canaan be their servant!
> May God extend Japheth,
> And may he dwell in the tents of Shem!
> And let Canaan be their servant.   (Genesis 9. 25–27)

The inspired benedictions of the patriarchs Isaac (Genesis 27. 27–40) and Jacob are altogether of the same kind: and the great importance of these prophecies, not only to the destiny of the people of Israel, but to that of the whole human race, renders it highly probable that they were extant in this form before the time of Moses; and that they were afterwards committed to writing by the inspired historian, exactly as he had received them from his ancestors, without presuming to bestow on these sacred oracles any adventitious ornaments or poetical colouring.

The matter will appear yet clearer, if we advert to some other verses, a little different in kind, to which the same historian appeals (as well known and popular) in testimony of the truth of his narration. Thus, when he relates the first incursion of the Israelites into the country of the Amorites, in order to mark more precisely the boundaries of that state, and to explain more satisfactorily the nature of the victories not long before atchieved over the Moabites, he cites two fragments of poems; the one from the book of the Wars of Jehovah (Numbers 21. 14, 15), the other from the Sayings (*Mashalim*) of those who spoke in parables (Numbers 21. 27–30); that is, as appears from the nature of things, from some panegyrical or triumphal poem of the Amorites. To which we may add, what immediately follow, the prophecies of Balaam the Mesopotamian, pronounced also in the parabolic style, as appears from the extreme neatness of the composition, the metrical and parallel sentences, the sublimity of the language and sentiment, and the uncommon elegance of the verse. Hence it is easy to collect, that this kind of poetry, which appears perfectly analogous to all the rest of the Hebrew poetry that still remains, was neither originally the production of Moses, nor peculiar to the Jewish nation, but that it may be accounted among the first-fruits of human ingenuity, and was cultivated by the Hebrews and other Eastern nations from the first ages, as the recorder of events, the preceptor of morals, the historian of the past, and prophet of the future.

Concerning the utility of poetry, therefore, the Hebrews have maintained the same opinion throughout all ages. This being always accounted the highest commendation of science and erudition; 'To understand a proverb and the interpretation; the words of the wise and their dark sayings' (Proverbs 1. 6) under which titles two species of poetry seem to be particularly indicated, different indeed in many respects, yet agreeing in some. The one I call *didactic*, which expresses some moral precept in elegant and pointed verses, often illustrated by a comparison either direct or implied; similar to the *gnomai* and adages of the wise men: the other was truly poetical, adorned with all the more splendid colouring of language, magnificently sublime in the sentiments, animated by the most pathetic expression, and diversified and embellished by figurative diction and poetical imagery; such are almost all the remaining productions of the Prophets.

Brevity or conciseness was a characteristic of each of these forms of composition, and a degree of obscurity was not unfrequently attendant upon this studied brevity. Each consisted of metrical sentences; on which account chiefly the poetic and proverbial language seem to have obtained the same appellation: and in these two kinds of composition all knowledge human and divine was thought to be comprized.

The sententious[2] style, therefore, I define to be the primary characteristic of the Hebrew poetry, as being the most conspicuous and comprehensive of all. For although that style seems naturally adapted only to the didactic, yet it is found to pervade the whole of the poetry of the Hebrews. There are indeed many passages in the sacred writings highly figurative, and infinitely sublime; but all of them manifestly assume a sententious form. There are some too, and those not inelegant, which possess little more of the characteristics of poetry than the versification, and that terseness or adaptation of the sentences, which constitutes so important a part even of the harmony of verse. This is manifest in most of the didactic psalms, as well as in some others, the matter, order, diction, and thoughts of which are clearly historical; but the conformation of the sentences wholly poetical. There is indeed so strict an analogy between the structure of the sentences and the versification, that when the former chances to be confused or obscured, it is scarcely possible to form a conjecture concerning the division of the lines or verses; which is almost the only part of the Hebrew versification that remains. It was therefore necessary, before I could explain the mechanism of the Hebrew verse, to remark many particulars, which properly belong to the present topic.

The reason of this (not to detain you with what is obvious in almost every page of the sacred poetry) is as follows. The Hebrew poets frequently express a sentiment with the utmost brevity and simplicity, illustrated by no circumstances, adorned with no epithets (which in truth they seldom use); they afterwards call in the aid of ornament; they repeat, they vary, they amplify the same sentiment; and adding one or more sentences which run parallel to each other, they express the same or a similar, and often a contrary sentiment in nearly the same form of words. Of these three modes of ornament at least they make the most frequent use, namely, the amplification of the same ideas, the accumulation of others, and the opposition or antithesis of such as are contrary to each other; they dispose the corresponding sentences in regular distichs adapted to each other, and of an equal length, in which, for the most part, things answer to things, and words to words, as the Son of Sirach says of the works of

God, *two and two, one against the other.*[3] These forms again are diversified by notes of admiration, comparison, negation, and more particularly interrogation, whence a singular degree of force and elevation is frequently added to the composition.

Each language possesses a peculiar genius and character, on which depend the principles of the versification, and in a great measure the style or colour of the poetic diction. In Hebrew the frequent or rather perpetual splendour of the sentences, and the accurate recurrence of the clauses, seem absolutely necessary to distinguish the verse: so that what in any other language would appear a superfluous and tiresome repetition, in this cannot be omitted without injury to the poetry. This excellence therefore the sententious style possesses in the Hebrew poetry, that it necessarily prevents a prosaic mode of expression, and always reduces a composition to a kind of metrical form. For, as Cicero remarks, 'in certain forms of expression there exists such a degree of conciseness, that a sort of metrical arrangement follows of course. For when words or sentences directly correspond, or when contraries are opposed exactly to each other, or even when words of a similar sound run parallel, the composition will in general have a metrical cadence' (*Orator*). It possesses, however, great force in other respects, and produces several great and remarkable beauties of composition. For, as the sacred poems derive from this source a great part of their elegance, harmony, and splendour, so they are not unfrequently indebted to it for their sublimity and strength. Frequent and laconic sentences render the composition remarkably concise, harmonious, and animated; the brevity itself imparts to it additional strength, and being contracted within a narrower space, it has a more energetic and pointed effect.

Examples sufficient to evince the truth of these remarks will occur hereafter in the passages which will be quoted in illustration of other parts of our subject: and, in all probability, on a future occasion the nature of my undertaking will require a more ample discussion of this subject (see Lecture XIX).

Lecture V
Of the Figurative Style, and its Divisions

2 The Figurative Style; to be treated rather according to the genius of the Hebrew poetry than according to the forms and arrangements of Rhetoricians – The definition and constituent parts of the Figurative Style, META-

PHOR, ALLEGORY, COMPARISON, PERSONIFICATION – The reason of this mode of treating the subject: difficulties in reading the Hebrew poetry, which result from the Figurative Style; how to be avoided. 1 Of the META-PHOR, including a general disquisition concerning poetic imagery: the nature of which is explained; and four principal sources pointed out: Nature, Common Life, Religion, History.

* * *

It is the peculiar design of the figurative style, taken in the sense in which I have explained it, to exhibit objects in a clearer or more striking, in a sublimer or more forcible manner. Since, therefore, whatever is employed with a view to the illustration and elevation of another subject, ought itself to be as familiar and obvious, at the same time as grand and magnificent as possible, it becomes necessary to adduce images from those objects, with which both the writers and the persons they address are well acquainted, and which have been constantly esteemed of the highest dignity and importance. On the other hand, if the reader be accustomed to habits of life totally different from those of the author, and be conversant only with different objects; in that case many descriptions and sentiments, which were clearly illustrated and magnificently expressed by the one, will appear to the other mean and obscure, harsh and unnatural; and this will be the case more or less, in proportion as they differ or are more remote from each other in time, situation, customs sacred or profane, in fine, in all the forms of public and private life. On this account difficulties must occur in the perusal of almost every work of literature, and particularly in poetry, where every thing is depicted and illustrated with the greatest variety and abundance of imagery; they must be still more numerous in such of the poets as are foreign and ancient; in the Orientals above all foreigners, they being the farthest removed from our customs and manners; and of all the Orientals more especially in the Hebrews, theirs being confessedly the most ancient compositions extant. To all who apply themselves to the study of their poetry, for the reasons which I have enumerated, difficulties and inconveniencies must necessarily occur. Not only the antiquity of these writings forms a principal obstruction in many respects; but the manner of living, of speaking, of thinking, which prevailed in those times, will be found altogether different from our customs and habits. There is therefore great danger, lest viewing them from an improper situation, and rashly estimating all things by our own standard, we form an erroneous judgment.

Of this kind of mistake we are to be always aware, and these inconveniencies are to be counteracted by all possible diligence: nor is it enough to be acquainted with the language of this people, their manners, discipline, rites and ceremonies; we must even investigate their inmost sentiments, the manner and connexion of their thoughts; in one word, we must see all things with their eyes, estimate all things by their opinions: we must endeavour as much as possible to read Hebrew as the Hebrews would have read it. We must act as the Astronomers with regard to that branch of their science which is called comparative, who, in order to form a more perfect idea of the general system, and its different parts, conceive themselves as passing through, and surveying the whole universe, migrating from one planet to another, and becoming for a short time inhabitants of each. Thus they clearly contemplate, and accurately estimate what each possesses peculiar to itself with respect to situation, celerity, satellites, and its relation to the rest; thus they distinguish what and how different an appearance of the universe is exhibited according to the different situations from which it is contemplated. In like manner, he who would perceive and feel the peculiar and interior elegancies of the Hebrew poetry, must imagine himself exactly situated as the persons for whom it was written, or even as the writers themselves; he must not attend to the ideas which on a cursory reading certain words would obtrude upon his mind; he is to feel them as a Hebrew, hearing or delivering the same words, at the same time, and in the same country.[+] As far as he is able to pursue this plan, so far he will comprehend their force and excellence. This indeed in many cases it will not be easy to do; in some it will be impossible; in all, however, it ought to be regarded, and in those passages particularly in which the figurative style is found to prevail.

In the Metaphor for instance (and what I remark concerning it may be applied to all the rest of the figures, since they are all naturally allied to each other) two circumstances are to be especially regarded, on which its whole force and elegance will depend: first, that resemblance which is the ground-work of the figurative and parabolic style, and which will perhaps be sufficiently apparent, even from a common and indistinct knowledge of the objects; and secondly, the beauty or dignity of the idea which is substituted for another; and this is a circumstance of unusual nicety. An opinion of grace and dignity results frequently, not so much from the objects themselves, in which these qualities are supposed to exist, as from the disposition of the spectator; or from some slight and obscure relation or connexion which they have with some other things. Thus it sometimes happens, that the external form and lineaments may be sufficiently apparent, though the original and intrinsic beauty and elegance be totally erased by time.

For these reasons, it will perhaps not be an useless undertaking, when we treat of the Metaphors of the sacred poets, to enter more fully into the nature of their poetical imagery in general, of which the Metaphor constitutes so principal a part. By this mode of proceeding, we shall be enabled not only to discern the general beauty and elegance of this figure in the Hebrew poetry, but the peculiar elegance, which it frequently possesses, if we only consider how forcible it must have appeared to those for whom it was originally intended; and what a connexion and agreement these figurative expressions must have had with their circumstances, feelings, and opinions. Thus many expressions and allusions, which even now appear beautiful, must, when considered in this manner, shine with redoubled lustre; and many, which now strike the superficial reader as coarse, mean, or deformed, must appear graceful, elegant, and sublime.

The whole course of nature, this immense universe of things, offers itself to human contemplation, and affords an infinite variety, a confused assemblage, a wilderness, as it were, of images, which being collected as the materials of poetry, are selected and produced as occasion dictates. The mind of man is that mirror of Plato (*Republic*: 10), which as he turns about at pleasure, and directs to a different point of view, he creates another sun, other stars, planets, animals, and even another self. In this shadow or image of himself, which man beholds when the mirror is turned inward towards himself, he is enabled in some degree to contemplate the souls of other men: for, from what he feels and perceives in himself, he forms conjectures concerning others; and apprehends and describes the manners, affections, conceptions of others from his own. Of this assemblage of images, which the human mind collects from all nature, and even from itself, that is, from its own emotions and operations, the least clear and evident are those which are explored by reason and argument; the more evident and distinct are those which are formed from the impressions made by external objects on the senses; and of these, the clearest and most vivid are those which are perceived by the eye.[5] Hence poetry abounds most in those images which are furnished by the senses, and chiefly those of the sight; in order to depict the obscure by the more manifest, the subtile by the more substantial; and, as far as simplicity is its object, it pursues those ideas which are most familiar and most evident; of which there is such an abundance, that they serve as well the purpose of ornament and variety, as that of illustration.

*   *   *

Lecture XIV
Of the Sublime in General, and of Sublimity of Expression in Particular

III In what manner the word *Mashal* implies the idea of Sublimity – Sublimity of language and sentiment – On what account the poetic diction of the Hebrews, either considered in itself, or compared with prose composition, merits an appellation expressive of sublimity – The sublimity of the poetic diction arises from the passions – How far the poetic diction differs from prose among the Hebrews – Certain forms of poetic diction and construction exemplified from Job, Ch. 3.

HAVING in the preceding Lectures given my sentiments at large on the nature of figurative style, on its use and application in poetry, and particularly in the poetry of the Hebrews; I proceed to treat of the Sublimity of the sacred poets; a subject which has been already illustrated by many examples quoted upon other occasions; but which, since we have admitted it as a third characteristic of the poetic style, now requires to be distinctly explained. We have already seen, that this is implied in one of the senses of the word *Mashal*,[6] it being expressive of power, or supreme authority, and when applied to style, seems particularly to intimate something eminent or energetic, excellent or important. This is certainly understood in the phrase 'to take (or lift) up his parable;' that is, to express a great or lofty sentiment. The very first instance, in which the phrase occurs, will serve as an example in point. For in this manner Balaam 'took up,' as our translation renders it, 'his parable, and said:'

> From Aram I am brought by Balak,
> By the king of Moab from the mountains of the East:
> Come, curse me Jacob;
> And come, execrate Israel.
> How shall I curse whom God hath not cursed?
> And how shall I execrate whom God hath not execrated?
> For from the tops of the rocks I see him,
> And from the hills I behold him;
> Lo! the people, who shall dwell alone,
> Nor shall number themselves among the nations!
> Who shall count the dust of Jacob?
> Or the number of the fourth of Israel?
> Let my soul die the death of the righteous,
> And let my end be as his. (Numbers 23. 7–10)

Let us now consider, on what account this address of the prophet is entitled *Mashal*. The sentences are indeed accurately distributed in parallelisms, as may be discovered even in the translation, which has not entirely obscured the elegance of the arrangement: and compositions in this form, we have already remarked, are commonly classed among the proverbs and adages, which are properly called *Mashalim*, though perhaps they contain nothing of a proverbial or didactic nature. But if we attentively consider this very passage, or others introduced by the same form of expression, we shall find, in all of them, either an extraordinary variety of figure and imagery; or an elevation of style and sentiment; or perhaps an union of all these excellencies; which will induce us to conclude, that something more is meant by the term to which I am alluding than the bare merit of a sententious neatness. If again we examine the same passage in another point of view, we shall discover in it little or nothing of the figurative kind, at least according to our ideas, or according to that acceptation of the word *Mashal* which denotes figurative language; there is evidently nothing in it of the mystical kind, nothing allegorical, no pomp of imagery, no comparison, and in fourteen verses but a single metaphor: as far, therefore, as figurative language is a characteristic of the parabolic style, this is no instance of it. We must then admit the word Parable, when applied to this passage, to be expressive of those exalted sentiments, that spirit of sublimity, that energy and enthusiasm, with which the answer of the prophet is animated. By this example I wished to explain on what reasons I was induced to suppose that the term *Mashal*, as well from its proper power or meaning, as from its usual acceptation, involves an idea of sublimity; and that the Hebrew poetry expresses in its very name and title, the particular quality in which it so greatly excels the poetry of all other nations.

The word Sublimity I wish in this place to be understood in its most extensive sense: I speak not merely of that sublimity, which exhibits great objects with a magnificent display of imagery and diction; but that force of composition, whatever it be, which strikes and overpowers the mind, which excites the passions, and which expresses ideas at once with perspicuity and elevation; not solicitous whether the language be plain or ornamented; refined or familiar: in this use of the word I copy Longinus, the most accomplished author on this subject, whether we consider his precepts or his example.

The sublime consists either in language or sentiment, or more frequently in an union of both, since they reciprocally assist each other, and since there is a necessary and indissoluble connexion between them: this, however, will not prevent our considering them apart with convenience and advantage. The first object, therefore, which presents itself for our investigation, is, upon what grounds the poetic diction of the Hebrews, whether considered in itself, or in comparison with prose composition, is deserving of an appellation immediately expressive of sublimity.

The poetry of every language has a style and form of expression peculiar to itself; forcible, magnificent, and sonorous; the words pompous and energetic; the composition singular and artificial; the whole form and complexion different from what we meet with in common life, and frequently (as with a noble indignation) breaking down the boundaries by which the popular dialect is confined. The language of Reason is cool, temperate, rather humble than elevated, well arranged and perspicuous, with an evident care and anxiety lest any thing should escape which might appear perplexed or obscure. The language of the Passions is totally different: the conceptions burst out in a turbid stream, expressive in a manner of the internal conflict; the more vehement break out in hasty confusion; they catch (without search or study) whatever is impetuous, vivid, or energetic. In a word, Reason speaks literally, the Passions poetically. The mind, with whatever passion it be agitated, remains fixed upon the object that excited it; and while it is earnest to display it, is not satisfied with a plain and exact description; but adopts one agreeable to its own sensations, splendid or gloomy, jocund or unpleasant. For the passions are naturally inclined to amplification; they wonderfully magnify and exaggerate whatever dwells upon the mind, and labour to express it in animated, bold, and magnificent terms. This they commonly effect by two different methods; partly by illustrating the subject with splendid imagery, and partly by employing new and extraordinary forms of expression, which are indeed possessed of great force and efficacy in this respect especially, that they in some degree imitate or represent the present habit and state of the soul. Hence those theories of Rhetoricians, which they have so pompously detailed, attributing that to art, which above all things is due to nature alone:

> For nature to each change of fortune forms
> The secret soul, and all its passions warms:
> Transports to rage, dilates the heart with mirth,
> Wrings the sad soul, and bends it down to earth.
> The tongue these various movements must express.
>
> (Francis's Horace, *Art of Poetry*, v. 155, etc.)

A principle which pervades all poetry, may easily be conceived to prevail even in a high degree in the poetry of the Hebrews. Indeed we have already seen how daring these writers are in the selection of their imagery, how forcible in the application of it; and what elegance, splendour, and sublimity they have by these means been enabled to infuse into their compositions. With respect to the diction also, we have had an opportunity of remarking the peculiar force and dignity of their poetic dialect; as well as the artificial distribution of the sentences, which appears to have been originally closely connected with the metrical arrangement, though the latter be now totally lost. We are therefore in the next place to consider whether there be any other remarkable qualities in the poetical language of the Hebrews, which serve to distinguish it from prose composition.

It is impossible to conceive any thing more simple and unadorned than the common language of the Hebrews. It is plain, correct, chaste, and temperate; the words are uncommon neither in their meaning nor application; there is no appearance of study, nor even of the least attention to the harmony of the periods. The order of the words is generally regular and uniform. The verb is the first word in the sentence, the noun, which is the agent, immediately succeeds, and the other words follow in their natural order. Each circumstance is exhibited at a single effort, without the least perplexity or confusion of the different parts: and, what is remarkable, by the help of a simple particle, the whole is connected from the beginning to the end in a continued series, so that nothing appears inconsistent, abrupt, or confused. The whole composition, in fine, is disposed in such an order, and so connected by the continued succession of the different parts, as to demonstrate clearly the regular state of the author, and to exhibit the image of a sedate and tranquil mind. But in the Hebrew poetry the case is different, in part at least, if not in the whole. The free spirit is hurried along, and has neither leisure nor inclination to descend to those minute and frigid attentions. Frequently, instead of disguising the secret feelings of the author, it lays them quite open to public view; and the veil being as it were suddenly removed, all the affections and emotions of the soul, its sudden impulses, its hasty sallies and irregularities, are conspicuously displayed.

Should the curious inquirer be desirous of more perfect information upon this subject, he may satisfy himself, I apprehend, with no great labour or difficulty. Let him take the book of Job; let him read the historical proem of that book; let him proceed to the metrical parts, and let him diligently attend to the first speech of Job. He will, I dare believe, confess, that, when arrived at the metrical part, he feels as if he were reading another language; and is surprized at the dissimilarity in the style of the two passages much greater than between that of Livy and Virgil, or even Herodotus and Homer.[7] Nor indeed could the fact be otherwise according to the nature of things; since in the latter passage the most exquisite pathos is displayed, such indeed as has not been exceeded, and scarcely equalled by any effort of the Muses. Not only the force, the beauty, the sublimity of the sentiments are unrivalled; but such is the character of the diction in general, so vivid is the expression, so interesting the assemblage of objects, so close and connected the sentences, so animated and passionate the whole arrangement, that the Hebrew literature itself contains nothing more poetical. The greater part of these beauties are so obvious, that they cannot possibly escape the eye of a diligent reader; there are some, however, which, depending chiefly upon the arrangement and construction, are of a more abstruse nature. It also sometimes happens, that those beauties which may be easily conceived, are very difficult to be explained: while we simply contemplate them, they appear sufficiently manifest; if we approach nearer, and attempt to touch and handle them, they vanish and escape. Since, however, it would not be consistent with my duty on the present occasion to pass them by totally unregarded, I shall rely, Gentlemen, upon your accustomed candour, while I attempt to render, if possible, some of these elegancies more obvious and familiar.

The first thing that arrests the attention of the reader in this passage, is the violent sorrow of Job, which bursts forth on a sudden, and flows from his heart, where it had long been confined and suppressed:

> Let the day perish, I was born in it; (i.e. in which I was born)
> And the night (which) said a man is conceived.   (Job 3. 3)

Observe here the concise and abrupt form of the first verse; and in the second the boldness of the figure, and the still more abrupt conclusion. Let the reader then consider, whether he could endure such a spirited, vehement, and perplexed form of expression in any prose composition; or even in verse, unless it were expressive of the deepest pathos. He will nevertheless, I doubt not, acknowledge that the meaning of this sentence is extremely clear, so clear indeed, that if any person should attempt to make it more copious and explanatory, he would render it less expressive of the mind and feelings of the speaker. It happens fortunately that we have an opportunity of making the experiment upon this very sentiment. There is a passage of Jeremiah so exactly similar, that it might almost be imagined a direct imitation: the meaning is the same, nor is there any very great difference in the phraseology; but Jeremiah fills up the ellipses, smooths and harmonizes the rough and uncouth language of Job, and dilates a short distich into two equal distichs, consisting of somewhat longer verses, which is the measure he commonly makes use of:

> Cursed be the day on which I was born,
> The day on which my mother bare me, let it not be blessed.
> Cursed be the man who brought the news to my father,
> Saying, there is a male child born unto thee;
> Making him exceedingly glad. (Jeremiah 20. 14, 15)

Thus it happens, that the imprecation of Jeremiah has more in it of complaint than of indignation; it is milder, softer, and more plaintive, peculiarly calculated to excite pity, in moving which the great excellence of this prophet consists: while that of Job is more adapted to strike us with terror than to excite our compassion.

But to proceed. I shall not trouble you with a tedious discussion of those particulars which are sufficiently apparent; the crouded and abrupt sentences, which seem to have little connexion, bursting from the glowing bosom with matchless force and impetuosity; the bold and magnificent expressions, which the eloquence of indignation pours forth, four instances of which occur in the space of twice as many verses, and which seem to be altogether poetical: two of them indeed are found continually in the poets, and in them only; the others are still more uncommon. Omitting these, therefore, the object which at present seems more worthy of examination, is, that redundancy of expression, which in a few lines takes place of the former excessive conciseness:

> That night – let darkness seize upon it. (Job 3. 6)

In this also there is the strongest indication of passion, and a perturbid mind. He doubtless intended at first to express himself in this manner:

> Be that night darkness (Job 3. 4)

But in the very act of uttering it, he suddenly catches at an expression, which appears more animated and energetic. I do not know that I can better illustrate this observation than by referring to a passage in Horace, in which a similar transition and redundancy falls from the indignant poet:

> He who – (bane of the fruitful earth!
> Curst was the hour that gave thee birth!)
> He – O vile pernicious tree!

> Was surely curst who planted thee,
> Well may I think the parricide
> In blood his guilty soul had dy'd,
> Or plung'd his dagger in the breast,
> At midnight, of his sleeping guest,
> Or temper'd every baleful juice,
> Which pois'nous Cholchian glebes produce,
> Or if a blacker crime be known,
> That crime the wretch had made his own.
>
> (Francis, B. ii. Ode xiii. with some little alteration)

For undoubtedly the poet begun, as if he intended to pursue the subject in a regular order, and to finish the sentence in this form. 'He who – planted thee; he was accessory to the murder of his parents, and sprinkled his chambers with the blood of his guest; he dealt in the poison of Cholchis,' etc. But anger and vexation dissipated the order of his ideas, and destroyed the construction of this sentence. But should some officious Grammarian take in hand the passage, (for this is a very diligent race of beings, and sometimes more than sufficiently exact and scrupulous) and attempt to restore it to its primitive purity and perfection, the whole grace and excellence of that beautiful exordium would be immediately annihilated, all the impetuosity and ardour would in a moment be extinguished. But to return to Job:

> Lo! that night, may it be fruitless! (Job 3. 7)

He appears to have a direct picture or image of that night before his eyes, and to point it out with his finger. 'The doors of my womb' for 'the doors of my mother's womb' (Job 3. 10) is an elliptical form of expression, the meaning of which is easily cleared up, but which no person in a tranquil state of mind, and quite master of himself, would venture to employ. Not to detain you too long upon this subject, I shall produce only one passage more, which is about the conclusion of this animated speech:

> Wherefore should he give light to the miserable?
> And life to those who are in bitterness of soul?
> Who call aloud for death, but it cometh not;
> Who dig for it more than for hidden treasures.
> Who would rejoice even to exultation,
> And be in raptures, if they had found the grave.
> Well might it befit the man whose way is sheltered,
> And whom God hath surrounded with an hedge.
> But my groaning cometh like my daily food,
> And my roarings are poured out like water.
>
> (Job 3. 20–24)

The whole composition of this passage is admirable, and deserves a minute attention. 'Wherefore should he give light to the miserable?' But who is the giver alluded to? Certainly God himself, whom Job has indeed in his mind; but it escaped his notice that no mention is made of him in the preceding lines. He seems to speak of the miserable in general, but by a violent and sudden transition he applies the whole to himself, 'But my groaning cometh like my daily food.' It is plain, therefore, that in all the preceding reflexions he has himself only in view. He makes a transition from the singular to the plural, and back again, a remarkable amplification intervening, expressive of his desire of death, the force and boldness of which is incomparable; at last, as if suddenly recollecting himself, he returns to the former subject, which he had apparently quitted, and resumes the detail of his own misery. From these observations I think it will be manifest, that the agitated and disordered state of the speaker's mind is not more evidently demonstrated by a happy boldness of sentiment and imagery, and an uncommon force of language, than by the very form, conduct, and arrangement of the whole.

The peculiar property which I have laboured to demonstrate in this passage, will, I apprehend, be found to prevail as a characteristic of the Hebrew poetry, making due allowance for different subjects and circumstances; I mean that vivid and ardent style, which is so well calculated to display the emotions and passions of the mind. Hence the poetry of the Hebrews abounds with phrases and idioms totally unsuited to prose composition, and which frequently appear to us harsh and unusual, I had almost said unnatural and barbarous; which, however, are destitute neither of meaning, nor of force, were we but sufficiently informed to judge of their true application. It will, however, be worth our while, perhaps, to make the experiment on some other passages of this nature, and to try at least what can be done towards the further elucidation of this point.

Lecture XVII
Of the Sublime of Passion

Sublimity of sentiment as arising from the vehement affections of the mind – What is commonly called Enthusiasm is the natural effect of passion: the true Enthusiasm arises from the impulse of the Divine Spirit, and is peculiar to the sacred poets – The principal force of poetry is displayed in the expression of passion: in exciting the passions poetry best atchieves its purpose, whether

Robert Lowth

it be utility or pleasure – How the passions are excited to the purpose of utility; how to that of pleasure – The difference and connexion between the pathetic and the sublime – That sublimity, which in the sacred poetry proceeds from the imitation of the passions of admiration, of joy, indignation, grief, and terror; illustrated by examples.

* * *

The language of poetry I have more than once described as the effect of mental emotion. Poetry itself is indebted for its origin, character, complexion, emphasis, and application, to the effects which are produced upon the mind and body, upon the imagination, the senses, the voice, and respiration by the agitation of passion. Every affection of the human soul, while it rages with violence, is a momentary phrenzy. When therefore a poet is able by the force of genius, or rather of imagination, to conceive any emotion of the mind so perfectly as to transfer to his own feelings the instinctive passion of another, and, agreeably to the nature of the subject, to express it in all its vigour, such a one, according to a common mode of speaking, may be said to possess the true poetic enthusiasm, or, as the ancients would have expressed it, 'to be inspired; full of the God:' not however implying, that their ardour of mind was imparted by the Gods, but that this extatic impulse became the God of the moment.[8]

This species of enthusiasm I should distinguish by the term *natural*, were it not that I should seem to connect things which are really different, and repugnant to each other: the true and genuine enthusiasm, that which alone is deserving of the name, that I mean with which the sublimer poetry of the Hebrews, and particularly the prophetic, is animated, is certainly widely different in its nature, and boasts a much higher origin.

As poetry, however, derives its very existence from the more vehement emotions of the mind, so its greatest energy is displayed in the expression of them; and by exciting the passions it more effectually attains its end.

Poetry is said to consist in imitation: whatever the human mind is able to conceive, it is the province of poetry to imitate; things, places, appearances natural and artificial, actions, passions, manners and customs: and since the human intellect is naturally delighted with every species of imitation, that species in particular, which exhibits its own image, which displays and depicts those impulses, inflexions, perturbations, and secret emotions, which it perceives and knows in itself, can scarcely fail to astonish and to delight above every other. The delicacy and difficulty of this kind of imitation are among its principal commendations; for to effect that which appears almost

impossible naturally excites our admiration. The understanding
slowly perceives the accuracy of the description in all other subjects,
and their agreement to their archetypes,[9] as being obliged to
compare them by the aid and through the uncertain medium, as it
were, of the memory: but when a passion is expressed, the object is
clear and distinct at once; the mind is immediately conscious of itself
and its own emotions; it feels and suffers in itself a sensation, either
the same or similar to that which is described. Hence that sublimity,
which arises from the vehement agitation of the passions, and the
imitation of them, possesses a superior influence over the human
mind; whatever is exhibited to it from without, may well be supposed to move and agitate it less than what it internally perceives, of
the magnitude and force of which it is previously conscious.

And as the imitation or delineation of the passions is the most
perfect production of poetry, so by exciting them it most completely
effects its purpose. The intent of poetry is to profit while it entertains
us; and the agitation of the passions, by the force of imitation, is in
the highest degree both useful and pleasant.

This method of exciting the passions is in the first place useful,
when properly and lawfully exercised; that is, when these passions are
directed to their proper end, and rendered subservient to the dictates
of nature and truth; when an aversion to evil, and a love of goodness
is excited; and if the poet deviate on any occasion from this great end
and aim, he is guilty of a most scandalous abuse and perversion of his
art. For the passions and affections are the elements and principles of
human action; they are all in themselves good, useful, and virtuous;
and, when fairly and naturally employed, not only lead to useful ends
and purposes, but actually prompt and stimulate to virtue. It is the
office of poetry to incite, to direct, to temper the passions, and not to
extinguish them. It professes to exercise, to amend, to discipline the
affections: it is this which is strictly meant by Aristotle, when he
speaks of the *pruning of the passions*,[10] though certain commentators
have strangely perverted his meaning.

But this operation on the passions is also more immediately useful,
because it is productive of pleasure. Every emotion of the mind, (not
excepting even those which in themselves are allied to pain) when
excited through the agency of the imitative arts, is ever accompanied
with an exquisite sensation of pleasure. This arises partly from the
contemplation of the imitation itself; partly from the consciousness
of our own felicity, when compared with the miseries of others; but
principally from the moral sense. Nature has endued man with a
certain social and generous spirit; and commands him not to confine

his cares to himself alone, but to extend them to all his fellow-creatures; to look upon nothing which relates to mankind as foreign to himself. Thus, 'to rejoice with them that do rejoice, and to weep with them that weep;' to love and to respect piety and benevolence; to cherish and retain an indignant hatred of cruelty and injustice; that is, to obey the dictates of nature; is right, is honest, is becoming, is pleasant.

The sublime and the pathetic are intrinsically very different; and yet have in some respects a kind of affinity or connexion. The pathetic includes the passions which we feel, and those which we excite. Some passions may be expressed without any thing of the sublime; the sublime also may exist, where no passion is directly expressed: there is however no sublimity where no passion is excited. That sensation of sublimity, which arises from the greatness of the thoughts and imagery, has admiration for its basis, and that for the most part connected with joy, love, hatred, or fear; and this I think is evident from the instances which were so lately under our consideration.

How much the sacred poetry of the Hebrews excels in exciting the passions, and in directing them to their noblest end and aim; how it exercises them upon their proper objects; how it strikes and fires the admiration by the contemplation of the Divine Majesty; and, forcing the affections of love, hope, and joy, from unworthy and terrestrial objects, elevates them to the pursuit of the supreme good: How it also stimulates those of grief, hatred, and fear, which are usually employed upon the trifling miseries of this life to the abhorrence of the supreme evil, is a subject, which at present wants no illustration, and which, though not unconnected with sublimity in a general view, would be improperly introduced in this place. For we are not at present treating of the general effects of sublimity on the passions; but of that species of the sublime which proceeds from vehement emotions of the mind, and from the imitation or representation of passion.

Here indeed a spacious field presents itself to our view: for by far the greater part of the sacred poetry is little else than a continued imitation of the different passions. What in reality forms the substance and subject of most of these poems but the passion of admiration, excited by the consideration of the Divine power and majesty; the passion of joy, from the sense of the Divine favour, and the prosperous issue of events; the passion of resentment and indignation against the contemners of God; of grief, from the consciousness of sin; and terror, from the apprehension of the Divine judgment? Of all these, and if there be any emotions of the mind beyond these, exquisite examples may be found in the Book of Job, in the Psalms, in the Canticles, and in every part of the prophetic writings.

*   *   *

Lecture XIX
The Prophetic Poetry is Sententious

The psalmody of the Hebrews. – The manner of chanting the hymns by alternate choirs: whence the origin of the poetical construction of the sentences, and that peculiar form, in which verses and distichs run parallel or correspondent to each other. – Three species of parallelism; the synonymous, the antithetic, and the synthetic: examples of each, first from the books generally allowed to be poetical, and afterwards from the writings of the prophets. – The sentiments of R. Azarias considered. – The great importance of an accurate attention to this poetical conformation of the sentences.

THE origin and earliest application of the Hebrew poetry have, I think, been clearly traced into the service of religion. To celebrate in hymns and songs the praises of Almighty God; to decorate the worship of the Most High with all the charms and graces of harmony; to give force and energy to the devout affections was the sublime employment of the Sacred Muse. It is more than probable, that the very early use of sacred music in the public worship of the Hebrews, contributed not a little to the peculiar character of their poetry, and might impart to it that appropriate form, which, though chiefly adapted to this particular purpose, it nevertheless preserves on every other occasion. But in order to explain this matter more clearly, it will be necessary to premise a few observations concerning the ancient Hebrew mode of chanting their sacred hymns.

Though we are rather at a loss for information, respecting the usual manner and ceremony of chanting their poems; and though the subject of their sacred music in general be involved in doubt and obscurity, thus far at least is evident from many examples, that the sacred hymns were alternately sung by opposite choirs (Nehemiah 12. 24–40), and that the one choir usually performed the hymn itself while the other sung a particular distich, which was regularly inter-posed at stated intervals, either of the nature of the proasm or epode of the Greeks.[11] In this manner we learn that Moses with the Israelites chanted the ode at the Red-sea; for 'Miriam the prophetess took a timbrel in her hand, and all the women followed her with timbrels, and with dances; and Miriam answered them,' that is, she and the women sung the response to the chorus of men (Exodus 15. 20, 21);

> Sing to JEHOVAH, for he is greatly exalted;
> The horse and the rider he hath cast into the sea.

The same is observable in some of the Psalms, which are composed in this form. The musical performance was on some occasions differently conducted: for instance, one of the choirs sung a single verse to the other, while the other constantly added a verse in some respect correspondent to the former. Of this the following distich is an example,

> Sing praises to JEHOVAH, for he is good;
> Because his mercy endureth for ever:

which Ezra (Ezra 3. 11) informs us was sung by the Priests and Levites in alternate choirs at the command of David; as indeed may be collected from the Psalm itself (Psalm 136), in which the latter verse, sung by the latter choir, forms a perpetual epode. Of the same nature is the song of the women concerning Saul and David (I Samuel 18. 7), for 'the women who played answered one another;' that is, they chanted in two choirs the alternate song, the one choir singing,

> Saul hath smote his thousands,

The other answering,

> And David his ten thousands.

In the very same manner Isaiah describes the Seraphim chanting the praise of Jehovah (Isaiah 6. 3): they cried alternately,

> Holy, holy, holy, JEHOVAH God of Hosts!
> The whole earth is filled with his glory.

From the Jewish, the custom of singing in alternate chorus was transmitted to the Christian Church, and was continued in the latter from the first ages, it was called 'alternate or responsive' (Pliny x. Epist. 97), when the whole choir separated into two divisions sung the Psalm alternately by strophes; and when this was done by single verses, or lines, that is when the same division of the choir always sung the latter part of the distich, they were said to sing the choral response.

Now if this were the ancient and primitive mode of chanting their hymns, as indeed appears highly probable, the proximate cause will be easily explained, why poems of this kind are disposed in equal stanzas, indeed in equal distichs, for the most part; and why these distichs should in some measure consist of versicles or parallelisms[12] corresponding to each other. And this mode of composition being admirably adapted to the musical modulation of that kind of poetry, which was most in use among them from the very beginning, and at the same time being perfectly agreeable to the genius and cadence of the language, easily extended itself into the other species of poetry, though not designed for the same purpose; in fact, we find that it pervaded the whole of the poetry of the Hebrews; insomuch, that what was said of the Heathen Muses may still more strictly be applied to those of the Hebrews, 'they love alternate song.'[13] On this occasion also it may not be improper to remark, that the word *gnanah*, which properly signifies to answer, is used more generally to denote any song or poem (Exodus 32. 18, Numbers 21. 17, Hosea 2. 15, Psalm 147. 7); whence we can only infer, either that the word has passed from particular to general use, or that among the Hebrews almost every poem possesses a sort of responsive form.

Such appears to have been the origin and progress of that poetical and artificial conformation of the sentences, which we observe in the poetry of the Hebrews. That it prevailed no less in the Prophetic Poetry than in the Lyric and Didactic, to which it was, in the nature of things, most adapted, is evident from those very ancient specimens of poetical prophecy already quoted from the historical books; and it only remains to shew, that it is no less observable in those which are contained in the volumes of the prophets themselves. In order the more clearly to evince this point, I shall endeavour to illustrate the Hebrew parallelism according to its different species, first by examples taken from those books commonly allowed to be poetical, and afterwards by correspondent examples from the books of the prophets.

The poetical conformation of the sentences, which has been so often alluded to as characteristic of the Hebrew poetry, consists chiefly in a certain equality, resemblance, or parallelism between the members of each period; so that in two lines (or members of the same period) things for the most part shall answer to things, and words to words, as if fitted to each other by a kind of rule or measure. This parallelism has much variety and many gradations; it is sometimes more accurate and manifest, sometimes more vague and obscure: it may however, on the whole, be said to consist of three species.

The first species is the synonymous parallelism, when the same sentiment is repeated in different, but equivalent terms. This is the

most frequent of all, and is often conducted with the utmost accuracy
and neatness: examples are very numerous, nor will there be any
great difficulty in the choice of them: on this account I shall select
such as are most remarkable in other respects.

> When Israel went out from Egypt;
> The house of Jacob from a strange people:
> Judah was as his sacred heritage:
> Israel his dominion.
> The sea saw, and fled;
> Jordan turned back:
> The mountains leaped like rams;
> The hills like the sons of the flock.
> What ailed thee, O Sea, that thou fleddest;
> Jordan, that thou turnedst back:
> Mountains, that ye leaped like rams;
> And hills, like the sons of the flock?
> At the presence of the Lord tremble thou Earth;
> At the presence of the God of Jacob!
> Who turned the rock into a lake of waters;
> The flint into a water spring. (Psalm 114)

The Prophetic Muse is no less elegant and correct:

> Arise, be thou enlightened; for thy light is come;
> And the glory of JEHOVAH is risen upon thee.
> For behold darkness shall cover the earth;
> And a thick vapour the nations:
> But upon thee shall JEHOVAH arise;
> And his glory upon thee shall be conspicuous.
> And the nations shall walk in thy light;
> And kings in the brightness of thy rising. (Isaiah 60. 1–3)

Observe also that famous prophecy concerning the humiliation, and
expiatory sufferings of the Messiah:

> Who hath believed our report;
> And to whom hath the arm of JEHOVAH been manifested:
> For he groweth up in their sight like a tender sucker;
> And like a root from a thirsty soil;
> He hath no form, nor any beauty that we should regard him;
> Nor is his countenance such, that we should desire him.
> Despised, nor accounted in the number of men;
> A man of sorrows, and acquainted with grief;
> As one that hideth his face from us:
> He was despised, and we esteemed him not.
> Surely our infirmities he hath borne.
> And our sorrows he hath carried them.
> Yet we thought him judicially stricken;

Smitten of God and afflicted.
But he was wounded for our transgressions;
Was smitten for our iniquities:
The chastisement by which our peace was effected was laid upon
him;
And by his bruises we are healed.

(Isaiah 53. 1–12)

Isaiah is indeed excellent, but not unrivalled in this kind of composition: there are abundant examples in the other prophets; I shall, however, only add one from Hosea, which is exquisitely pathetic.

How shall I resign thee, O Ephraim!
How shall I deliver thee up, O Israel!
How shall I resign thee as Admah!
How shall I make thee as Zeboim!
My heart is changed within me;
I am warmed also with repentance towards thee.
I will not do according to the fervour of my wrath,
I will not return to destroy Ephraim:
For I am God, and not man;
Holy in the midst of thee, though I inhabit not thy cities.

(Hosea 11. 8, 9)

There is great variety in the form of the synonymous parallelism, some instances of which are deserving of remark. The parallelism is sometimes formed by the iteration of the former member, either in the whole or in part:

Much have they oppressed me from my youth up,
May Israel now say;
Much have they oppressed me from my youth,
Yet have they not prevailed against me.

(Psalm 129. 1, 2)

God of vengeance, JEHOVAH;
God of vengeance, shew thyself.
How long shall the wicked, O JEHOVAH,
How long shall the wicked triumph!

(Psalm 114. 1, 3)

With the jaw bone of an ass, heaps upon heaps;
With the jaw-bone of an ass a thousand men have I smitten.

(Judges 15. 16)

Thus, Isaiah:

Because in the night Ar is destroyed, Moab is undone!
Because in the night Kir is destroyed, Moab is undone.

(Isaiah 15. 1)

So Nahum also in the exordium of his sublime prophecy:

> JEHOVAH is a jealous and avenging God:
> JEHOVAH avengeth, and is wrathful:
> JEHOVAH avengeth his adversaries;
> And he reserveth *indignation* for his enemies.

(Nahum 1. 2)

There is frequently something wanting in the latter member, which must be repeated from the former to complete the sentence:

> The king sent and released him;
> The ruler of the people, and set him free.   (Psalm 105. 20)

In the same manner Isaiah:

> Kings shall see him and shall rise up;
> Princes, and they shall worship him:
> For the sake of JEHOVAH, who is faithful;
> Of the Holy One of Israel, for he hath chosen thee.

(Isaiah 49. 7)

Frequently the whole of the latter division answers only to some part of the former:

> JEHOVAH reigneth, let the earth rejoice:
> Let the multitude of islands be glad

(Psalm 97. 1)

> Arise, be thou enlightened; for thy light is come;
> And the glory of JEHOVAH is risen upon thee.

(Isaiah 60. 1)

Sometimes also there are triplet parallelisms. In these the second line is generally synonymous with the first, whilst the third either begins the period, or concludes it, and frequently refers to both the preceding:

> The floods have lifted up, O JEHOVAH,
> The floods have lifted up their voice;
> The floods have lifted up their waves.
> Than the voice of many waters,
> The glorious waves of the sea,
> JEHOVAH on high is more glorious.

(Psalm 93. 3, 4)

> Come and let us return unto JEHOVAH;
> For he hath torn, and he will heal us;
> He hath smitten, and he will bind us up:
> After two days he will revive us;
> On the third day he will raise us up;
> And we shall live in his sight.

(Hosea 6. 12)

In stanzas (if I may so call them) of five lines, the nature of which is nearly similar, the line that is not parallel is generally placed between the two distichs:

> Like as the lion growleth,
> Even the young lion over his prey;
> Though the whole company of shepherds be called together against him:
> At their voice he will not be terrified,
> Nor at their tumult will he be humbled.
>
> (Isaiah 31. 4)

> Askalon shall see it, and shall fear;
> Gaza shall also see it, and shall be greatly pained:
> And Ekron shall be pained, because her expectation is put to shame;
> And the king shall perish from Gaza;
> And Askalon shall not be inhabited.
>
> (Zechariah 9. 5)

Those which consist of four lines generally form two regular distichs; but there is sometimes a peculiar artifice to be perceived in the distribution of the sentences:

> From the Heavens JEHOVAH looketh down,
> He seeth all the children of men;
> From the seat of his rest he contemplateth
> All the inhabitants of the earth.
>
> (Psalm 33. 13, 14)

> I will drench my arrows in blood,
> And my sword shall devour flesh;
> In the blood of the slain and the captives;
> From the bushy head of the enemies.
>
> (Deuteronomy 32. 42)

In both the above passages, the latter members are to be alternately referred to the former. Isaiah too uses with great elegance this form of composition:

> For thy husband is thy maker;
> JEHOVAH God of Hosts is his name:
> And thy redeemer is the Holy One of Israel;
> The God of the whole earth shall he be called.
>
> (Isaiah 54. 5)

The sense has an alternate correspondence in these lines. In the following the form of the construction is alternate:

And his land is filled with silver and gold;
And there is no end to his treasures:
And his land is filled with horses,
Neither is there any end to his chariots.   (Isaiah 2. 7)

The following is perhaps a singular instance:

Who is like unto JEHOVAH our God?
Who is exalted to dwell on high,
Who humbleth himself to look down,
In the heavens, and in the earth.   (Psalm 113. 5, 6)

Here the two members of the latter line are to be referred severally to the two preceding lines; as if it were: 'Who is exalted to dwell in the heavens, and who humbleth himself to inspect the things that are in the earth.'

The Antithetic parallelism is the next that I shall specify, when a thing is illustrated by its contrary being opposed to it. This is not confined to any particular form: for sentiments are opposed to sentiments, words to words, singulars to singulars, plurals to plurals, etc. of which the following are examples:

The blows of a friend are faithful;
But the kisses of an enemy are treacherous.
The cloyed will trample upon an honey-comb;
But to the hungry every bitter thing is sweet.
There is who maketh himself rich, and wanteth all things;
Who maketh himself poor, yet hath much wealth.
The rich man is wise in his own eyes,
But the poor man that hath discernment to trace him out will
          despise him.   (Proverbs 27. 6, 7; 13. 7; 27. 11)

There is sometimes a contraposition of parts in the same sentence, such as occurs once in the above; and as appears in the following:

I am swarthy but comely, O daughters of Jerusalem;
As the tents of Kedar, as the pavilions of Solomon.
          (Song of Solomon 1. 5)

The last line here is also to be divided and separately applied to the preceding, 'swarthy as the tents of Kedar; comely as the pavilions of Solomon,' so likewise in the enigma of Sampson:

Out of the eater came forth meat;
And out of the strong came forth sweetness.
          (Judges 14. 14)

This form of composition, indeed, agrees best with adages and acute sayings: it is therefore very prevalent in the proverbs of Solomon, in some of which the principal force and elegance depend on the exactness of the antithesis. It is not however inconsistent with the superior kinds of Hebrew poetry; for we meet with it in the thanks-giving ode of Hannah, which is imitated in this particular, as well as in the general form of its composition in that of the Virgin Mary:

> The bows of the mighty are broken;
> And they that stumbled are girded with strength:
> The full have hired themselves for bread;
> And the hungry have ceased to hunger:
> The barren also hath borne seven;
> And she who had many children is become fruitless.
> JEHOVAH killeth and maketh alive;
> He casteth down to hell, and lifteth up.
> JEHOVAH maketh poor, and maketh rich;
> Depresseth, and also exalteth.

(I Samuel 2. 4–7; compare Luke 1. 52, 53)

The sublimer poetry seldom indeed adopts this style. Isaiah, however, by means of it, without departing from his usual dignity, adds greatly to the sweetness of his composition in the following instances:

> In a little anger have I forsaken thee;
> But with great mercies will I receive thee again:
> In a short wrath I hid my face for a moment from thee;
> But with everlasting kindness will I have mercy on thee.

(Isaiah 54. 7, 8)

> Behold my servants shall eat, but ye shall be famished;
> Behold my servants shall drink, but ye shall be thirsty;
> Behold my servants shall rejoice, but ye shall be confounded;
> Behold my servants shall sing aloud, for gladness of heart;
> But he shall cry aloud for grief of heart;
> And in the anguish of a broken spirit shall ye howl.

(Isaiah 65. 13, 14)

There is a third species of parallelism, in which the sentences answer to each other, not by the iteration of the same image or sentiment, or the opposition of their contraries, but merely by the form of con-struction. To this, which may be called the Synthetic or Constructive Parallelism, may be referred all such as do not come within the two former classes: I shall however produce a few of the most remarkable instances:

The law of JEHOVAH is perfect, restoring the soul;
The testimony of JEHOVAH is sure, making wise the simple:
The precepts of JEHOVAH are right, rejoicing the heart;
The commandment of JEHOVAH is clear, enlightening the eyes:
The fear of JEHOVAH is pure, enduring for ever;
The judgments of JEHOVAH are truth, they are just altogether.
More desirable than gold, or than much fine gold;
And sweeter than honey, or the dropping of honey-combs.

(Psalm 19. 8–11)

This kind of parallelism generally consists of verses somewhat longer than usual, of which there are not wanting examples in the prophets:

How hath the oppressor ceased! the exactress of gold ceased!
JEHOVAH hath broken the staff of the wicked, the sceptre of
the rulers.
He that smote the people in wrath with a stroke unremitted;
He that ruled the nations in anger is persecuted, and none
hindereth.
The whole earth is at rest, is quiet; they burst forth into a
joyful shout;
Even the fir-trees rejoice over thee, the cedars of Lebanon:
Since thou art fallen, no feller hath come up against us.
Hades from beneath is moved because of thee, to meet thee at
thy coming:
He rouseth for thee the mighty dead, all the great chiefs of the
earth;
He maketh to rise up from their thrones all the kings of the
nations.

(Isaiah 14. 4–9)

Triplets are frequently formed of this kind of parallelism:

The clouds overflowed with water;
The atmosphere resounded;
Thine arrows also issued forth;
The voice of thy thunder was in the skies;
The lightnings enlightened the world;
The earth trembled and shook.

(Psalm 77. 18, 19)

I will be as the dew to Israel:
He shall blossom as the lily;
And he shall strike his roots like Lebanon,
His suckers shall spread,
And his glory shall be as the olive-tree,
And his smell as Lebanon.

(Hosea 14. 6, 7)

Frequently one line or member contains two sentiments:

The nations raged; the kingdoms were moved;

He uttered a voice; the earth was dissolved:
Be still, and know that I am God:
I will be exalted in the nations, I will be exalted in the earth.

(Psalm 46. 6, 10)

When thou passest through waters I am with thee;
And through rivers, they shall not overwhelm thee:
When thou walkest in the fire thou shalt not be scorched;
And the flame shall not cleave to thee. (Isaiah 43. 2)

There is a peculiar figure which is frequently made use of in this species of parallelism, and which seems altogether poetical: that is, when a definite number is put for an indefinite, principally, it should seem, for the sake of the parallelism: for it sometimes happens, that the circumstances afterwards enumerated do not accurately accord with the number specified:

In six troubles will he deliver thee;
And in seven there shall no evil touch thee.

(Job 5. 19)

God hath said once;
Twice also have I heard the same.

(Psalm 42. 12)

That frequently-repeated passage of Amos is well-known:

For three transgressions of Damascus,
And for four, I will not restore it. (Amos 1. 3 etc.)

The variety in the form of this synthetic parallelism is very great, and the degrees of resemblance almost infinite: so that sometimes the scheme of the parallelism is very subtile and obscure, and must be developed by art and ability in distinguishing the different members of the sentences, and in distributing the points, rather than by depending upon the obvious construction. How much this principle pervades the Hebrew poetry, and how difficult of explication it is, may in some degree be illustrated by one example. This appears to consist of a single line, if the sentiment only be considered:

I also have anointed my King on Sion, the mountain of my
sanctity. (Psalm 2. 6)

But the general form and nature of the Psalm requires that it should be divided into two parts or versicles; as if it were,

I also have anointed my king;
I have anointed him in Sion, the mountain of my sanctity.

Which indeed the Masorites¹⁴ seem to have perceived in this as well as in other places. For they mark the word *mlf* with the distinctive accent *Athnac*, by which they generally distinguish the members of the distichs. (See 17. 7; 32. 3; 33. 14; 102, 8; 116. 1, 9, 12, 14, 15, 18; 137. 2.)

In this peculiar conformation, or parallelism of the sentences, I apprehend a considerable part of the Hebrew metre to consist; though it is not improbable that some regard was also paid to the numbers and feet. But of this particular we have at present so little information, that it is utterly impossible to determine, whether it were modulated by the ear alone, or according to any settled or definite rules of prosody. Since however this, and other marks or vestiges, as it were, of the metrical art are alike extant in the writings of the prophets, and in the books which are commonly allowed to be poetical, I think there is sufficient reason to rank them in the same class.

*   *   *

But should all that has been remarked concerning the members and divisions of the sentences appear light and trifling to some persons, and utterly undeserving any labour or attention; let them remember that nothing can be of greater avail to the proper understanding of any writer, than a previous acquaintance with both his general character, and the peculiarities of his style and manner of writing: let them recollect that translators and commentators have fallen into errors upon no account more frequently, than for want of attention to this article; and indeed, I scarcely know any subject which promises more copiously to reward the labour of such as are studious of sacred criticism, than this one in particular.

4. William Blake, 'The Marriage of Heaven and Hell' (1790), 'A Memorable Fancy'

Three years after the publication of Gregory's translation of Lowth, Blake engraved *The Marriage of Heaven and Hell*. In that time the French Revolution had begun. Blake greeted it with his poem 'The French Revolution', cast in the prophetic Hebrew verse and imagery which Lowth had described to a wide readership, e.g.:

> For the commons convene in the Hall of the Nation.
> France shakes! And the heavens of France
> Perplexed vibrate round each careful countenance!
> Darkness of old time around them ...   (lines 16 ff.)

Blake must have known Lowth. There is no documentary evidence for it, but the internal evidence of *The Marriage of Heaven and Hell* alone is overwhelming. The 'Memorable Fancy' which is printed from it here occupies its plates 12 and 13. Plate 4, 'The Voice of the Devil', was subversive biblical interpretation. Plates 7 to 10, 'Proverbs of Hell', took the further step of biblical imitation. Plate 11 played off 'the ancient poets', who showed that 'all deities reside in the human breast' (Lowth not much radicalised), against that conventional target of Enlightenment biblical criticism, priestly system.

A third influence on *The Marriage of Heaven and Hell*, along with Lowth and revolution, was Swedenborg. But this was an influence exerted at the point of being disowned by means of satire. Blake turned Swedenborg's airy equilibriums into contraries, his vertical and static apocalyptic manner into the horizontal of current apocalyptic history. Lowth's legacy is much more active and central. Lowthian are the prophetic use of common imagery to express passion ('honest indignation is the voice of God') in a creative mental coup ('the firm persuasion removed mountains'), and Ezekiel's assertion that 'the philosophy of the east taught the first principles of human perception'. Blake moves Lowth into the theological centre which the bishop himself had sedulously avoided by making 'the poetic genius' into the Creator God without remainder. Blake can do this because he *is* the sort of man whom Lowth described. Biblical criticism here enables biblical creativity, and in the mind of a poet who understands (from a bishop of the established church) the structures of the canonical books and will not 'resist his genius', the bounds of canon are splendidly broken.

Ezekiel was Blake's favourite prophet and history tutor. His sign of eating dung comes from Ezekiel 4. Isaiah's going naked and barefoot comes from Isaiah 20. Both signs are, in accordance with Blake's apocalyptic mode, of unfolding apocalyptic events. The exchange about the unimportance of their lost works reflects Lowth's conviction that the authority of a text is not impugned by its textual defects. The North American tribes, to which Blake refers in his last sentence here, have not been identified precisely.

A Memorable Fancy

The prophets Isaiah and Ezekiel dined with me, and I asked them how they dared so roundly to assert that God spake to them; and whether they did not think at the time that they would be misunderstood, and so be the cause of imposition.

Isaiah answered, 'I saw no God, nor heard any, in a finite organical perception; but my senses discovered the infinite in everything, and as I was then persuaded, and remain confirmed, that the voice of honest indignation is the voice of God, I cared not for consequences but wrote.'

Then I asked: 'Does a firm persuasion that a thing is so, make it so?'

He replied, 'All poets believe that it does, and in ages of imagination the firm persuasion removed mountains; but many are not capable of a firm persuasion of anything.'

Then Ezekiel said, 'The philosophy of the east taught the first principles of human perception; some nations held one principle for the origin and some another. We of Israel taught that the Poetic Genius (as you now call it) was the first principle, and all the others merely derivative – which was the cause of our despising the priests and philosophers of other countries, and prophesying that all gods would at last be proved to originate in ours and to be the tributaries of the Poetic Genius. It was this that our great poet King David desired so fervently and invoked so pathetically, saying by this he conquers enemies and governs kingdoms. And we so loved our God, that we cursed in his name all the deities of surrounding nations, and asserted that they had rebelled; from these opinions the vulgar came to think that all nations would at last be subject to the Jews.

'This,' said he, 'like all firm persuasions, is come to pass, for all nations believe the Jews' code and worship the Jews' God, and what greater subjection can be?'

I heard this with some wonder, and must confess my own conviction. After dinner I asked Isaiah to favour the world with his lost works; he said none of equal value was lost. Ezekiel said the same of his.

I also asked Isaiah what made him go naked and barefoot for three years. He answered, 'The same that made our friend Diogenes the Grecian.'

I then asked Ezekiel why he ate dung, and lay so long on his right and left side. He answered, 'The desire of raising other men into a perception of the infinite. This the North American tribes practise, and is he honest who resists his genius or conscience only for the sake of present ease or gratification?'

5. Samuel Taylor Coleridge, 'Confessions of an Inquiring Spirit' (1825), Letters V, VI, VII

Confessions is a text from Coleridge's later life. After twenty years of turbulence, he was living at Highgate, to the north of London, in the house of the surgeon, James Gillman. Surrounded by his books and with his opium addiction kept within bounds, he was a venerable figure who read, wrote, annotated and conversed – all widely and wonderfully. He hoped that his immense stores of learning and experience – not least experience – could be unified in the frame of Christian theism. Christianity, as no modern writer knew more vividly and richly than Coleridge, is a universal religion. Therefore its truth, in which he believed more ardently than ever before, could only be realised on this big scale. And its truth meant that such a project must be possible. His unequalled knowledge of the things that had to be unified – philosophy, theology, history, poetry, science, politics – equipped him to do it. It was never written, unless the unpublished scientific treatise called (not by him) 'opus maximum' is it or its prototype. But plentiful *hors d'oeuvres* survive, and *Confessions* is the best of them. *The Statesman's Manual* peters out, and *Aids to Reflection*, though so influential and popular in the nineteenth century, seems to modern readers to go on and on. In *Confessions* he hit on the right genre. Its short letters are near to his genius as a talker. They contain urgent passion and sustain practical concern. They were the humble, apparently off-hand, ruse by which he got round the self-imposed duty of the great project. And being about the inspiration of the Bible, they evoked his experience as a poet and his mastery as a literary critic.

In a letter of 1820 to his friend Thomas Allsop Coleridge described four works almost ready for the press. One of them was 'Letters on the Old and New Testaments'. The others were three volumes on Shakespeare, two volumes on the history of philosophy, and 'A Philosophical Analysis of the Genius and Works of Dante, Spenser, Milton, Cervantes and Calderon' – an astounding glimpse of the hopes and contents of his mind at the time (Walter Jackson Bate, *Coleridge*, p. 209).

The manuscript of *Confessions* was with Hessey the publisher in 1824. Coleridge then saw it as a supplement to *Aids to Reflection*, but it proved to be too long for that. In the summer of 1825 he asked to have it back. Either he was anxious about its effect, or wanted to revise it, or both. The publishers had lost it, but eventually found it and returned it (*Collected Letters*, 1447 and 1480). The manuscript (BL Add. MS 34225) has many slight variations from the printed text of 1840 used here and is at present being edited by Robin Jackson for the Princeton/Bollingen edition of Coleridge's works.

In his last years Coleridge was more orthodox than before. He knew plenty now about the moral hopelessness to which the orthodox Sherlock had addressed himself. He had experienced deeply what he had long before described in *The Ancient Mariner*. But this orthodox tendency, this need for something more psychologically penetrating and more redemptive than the Lockean inheritance provided, had to struggle with his knowledge of the power of German biblical criticism. He knew it well. He had visited Göttingen in 1799 and met Baumgarten, who introduced the biblical work of the English Deists there, and Eichhorn. Dialogue with the German masters of philosophy and biblical criticism was a constant constituent of his Highgate years. It was the tilling of the soil out of which *Confessions* grew.

He had accumulated a debt to Lessing so large as to raise the suspicion, so recurrent to studious readers of Coleridge, of plagiarism. The charge was confronted by J. H. Green in the 'Introduction' which he contributed to the second edition of *Confessions* in 1849. It is reprinted in H. St J. Hart's edition of 1956. Green dealt with it well. He realised that the fundamental difficulty lay in Coleridge's capacity for sympathetic absorption: enhanced, one might add, by self-distrust. He noticed passages which are so similar to passages in Lessing – using the same references to illustrate the same argument – that plagiarism is a real issue. Green tactfully forbears from dwelling on Coleridge's spectacular withholding of acknowledgement, which might be thought to justify the charge. However, Coleridge's most important debt to Lessing is in ideas. He owes him the distinction between the Bible and religion, which cracks the old protestant certainty that they are coterminous by showing that religion has its own internal life and evidence and energy. This is reinforced by the distinction between letter and spirit which goes back to St Paul. Lessing used it historically: spirited Christianity existed before the New Testament. This highlights apostolic tradition as the bridge between the two. It is here that the difference Coleridge makes to Lessing comes out. Lessing emphasised the difference, even disjunction, between apostolic teaching and the New Testament records. Coleridge emphasised the continuity between them. It was characteristic of him to do so. And as a member of the Church of England with its allegiance to scripture *and* tradition, he could see himself as correcting a bibliolatrous distortion of Anglicanism. Green's judgement that Coleridge had done nothing more culpable with Lessing than to take his ideas, absorb them, and adapt them to his own fertile thinking, seems fair and good. But it is a pity that he concealed his debt from the reader of *Confessions*, leaving Green to put the record straight.

Coleridge annotated Eichhorn's *Introductions* to the Old and New Testaments – usually indignantly. Eichhorn believed that the canonical gospels were enlargements of a single primal gospel (*Urevangelium*). Of the infancy narratives in Matthew and Luke he asked, since they were no part of the *Urevangelium*, 'can they be regarded as anything more than sagas which, to be sure, may have a basis in fact, but a basis which can no longer be distinguished from the embellishments with which tradition has clothed it?'

(*Einleitung in das Neue Testament*, I, 458). Coleridge took frequent issue with Eichhorn's notions of facts and adornments. The facts were too often, like the *Urevangelium* itself, historical guesses by an interpreter turned interpolator. As for the 'adornments', Coleridge's English empiricism was offended by the suggestion that the evangelists were lying; and as a poet he found the description too shallow and trivial to match the mystery of inspiration. 'What remains after he has taken away the Divinity, Incarnation, mysterious Redemption and all the miraculous colouring of the facts?' (*Marginalia*, pp. 453–4).

That conservative *cri de coeur* in the margin of Eichhorn is part of the motivation of *Confessions*. Coleridge wanted a doctrine of inspiration both less flattering and less speculative than Eichhorn's. It would also, by virtue of having much more religious juice in it than Eichhorn's 'neology', be a vivid and superior alternative to the fundamentalist 'Doctrine' of the verbal dictation of the scriptures by God, which held the field in England and reduced the inspired writers to mere ventriloquist's dummies. His doctrine turned on distinguishing the revealed from the inspired. Revelation was then left where it was, unquestioned, while he explored inspiration. Coleridge was mediating, with sharp modifications, German thought to the English public, and biblical piety to modern minds. And mediation was for him more than a ploy. It was a belief. Fundamental to *Confessions* is the Christian mediation between the divine and the human, as set out in the doctrine of the Trinity – a Coleridgean version of which was prefaced to *Confessions*. The 'Doctrine' crushed the human under the authoritarian weight of divine utterance. Coleridge's divine Logos was mediatory. Eichhorn disinherited the human of its birthright: its capacity for God. For Coleridge, following Paul, to be human was to have a spirit which bore witness to divine Spirit – which 'corresponded'. So the Bible became a meeting-place: something Coleridge achieved, not by excluding revelation but by distinguishing it from inspiration and tacitly giving inspiration the bigger and better part. Then the play of correspondences could begin: 'the spirit in each true believer' finding objective correlatives, in rich diversity, in the inspired text. '*Imagination*, or the *modifying*, and *co-adunating* Faculty' (*Collected Letters*, 2: 866) discoverd the inter-relatedness of things, and so met its theological correspondent, the Logos, the unifying spiritual ground of all matter. Kant's reason became a threshold to theology.

What apter form for all this correspondence than letters? That is what Coleridge himself always called them. *Confessions of an Inquiring Spirit* is not his title, but was given by his nephew, H. N. Coleridge, when he published them in 1840. But it is apt. The first letter took as starting point Coleridge's recent reading of 'The Confessions of a Fair Saint' in Goethe's *Wilhelm Meister*, translated by Carlyle, and presented by him to Coleridge in June 1824. Goethe's confessional novel-within-a-novel is moved by the same feelings, the same sense of developing process, as Coleridge's letters on the Bible. It is an Odyssey, the quest of a person like Coleridge who 'feels the want, the necessity, of religious support' (Letter 1); finds it neither in the harsh objectivities of doctrine alone, nor in the labile subjectivities of feelings alone; but achieves a faith which sustains personal growth and makes the person useful to others. Goethe's text, by virtue of its narrative process, is really the best introduction to Coleridge's, in which Coleridge attempts, as he said elsewhere, 'to delineate an arc of oscillation'.

Letter V

Yes! my dear Friend, it is my conviction that in all ordinary cases the knowledge and belief of the Christian Religion should precede the study of the Hebrew Canon. Indeed with regard to both Testaments, I consider oral and catechismal instruction as the preparative provided by Christ himself in the establishment of a visible Church. And to make the Bible, apart from the truths, doctrines, and spiritual experiences contained therein, the subject of a special article of faith, I hold an unnecessary and useless abstraction, which in too many instances has the effect of substituting a barren acquiescence in the letter for the lively *faith that cometh by hearing;* even as the hearing is productive of this faith, because it is the word of God that is heard and preached (Rom. 10. 8, 17). And here I mean the written word preserved in the armoury of the Church to be the sword of faith *out of the mouth* of the preacher, as Christ's ambassador and representative (Rev. 1. 16), and out of the heart of the believer, from generation to generation. Who shall dare dissolve or loosen this holy bond, this divine reciprocality, of Faith and Scripture? Who shall dare enjoin aught else as an object of saving faith, beside the truths that appertain to salvation? The imposers take on themselves a heavy responsibility, however defensible the opinion itself, as an opinion, may be. For by imposing it, they counteract their own purposes. They antedate questions, and thus in all cases aggravate the difficulty of answering them satisfactorily. And not seldom they create difficulties that might never have occurred. But, worst of all, they convert things trifling or indifferent into mischievous pretexts for the wanton, fearful, difficulties for the weak, and formidable objections for the inquiring. For what man *fearing God* dares think any the least point indifferent, which he is required to receive as God's own immediate word miraculously infused, miraculously recorded, and by a succession of miracles preserved unblended and without change? Through all the pages of a large and multifold volume, at each successive period, at every sentence, must the question recur: 'Dare I believe – do I in my heart believe – these words to have been dictated by an infallible reason, and the immediate utterance of Almighty God?' No! It is due to Christian charity that a question so awful should not be put unnecessarily, and should not be put out of time. The necessity I deny. And out of time the question must be put, if after enumerating the several articles of the Catholic Faith I am bound to add: 'and further you are to believe with equal faith, as having the same immediate and miraculous derivation from God, whatever else you shall hereafter read in any of the sixty six books collected in the Old and New Testaments.'

I would never say this. Yet let me not be misjudged as if I treated the Scriptures as a matter of indifference. I would not say this: but where I saw a desire to believe, and a beginning love of Christ, I would there say: 'There are likewise sacred Writings, which, taken in connection with the institution and perpetuity of a visible Church, all believers revere as the most precious boon of God, next to Christianity itself, and attribute both their communication and preservation to an especial Providence. In them you will find all the revealed truths, which have been set forth and offered to you, clearly and circumstantially recorded; and, in addition to these, examples of obedience and disobedience both in states and individuals, the lives and actions of men eminent under each dispensation, their sentiments, maxims, hymns, and prayers, their affections, emotions and conflicts; in all which you will recognize the influence of the Holy Spirit, with a conviction increasing with the growth of your own faith and spiritual experience.'

Farewell.

Letter VI

MY DEAR FRIEND,

IN my last two Letters I have given the state of the argument, as it would stand between a Christian thinking as I do, and a serious well-disposed Deist. I will now endeavour to state the argument, as between the former and the advocates for the popular belief, such of them, I mean, as are competent to deliver a dispassionate judgment in the cause. And again, more particularly, I mean the learned and reflecting part of them, who are influenced to the retention of the prevailing dogma by the supposed consequences of a different view, and, especially, by their dread of conceding to all alike, simple and learned, the privilege of picking and choosing the Scriptures that are to be received as binding on their consciences. Between these persons and myself the controversy[a] may be reduced to a single question:

Is it safer for the Individual, and more conducive to the interests of the Church of Christ, in its twofold character of pastoral and militant, to conclude thus: The Bible is the Word of God, and therefore true, holy, and in all parts unquestionable; or thus, The Bible, considered in reference to its declared ends and purposes, is true and holy, and for all who seek truth with humble spirits an unquestionable guide, and therefore it is the Word of God?

In every generation, and wherever the light of Revelation has shone, men of all ranks, conditions, and states of mind have found in this Volume a correspondent for every movement toward the Better felt in their own hearts. The needy soul has found supply, the feeble a help, the sorrowful a comfort; yea, be the recipiency the least that can consist with moral life, there is an answering grace ready to enter. The Bible has been found a spiritual World, spiritual, and yet at the same time outward and common to all. You in one place, I in another, all men somewhere or at some time, meet with an assurance that the hopes and fears, the thoughts and yearnings that proceed from, or tend to, a right spirit in us, are not dreams or fleeting singularities, no voices heard in sleep, or spectres which the eye suffers but not perceives. As if on some dark night a pilgrim, suddenly beholding a bright star moving before him, should stop in fear and perplexity. But lo! traveller after traveller passes by him, and each, being questioned whither he is going, makes answer, 'I am following yon guiding Star!' The pilgrim quickens his own steps, and presses onward in confidence. More confident still will he be, if by

[a] It is remarkable that both parties might appeal to the same text of St Paul, πᾶσα γραφὴ Θεόπνευστος καὶ ὠφέλιμος πρὸς διδασκαλίαν, κ. τ. λ. (II Tim. 3. 16), which favors the one or the other opinion accordingly as the words are construed; and which, again, is the more probable construction, depends in great measure on the preference given to one or other of two different readings, the one having and the other omitting the conjunction copulative καὶ.

[The English version is: *All Scripture is given by inspiration of God, and is profitable*, etc. And in this rendering of the original the English is countenanced by the established Version of the Dutch Reformed Church: *Alle de Schrift is van Godt ingegeven, ende is nuttigh* etc. And by Diodati: *Tutta la Scrittura è divinamente inspirata, ed util*, etc. And by Martin: *Toute l'Ecriture est divinement inspirée, et profitable*, etc. And by Beza: *Tota Scriptura divinitus est inspirata, et utilis*, etc.

The other rendering is supported by the Vulgate: *Omnis Scriptura, divinitus inspirata, utilis est ad*, etc. By Luther: *Denn alle Schrift von Gott eingegeben, ist nütze zur*, etc. And by Calmet: *Toute l'Ecriture, qui est inspirée de Dieu, est utile*, etc. And by the common Spanish translation: *Toda Escritura, divinamente inspirada, es util para enseñar* etc. This is also the rendering of the Syriac (Pesch.) and two Arabic Versions, and is followed by Clement of Alexandria, Origen, and most of the Fathers. See the note in Griesbach. Tertullian represents the sense thus: *Legimus, Omnem Scripturam, aedificationi habilem, divinitus inspirari.* De Habit. Mul. c. iii. Origen has it several times, Θεόπνευστος οὖσα, ὠφέλιμός ἐστι, and once as in the received text. *Ed.*]

the way side he should find, here and there, ancient monuments, each with its votive lamp, and on each the name of some former pilgrim, and a record that there he had first seen or begun to follow the benignant Star!

No otherwise is it with the varied contents of the Sacred Volume. The hungry have found food, the thirsty a living spring, the feeble a staff, and the victorious warfarer songs of welcome and strains of music; and as long as each man asks on account of his wants, and asks what he wants, no man will discover aught amiss or deficient in the vast and many-chambered storehouse. But if instead of this, an idler or a scoffer should wander through the rooms, peering and peeping, and either detects, or fancies he has detected, here a rusted sword or pointless shaft, there a tool of rude construction, and superseded by later improvements (and preserved, perhaps, to make us more grateful for them); which of two things will a sober-minded man, who from his childhood upward had been fed, clothed, armed, and furnished with the means of instruction from this very magazine, think the fitter plan? Will he insist that the rust is not rust, or that it is a rust *sui generis*, intentionally formed on the steel for some mysterious virtue in it, and that the staff and astrolabe of a shepherd astronomer are identical with, or equivalent to, the quadrant and telescope of Newton or Herschel?[1] Or will he not rather give the curious inquisitor joy of his mighty discoveries, and the credit of them for his reward?

Or lastly, put the matter thus. For more than a thousand years the Bible, collectively taken, has gone hand in hand with civilization, science, law, in short, with the moral and intellectual cultivation of the species, always supporting, and often leading the way. Its very presence, as a believed Book, has rendered the nations emphatically a chosen race, and this too in exact proportion as it is more or less generally known and studied. Of those nations, which in the highest degree enjoy its influences, it is not too much to affirm, that the differences public and private, physical, moral and intellectual, are only less than what might be expected from a diversity in species. Good and holy men, and the best and wisest of mankind, the kingly spirits of history, enthroned in the hearts of mighty nations, have borne witness to its influences, have declared it to be beyond compare the most perfect instrument, the only adequate organ, of Humanity; the organ and instrument of all the gifts, powers, and tendencies, by which the individual is privileged to rise above himself – to leave behind, and lose his dividual phantom self, in order to find his true Self in that Distinctness where no division can be, in the

Eternal I AM, the Ever-living WORD, of whom all the elect from the
archangel before the throne to the poor wrestler with the Spirit *until
the breaking of day*[2] are but the fainter and still fainter echoes. And are
all these testimonies and lights of experience to lose their value and
efficiency, because I feel no warrant of history, or Holy Writ, or of
my own heart for denying, that in the framework and outward case
of this instrument a few parts may be discovered of less costly
materials and of meaner workmanship? Is it not a fact that the Books
of the New Testament were tried by their consonance with the rule,
and according to the analogy, of Faith? Does not the universally
admitted canon – that each part of Scripture must be interpreted by
the spirit of the whole – lead to the same practical conclusion as that
for which I am now contending; namely, that it is the spirit of the
Bible, and not the detached words and sentences, that is infallible and
absolute? Practical, I say, and spiritual too; and what knowledge not
practical or spiritual are we entitled to seek in our Bibles? Is the grace
of God so confined, the evidences of the present and actuating Spirit
so dim and doubtful, that to be assured of the same we must first take
for granted that all the life and co-agency of our humanity is miraculously suspended?

Whatever is spiritual, is *eo nomine*[3] supernatural; but must it be
always and of necessity miraculous? Miracles could open the eyes of
the body; and he that was born blind beheld his Redeemer. But
miracles, even those of the Redeemer himself, could not open the
eyes of the self-blinded, of the Sadducean sensualist[4] or the self-
righteous Pharisee; while to have said, *I saw thee under the fig tree*,[5]
sufficed to make a Nathanael believe.

To assert and to demand miracles without necessity was the vice of
the unbelieving Jews of old; and from the Rabbis and Talmudists[6]
the infection has spread. And would I could say that the symptoms of
the disease are confined to the Churches of the Apostasy! But all the
miracles, which the legends of Monk or Rabbi contain, can scarcely
be put in competition, on the score of complication, inexplicableness,
the absence of all intelligible use or purpose, and of circuitous self-
frustration, with those that must be assumed by the maintainers of
this doctrine, in order to give effect to the series of miracles, by which
all the nominal composers of the Hebrew nation before the time of
Ezra, of whom there are any remains, were successively transformed
into *automaton* compositors, so that the original text should be in
sentiment, image, word, syntax, and composition an exact impression of the divine copy! In common consistency the theologians,
who impose this belief on their fellow Christians, ought to insist

equally on the superhuman origin and authority of the Masora,[7] and to use more respectful terms, than has been their wont of late, in speaking of the false Aristeas's legend concerning the Septuagint.[8] And why the miracle should stop at the Greek Version, and not include the Vulgate, I can discover no ground in reason. Or if it be an objection to the latter, that this belief is actually enjoined by the Papal Church, yet the number of Christians who read the Lutheran, the Genevan, or our own authorized, Bible, and are ignorant of the dead languages, greatly exceeds the number of those who have access to the Septuagint. Why refuse the writ of consecration to these, or to the one at least appointed by the assertors' own Church? I find much more consistency in the opposition made under pretext of this doctrine to the proposals and publications of Kennicot, Mill, Bentley, and Archbishop Newcome.[9]

But I am weary of discussing a tenet, which the generality of divines and the leaders of the Religious Public have ceased to defend, and yet continue to assert or imply. The tendency manifested in this conduct, the spirit of this and the preceding century, on which, not indeed the tenet itself, but the obstinate adherence to it against the clearest light of reason and experience, is grounded, this it is which, according to my conviction, gives the venom to the error, and justifies the attempt to substitute a juster view. As long as it was the common and effective belief of all the Reformed Churches, (and by none was it more sedulously or more emphatically enjoined than by the great Reformers of our Church), that by the good Spirit were the spirits tried, and that the light, which beams forth from the written Word, was its own evidence for the children of light; as long as Christians considered their Bible as a plenteous entertainment, where every guest, duly called and attired, found the food needful and fitting for him, and where each – instead of troubling himself about the covers not within his reach – beholding all around him glad and satisfied, praised the banquet and thankfully glorified the Master of the feast, so long did the Tenet – that the Scriptures were written under the special impulse of the Holy Ghost remain safe and profitable. Nay, in the sense, and with the feelings, in which it was asserted, it was a truth – a truth to which every spiritual believer now and in all times will bear witness by virtue of his own experience. And if in the overflow of love and gratitude they confounded the power and presence of the Holy Spirit, working alike in weakness and in strength, in the morning mists and in the clearness of the full day; if they confounded this communion and co-agency of divine grace, attributable to the Scripture generally, with those express, and expressly recorded, communications and messages of the Most High, which form so large and prominent a portion of the same Scriptures; if, in short, they did not always duly distinguish the inspiration, the imbreathment, of the predisposing and assisting SPIRIT from the revelation of the informing WORD, it was at worst a harmless hyperbole. It was holden by all, that if the power of the Spirit from without furnished the text, the grace of the same Spirit from within must supply the comment.

In the sacred Volume they saw and reverenced the bounden wheat-sheaf that *stood upright*, and had *obeisance* from all the other sheaves[10] (the writings, I mean, of the Fathers and Doctors of the Church) sheaves depreciated indeed, more or less, with tares,

> and furrow-weeds,
> Darnel and many an idle flower that grew
> Mid the sustaining corn;[11]

yet sheaves of the same harvest, the sheaves of brethren! Nor did it occur to them, that, in yielding the more full and absolute honor to the sheaf of the highly favoured of their Father, they should be supposed to attribute the same worth and quality to the straw-bands which held it together. The bread of life was there. And this in an especial sense was *bread from heaven;* for no where had the same been found wild; no soil or climate dared claim it for its natural growth. In simplicity of heart they received the Bible as the precious gift of God, providential alike in origin, preservation, and distribution, without asking the nice question, whether all and every part were likewise miraculous. The distinction between the providential and the miraculous, between the divine Will working with the agency of natural causes, and the same Will supplying their place by a special *fiat* – this distinction has, I doubt not, many uses in speculative divinity. But its weightiest practical application is shown, when it is employed to free the souls of the unwary and weak in faith from the nets and snares, the insidious queries and captious objections, of the Infidel by calming the flutter of their spirits. They must be quieted, before we can commence the means necessary for their disentanglement. And in no way can this be better effected than when the frightened captives are made to see in how many points the disentangling itself is a work of expedience rather than of necessity; so easily and at so little loss might the web be cut or brushed away!

First, let their attention be fixed on the history of Christianity as learnt from universal tradition, and the writers of each successive generation. Draw their minds to the fact of the progressive and still continuing fulfilment of the assurance of a few fishermen, that both their own religion, though of divine origin, and the religion of their conquerors, which included or recognized all other religions of the known world, should be superseded by the faith in a man recently and ignominiously executed. Then induce them to meditate on the universals of Christian Faith, on Christianity, taken as the sum of belief common to Greek and Latin, to Romanist and Protestant. Shew them that this and only this is the *ordo traditionis, quam tradiderunt Apostoli iis quibus committebant ecclesias*, and which we should have been bound to follow, says Irenæus, *si neque Apostoli quidem Scripturas reliquissent.*[12] This is that *regula fidei*, that *sacramentum symboli memoriæ mandatum*, of which St Augustine says; *noveritis hoc esse Fidei Catholicæ fundamentum super quod edificium surrexit Ecclesiæ.*[13] This is the *norma Catholici et Ecclesiastici sensus*,[14] determined and explicated, but not augmented, by the Nicene Fathers, as Waterland[15] has irrefragably shewn; a norm or model of Faith grounded on the solemn affirmations of the Bishops collected from all parts of the Roman Empire, that this was the essential and unalterable Gospel received by them from their predecessors in all the Churches as the παράδοσις ἐκκλησιαστικὴ, *cui*, says Irenæus, *assentiunt multæ gentes eorum qui in Christum credunt sine charta et atramento, scriptam habentes per Spiritum in cordibus suis salutem, et veterum traditionem diligenter custodientes.*[16] Let the attention of such as have been shaken by the assaults of Infidelity be thus directed, and then tell me wherein a spiritual physician would be blameworthy, if he carried on the cure by addressing his patient in this manner:

'All men of learning, even learned unbelievers, admit that the greater part of the objections, urged in the popular works of Infidelity, to this or that verse or chapter of the Bible prove only the ignorance or dishonesty of the objectors. But let it be supposed for a moment that a few remain hitherto unanswered, nay, that to your judgment and feelings they appear unanswerable. What follows? That the Apostles' and Nicene Creed is not credible, the Ten Commandments not to be obeyed, the clauses of the Lord's Prayer not to be desired, or the Sermon on the Mount not to be practised? – See how the logic would look. David cruelly tortured the inhabitants of Rabbah (II Sam. 12. 31. Chr. 20. 3) and in several of the Psalms he invokes the bitterest curses on his enemies: therefore it is not to be believed that *the love of God toward us was manifested in sending his only-begotten Son into the world that we might live through him* (I John 4. 9). Or: Abijah is said to have collected an army of 400,000 men, and Jeroboam to have met him with an army of 800,000, each army consisting of chosen men (II Chr. 13. 3), and making together a host of 1,200,000, and Abijah to have slain 500,000 out of the 800,000: therefore, the words which admonish us that *if God so loved us, we ought also to love one another* (I John 4. 11), even our enemies, yea, *to bless them that curse* us, and to *do good to them that hate* us (Matt. 5. 44), cannot proceed from the Holy Spirit. Or: The first six chapters of the Book of Daniel contain several words and phrases irreconcilable with the commonly received dates, and those chapters and the Book of Esther have a traditional and legendary character unlike that of the other historical books of the Old Testament: therefore, those other books, by contrast with which the former appear suspicious, and the historical document, I Cor. 15. 1–8, are not to be credited!'

We assuredly believe that the Bible contains all truths necessary to salvation, and that therein is preserved the undoubted Word of God.[17] We assert likewise that, besides these express oracles and immediate revelations, there are Scriptures which to the soul and conscience of every Christian man bear irresistible evidence of the Divine Spirit assisting and actuating the authors; and that both these and the former are such as to render it morally impossible that any passage of the small inconsiderable portion, not included in one or other of these, can supply either ground or occasion of any error in faith, practice, or affection, except to those who wickedly and wilfully seek a pretext for their unbelief. And if in that small portion of the Bible which stands in no necessary connection with the known and especial ends and purposes of the Scriptures, there should be a few apparent errors resulting from the state of knowledge then existing – errors which the best and holiest men might entertain uninjured, and which without a miracle those men must have entertained; if I find no such miraculous prevention asserted, and see no reason for supposing it – may I not, to ease the scruples of a perplexed inquirer, venture to say to him: 'Be it so. What then? The absolute infallibility even of the inspired writers in matters altogether incidental and foreign to the objects and purposes of their inspiration is no part of my Creed; and even if a professed divine should follow the doctrine of the Jewish Church so far as not to attribute to the *Hagiographi*,[18] in every word and sentence, the same height and fullness of inspiration as to the Law and the Prophets, I feel no warrant to brand him as a heretic for an opinion, the admission of which disarms the Infidel without endangering a single article of the Catholic Faith. If to an unlearned but earnest and thoughtful neighbour, I give the advice; 'Use the Old Testament to express the affections excited, and to confirm the faith and morals taught you, in the New, and leave all the rest to the students and professors of theology and Church history! You profess only to be a Christian:' am I misleading my brother in Christ?

This I believe by my own dear experience, that the more tranquilly an inquirer takes up the Bible as he would any other body of ancient writings, the livelier and steadier will be his impressions of its superiority to all other books, till at length all other books and all other knowledge will be valuable in his eyes in proportion as they help him to a better understanding of his Bible. Difficulty after difficulty has been overcome from the time that I began to study the Scriptures with free and unboding spirit, under the conviction that my faith in the Incarnate Word and his Gospel was secure, whatever the result might be; the difficulties that still remain being so few and insignificant in my own estimation, that I have less personal interest in the question than many of those who will most dogmatically condemn me for presuming to make a question of it.

So much for scholars – for men of like education and pursuits as myself. With respect to Christians generally, I object to the consequence drawn from the Doctrine rather than to the Doctrine itself; a consequence not only deducible from the premises, but actually and imperiously deduced; according to which every man that can but read is to sit down to the consecutive and connected perusal of the Bible under the expectation and assurance that the whole is within his comprehension, and that, unaided by note or comment, catechism or liturgical preparation, he is to find out for himself what he is bound to believe and practise, and that whatever he conscientiously understands by what he reads, is to be *his* religion. For he has found it in his Bible, and the Bible is the Religion of Protestants![19]

Would I then withhold the Bible from the Cottager and the Artisan? Heaven forefend! The fairest flower that ever clomb up a cottage window is not so fair a sight to my eyes, as the Bible gleaming through the lower panes. Let it but be read as by such men it used to be read; when they came to it as to a ground covered with manna, even the bread which the Lord had given for his people to eat; where he that gathered much had nothing over, and he that gathered little had no lack. They gathered every man according to his eating.[20] They came to it as to a treasure-house of Scriptures; each visitant taking what was precious and leaving as precious for others; Yea, more, says our worthy old Church-historian, Fuller, where 'the same man at several times may in his apprehension prefer several Scriptures as best, formerly most affected with one place, for the present more delighted with another, and afterwards, conceiving comfort therein not so clear, choose other places as more pregnant and pertinent to his purpose. Thus God orders it, that divers men, (and perhaps the same man at divers times) make use of all his gifts, gleaning and gathering comfort, as it is scattered through the whole field of the Scripture.'[21]

Farewell.

Letter VII

You are now, my dear Friend, in possession of my whole mind on this point, one thing only excepted which has weighed with me more than all the rest, and which I have therefore reserved for my concluding Letter. This is the impelling principle, or way of thinking, which I have in most instances noticed in the assertors of what I have ventured to call Bibliolatry, and which I believe to be the main ground of its prevalence at this time, and among men whose religious views are any thing rather than enthusiastic.[22] And I here take occasion to declare, that my conviction of the danger and injury of this principle was and is my chief motive for bringing the Doctrine itself into question; the main error of which consists in the confounding of two distinct conceptions, revelation by the Eternal Word, and actuation of the Holy Spirit. The former indeed is not always or necessarily united with the latter – the prophecy of Balaam[23] is an instance of the contrary – but yet being ordinarily, and only not always, so united, the term, Inspiration, has acquired a double sense.

First, the term is used in the sense of Information miraculously communicated by voice or vision; and secondly, where without any sensible addition or infusion, the writer or speaker uses and applies his existing gifts of power and knowledge under the predisposing, aiding, and directing actuation of God's Holy Spirit. Now, between the first sense, that is, inspired revelation, and the highest degree of that grace and communion with the Spirit, which the Church under all circumstances, and every regenerate member of the Church of Christ, is permitted to hope, and instructed to pray, for – there is a positive difference of kind, a chasm, the pretended overleaping of which constitutes imposture, or betrays insanity. Of the first kind are the Law and the Prophets, no jot or tittle of which can pass unfulfilled, and the substance and last interpretation of which passes not away; for they wrote of Christ, and shadowed out the everlasting Gospel. But with regard to the second, neither the holy writers – the so called *Hagiographi* – themselves, nor any fair interpretations of Scripture, assert any such absolute diversity, or enjoin the belief of any greater difference of degree, than the experience of the Christian World, grounded on, and growing with, the comparison of these Scriptures with other works holden in honor by the Churches, has established. And *this* difference I admit; and doubt not that it has in every generation been rendered evident to as many as read these Scriptures under the gracious influence of the spirit in which they were written.

But alas! this is not sufficient; this cannot but be vague and unsufficing to those, with whom the Christian Religion is wholly objective, to the exclusion of all its correspondent subjective. It must appear vague, I say, to those whose Christianity, as matter of belief, is wholly external, and, like the objects of sense, common to all alike; altogether historical, an *opus operatum*,[24] its existing and present operancy in no respect differing from any other fact of history, and not at all modified by the supernatural principle in which it had its origin in time. Divines of this persuasion are actually, though without their own knowledge, in a state not dissimilar to that, into which the Latin Church sank deeper and deeper from the sixth to the fourteenth century; during which time religion was likewise merely objective and superstitious, a letter proudly emblazoned and illuminated, but yet a dead letter that was to be read by its own outward glories without the light of the Spirit in the mind of the believer. The consequence was too glaring not to be anticipated and, if possible, prevented. Without that spirit in each true believer, whereby we know the spirit of truth and the spirit of error in all things appertaining to salvation, the consequence must be – So many men, so many minds! And what was the antidote which the Priests and Rabbis of this purely objective Faith opposed to this peril? Why, an objective, outward Infallibility; concerning which, however, the differences were scarcely less or fewer than those which it was to heal; an Infallibility, which, taken literally and unqualified, became the source of perplexity to the well-disposed, of unbelief to the wavering, and of scoff and triumph to the common enemy; and which was, therefore, to be qualified and limited, and then it meant so much and so little, that to men of plain understandings and single hearts it meant nothing at all. It resided here. No! there. No! but in a third subject. Nay! neither here, nor there, nor in the third, but in all three conjointly!

But even this failed to satisfy; and what was the final resource, the doctrine of those who would not be called a Protestant Church, but in which doctrine the Fathers of Protestantism in England would have found little other fault, than it might be affirmed as truly of the decisions of any other Bishop as of the Bishop of Rome? The final resource was to restore what ought never to have been removed – the correspondent subjective, that is, the assent and confirmation of the Spirit promised to all true believers, as proved and manifested in the reception of such decision by the Church Universal in all its rightful members.

I comprise and conclude the sum of my conviction in this one sentence. Revealed Religion (and I know of no religion not revealed) is in its highest contemplation the unity, that is, the identity or co-inherence, of Subjective and Objective. It is in itself, and irrelatively, at once inward Life and Truth, and outward Fact and Luminary. But as all Power manifests itself in the harmony of correspondent Opposites, each supposing and supporting the other, so has Religion its objective, or historic and ecclesiastical pole, and its subjective, or spiritual and individual pole. In the miracles, and miraculous parts of religion – both in the first communication of divine truths, and in the promulgation of the truths thus communicated – we have the union of the two, that is, the subjective and supernatural displayed objectively – outwardly and phenomenally – *as* subjective and supernatural.

Lastly, in the Scriptures, as far as they are not included in the above as miracles, and in the mind of the believing and regenerate Reader and Meditater, there is proved to us the reciprocity, or reciprocation, of the Spirit as subjective and objective, which in conformity with the Scheme proposed by me, in aid of distinct conception and easy recollection, I have named the Indifference.[a] What I mean by this, a familiar acquaintance with the more popular parts of Luther's Works, especially his Commentaries, and the delightful volume of his Table Talk, would interpret for me better than I can do for myself. But I do my best, when I say that no Christian probationer, who is earnestly working out his salvation, and experiences the conflict of the spirit with the evil and the infirmity within him and around him, can find his own state brought before him and, as it were, antedated, in writings reverend even for their antiquity and enduring permanence, and far more, and more abundantly, consecrated by the reverence, love, and grateful testimonies of good men through the

---

[a] The Papacy elevated the Church to the virtual exclusion or suppression of the Scriptures: the modern Church of England, since Chillingworth, has so raised up the Scriptures as to annul the Church: both alike have quenched the Holy Spirit, as the *mesothesis* or indifference of the two, and substituted an alien compound for the genuine Preacher, which should be the *synthesis* of the Scriptures and the Church, and the sensible voice of the Holy Spirit. *Lit. Rem.* v. iii. p. 93. *Ed.*

long succession of ages, in every generation, and under all states of minds and circumstances of fortune, that no man, I say, can recognize his own inward experiences in such Writings, and not find an objectiveness, a confirming and assuring outwardness, and all the main characters of reality, reflected therefrom on the spirit, working in himself and in his own thoughts, emotions, and aspirations – warring against sin, and the motions of sin. The unsubstantial, insulated Self passes away as a stream; but these are the shadows and reflections of the Rock of Ages, and of the Tree of Life that starts forth from its side.

On the other hand, as much of reality, as much of objective truth, as the Scriptures communicate to the subjective experiences of the Believer, so much of present life, of living and effective import, do these experiences give to the letter of these Scriptures. In the one *the Spirit itself beareth witness with our spirit*, that we have received the *spirit of adoption*;[25] in the other our spirit bears witness to the power of the Word, that it is indeed the Spirit that proceedeth from God. If in the holy men thus actuated all imperfection of knowledge, all participation in the mistakes and limits of their several ages had been excluded, how could these Writings be or become the history and example, the echo and more lustrous image of the work and warfare of the sanctifying Principle in us? If after all this, and in spite of all this, some captious litigator should lay hold of a text here or there – St Paul's *cloak left at Troas with Carpus*,[26] or a verse from the Canticles, and ask: 'Of what spiritual use is this?' – the answer is ready: It proves to us that nothing can be so trifling as not to supply an evil heart with a pretext for unbelief.

Archbishop Leighton has observed that the Church has its extensive and intensive states, and that they seldom fall together.[27] Certain it is that since kings have been her nursing fathers, and queens her nursing mothers, our theologians seem to act in the spirit of fear rather than in that of faith; and too often instead of inquiring after the Truth in the confidence, that whatever is truth must be fruitful of good to all who *are in Him that is true*, they seek with vain precautions *to guard against the possible inferences* which perverse and distempered minds may pretend, whose whole Christianity – do what we will – is and will remain nothing but a Pretence.

You have now my entire mind on this momentous Question, the grounds on which it rests, and the motives which induce me to make it known; and I now conclude by repeating my request – Correct me, or confirm me.

Farewell.

6. *Thomas Arnold, 'On the Right Interpretation and Understanding of the Scriptures' (1829) (ending at page xl of the 1874 edition)*

The first two-thirds of Thomas Arnold's essay on the interpretation of scripture is printed here. It propounds the liberal Anglican view of history which was explored by J. C. Hare, H. H. Milman, Connop Thirlwall and Arnold's pupil and biographer, A. P. Stanley. 'It was Thomas Arnold', says Duncan Forbes 'who pursued the possibility of a science of history most ardently, and who alone gave his ideas of the subject any formal shape' (*The Liberal Anglican Idea of History*, Cambridge 1952, p. 12).

Arnold was a romantic and a Lakist. He consulted Wordsworth about the building of his Lakeland home, Fox How, and he admired Coleridge. So his historical vision was formed by their convictions, particularly Coleridge's, which were ripe for development by historians: the universal scope, the unity, the development through time, and the duty to empathise with the apparent strangeness of the past. The all-important unity was guaranteed by robust theism. We shall see this become etiolated in the work of his son, Matthew Arnold. But for Thomas himself, divine providence was a bulwark against rationalistic historiography with its secularised belief in progress and 'the march of mind'. Yet Arnold was not reactionary, nor even conservative. He was actively and radically concerned about the condition of England, and his emphasis on development and universality was opposed to the essentially unhistorical and decidedly reactionary thought of the Oxford Movement – polemic in which Matthew followed him vigorously. Arnold likened the biblical Melchizedek to the priest-kings of ancient Greece; Stanley, the time of the Book of Judges to the European middle ages. Such comparisons incensed Tractarians.

Before he wrote this essay Arnold had read Niebuhr, learning German for the purpose, and got a sense of the development of nations from within as they went through similar sequences of development. He had got acquainted with the calm and objective view of universal history in Vico's *Scienza Nuova*. The Bible was, in a quite precise sense, waiting for interpretation in terms of historical development. St Paul rethought biblical history into a series of epochs in order to accommodate his conversion to Christianity. In Galatians, and more fully in Romans, he worked out a scheme whereby other things were required of mankind by God before Christ came than He required of them after his coming. A favourite preaching text of Arnold's was Galatians

On Right Interpretation

3. 24: 'The law (sc. the whole Old Testament dispensation) was our school-master to bring us unto Christ.' The verse appealed to the headmaster as well as the historian in him. And Stanley plausibly hailed the writer of the Book of Daniel as the first philosopher of history (*Jewish Church*, III, p. 43): for in Daniel there is the apocalyptic division of historical process into contrasted but sequential ages or 'times' which Paul adapted.

'Accommodation', which plays such a large part in Arnold's thinking in this essay, must be seen in this grand frame. It is not merely special pleading on behalf of revolting episodes in the Old Testament. It is a serious theological attempt, grounded in scripture and Anglican theology ('accommodation' was a favourite idea of the late seventeenth-century divines), to see the relations of God and mankind as reciprocal. It was an historically serious attempt to explore the reciprocal relations of religion and culture. Last and not least, it had practical virtue for Arnold's work as the reforming headmaster of Rugby. His study was not just a bookroom, like Collins's. It was a place to which pupils came for counselling when Arnold signalled, by hoisting a flag, that he was free to talk to them. The development of nations and the development of individuals were, Arnold believed, parallel. So historical and educational endeavours coincided. Accommodation was as necessary when dealing with boys as with biblical history. In a famous letter of 2 March 1828 he wrote:

My object will be, if possible, to form Christian men, for Christian boys I can hardly hope to make; I mean that from the naturally imperfect state of boyhood they are not susceptible of Christian principles in their full development upon their practice, and I suspect that a low standard of morals in many respects must be tolerated among them, as it was on a larger scale in what I consider the boyhood of the human race.

Here is the moral and historical relativism which can still scandalise the orthodox when it is aired by biblical critics. But here the danger is defused by staunch belief in the providential direction of history which allowed for the differences which he noted in his book of themes, a manuscript at Rugby, in 1827:

of the use of examples in Argument and the cautions to be used in taking them from the history of other times and countries.

His introduction of history to the curriculum at Rugby was as much a Christian and moral as an academic reform. The sixth form, 'Christian men' whose relation to their juniors was comparable to the relation of the prophets to ancient Israel, read Guizot and Ranke. Arnold helped to bring up a generation for whom biblical interpretation and the new sense and study of history went hand in hand for the public good.

On the Right Interpretation and Understanding of the Scriptures

No question can be of greater importance to every man, than that which regards the right use of the Scriptures. The volume of the Old and New Testaments is received by Christians as their rule of life: they look to it as the source of all their religious knowledge, and all their hopes and fears beyond the grave; and as to the supreme guide of their principles and practice in this world. But that which holds good of God's natural gifts, holds good, also, of the revelation which he has been pleased to make to us of himself and of his will. It is not available to our use, without some efforts on our part: its benefits may remain hidden, nay, we may pervert it into absolute poison, unless we apply ourselves to it with a sound understanding, and a sincere and teachable heart.

As with God's other gifts also, so it is with the Scriptures, that the difficulties in applying them rightly become greater in proportion to our power of mastering them. This is a part of our trial, whose severity increases as we are able to bear it. A very ignorant man, therefore, and one who has no time to cultivate his understanding, is saved from perceiving the difficulty, which, if he did perceive it, he would be incapable of solving. Such a man, with the blessing of good elementary teaching, if he proceeds to read the Scriptures with a devout spirit and an honest purpose, finds in them all that is required for his own personal wants in belief and in conduct. There is much in them which he does not understand, many benefits which he cannot extract from them, many beautiful proofs of their divine original which he cannot discover or appreciate. But then he finds in them no perplexities, he does not see the apparent incongruities out of which their perfect harmony is composed; if there is much which he cannot interpret at all, there is little which he misinterprets. This state, however, is one which an educated man cannot remain in. With greater powers and opportunities of discovering truth, he gains, unavoidably, a greater sensitiveness to apparent error or inconsistency, a greater impatience of obscurity and confusion. It is vain for such a man to envy the peace of ignorance; God calls him to the painful pursuit of knowledge, and he must not disobey the call. Nor may he, as some do, strive to do violence to his understanding, and to the very nature of things, by trying to combine knowledge with an undisturbed tranquillity of belief, to enjoy the pleasures of a clear and active mind, without being subject to its pains. He may not say, 'Here I will have the comfort of a reasonable belief, and here of a blind one.' It must be all reasonable, or all blind; otherwise it will soon vanish altogether, and be succeeded by unbelief. Besides, he has not only himself to think of, but others. It is a fatal stumbling-block to many when they see a professed advocate of Christianity shrinking from inquiry, and manifestly replying to their doubts, and silencing his own, by considerations wholly inconclusive as to the point at issue.

But I wish to consider particularly the case of the great majority of young men of the educated classes of society; of all those, in short, who do not choose the ministry of the Church for their profession. Consider these men in the present age of intellectual activity; how much they will read, how much they will inquire, with what painful accuracy they will labour after truth in their several studies or pursuits. A mind thus disciplined, and acquiring, as it generally does in the process, an almost over-suspiciousness of every thing which it has not sifted to the bottom, turns from its professional or habitual studies to that of the Bible. I say nothing at present of the existence of any moral obstacles to belief; let us merely consider the intellectual difficulties of the case. From his own early education, from the practice of the Church, from the common language of Christians, a young man of this description is led to regard the volume of the Old and New Testaments as containing God's revelation of himself to mankind; he is taught that all its parts are of equal authority: but in what sense the revelation of the Old and New Testament is *one*, and all its parts of equal authority, he has probably never clearly apprehended nor thought of inquiring. He takes it then as *one*, in the simplest sense, and begins to read the Bible as if it were, like the Koran, all composed at one time, and addressed to persons similarly situated.[1] His habits of mind render it impossible for him to read without inquiry: obscurities, apparent contradictions, and still more, what he would feel to be immoralities, cannot pass without notice. He turns to commentators of reputation, anxious to read their solution of all the difficulties which bewilder him. He finds them too often greatly insufficient in knowledge, and perhaps still more so in judgment; often misapprehending the whole difficulty of a question, often answering it by repeating the mere assertions or opinions of others, and confounding the proper provinces of the intellect and the moral sense, so as to make questions of criticism, questions of religion, and to brand as profane, inquiries, to which the character of profaneness or devotion is altogether inapplicable. When the man is thus intellectually perplexed, undoubtedly all the moral obstacles within him to his embracing the Gospel beset him with tremendous advantage. I speak not only of positive obstacles, but of such as are negative; the absence of devotional habits, and the want of an experimental knowledge of the power and living truth of the Gospel. There may be, and how often is there an absence of these, without any hostile disposition towards Christianity; nay, with a general reverence and regard for it. For the time being, in many cases such as I have supposed, the struggle is mainly an intellectual one: the difficulty lies in the understanding, not in the heart. No doubt every day that this struggle continues, the foundation, at least, of moral difficulty is being laid: the heart cannot long hold aloof from being with Christ, without being seduced to turn against him. But, for the time the heart might be firmly won if the intellect were satisfied; or, more properly, if, without being fully satisfied, it were at least put in the right way of becoming so. Above all, it must be satisfied on those points where its difficulties have assumed a moral character; for here it feels itself warranted in requiring satisfaction: and even if it acknowledge the duty of submission on other points, it will insist that it never can be right to call evil, good, or to ascribe the encouragement of evil to God. It seems to me, then, to be a work of great usefulness to endeavour to meet the wants of a mind so circumstanced, to present such a view of the Scripture revelation as may enable a young man to read his Bible not only without constant perplexity, but with immense and increasing comfort and benefit.

In the first place, then, it should be remembered, that a command given to one man, or to one generation of men, is, and can be, binding upon other men, and other generations, only so far forth as the circumstances in which both are placed are similar. A commandment of eternal and universal obligation is one that relates to points in which all men at all times are alike, and which there is the same reason, therefore, for all obeying equally. Other commandments may be of a transitory nature, and binding only upon particular persons, or at particular times; but yet, when they proceed from the highest authority, their indirect use may be universal, even although their direct use be limited. That is, from knowing what was God's will under such and such circumstances, we may gather, by parity of reasoning, what it will be in all other circumstances; namely, the same when the circumstances are the same; analogous when the circumstances are analogous; and absolutely contrary, when they also are contrary.

It is these two rules, taken together, which will enable us to use the Old Testament, and, indeed, every part of God's revelation to man, at once fully and rightly. For while, on the one hand, they will prevent us from applying to ourselves commandments which we were never intended to obey; so, on the other hand, they will hinder us from neglecting any part of God's dealings with men, as if it was of no concern to us; whereas it is, in truth, of concern to us; and where it does not teach directly, it yet teaches according to the analogy of circumstances, that, as we should do the same under the same circumstances, so we should act analogously under analogous circumstances, and oppositely when the circumstances are opposite.

If it be said that all this renders the application of the Bible exceedingly difficult, and opens the door to a great deal of evasion, I answer, that undoubtedly the application of many parts of the Bible is difficult; and this is sufficiently proved by the discordant and unsatisfactory manner in which different persons have actually applied them. And as to wilful evasion of God's commandments, that will ever be easy; I may add, that God designs it to be easy to all those who, at their own peril, choose to practise it. That the word of God should furnish a ready occasion of perversion to those who wish to pervert it, can surely surprise no one who has a moderate acquaintance with God's manner of dealing with us, either as declared in the course of his providence, or in his own revelation.

But for those who really seek to know God's will, this method of discovering it will be exceedingly useful, inasmuch as it leads directly to an accurate knowledge both of the Scriptures on the one hand, and of themselves and their own condition on the other. Every one must have observed the difficulty which persons in general feel in bringing home to themselves what they read, even in the New Testament. They have but vague notions either of the state of things to which Christ's words applied in the first instance, or of those points in themselves to which they apply no less forcibly now; whereas the principle, on which I have laid so much stress, requires of us a very exact and lively perception, first, of all the features of the case to which the Divine command originally was addressed, and then of all the particulars of our own. It obliges us to consider carefully the purpose of the commandment when first given, what evil it was intended to check, and what particular form the evil at that time wore. Thus separating what is essential in it from what is accidental, we learn what is God's will; and then, by looking into ourselves and around us, and observing what is the actual form in our own case of the evil opposed to his will, we discover exactly to what parts in our own character or conduct his commandment is virtually and really directed.

II The revelations of God to man were gradual, and adapted to his state at the several periods when they were successively made. And, on the same principle, commands were given at one time which were not given at another; and which, according to God's method of dealing with mankind, not only were not, but *could not have been given*. This brings us to the famous doctrine of *accommodation*, which having been carried by some persons to an extravagant and offensive length, has fallen, consequently, with many good men into great suspicion. No doubt a man may abuse this doctrine, as the Nicolaitans did, and maintain that all God's commandments were but accommodations to man's imperfect state, which, in his riper knowledge, he might safely violate.[2] But I am not considering how a wicked man may pervert this doctrine, but how a good man may profit by it. The principle of accommodation is so expressly allowed by Christ himself, when he declares the liberty of divorce to have been given to the Jews 'on account of the hardness of their hearts,' that the question amongst Christians respecting it can only be one of degree. But perhaps it will be desirable to show more fully how *accommodation* must exist in every revelation from God to man, unless it were God's pleasure to change this world from a state of imperfection to one of perfection: in other words, he who argues against accommodation, as inconsistent with the Divine attributes, is but approaching unawares that great question of the origin of evil, which never has been solved by man, and probably never can be, until he be removed to a state where the *experience* of evil is no more.[3]

In any communication between a Being of infinite knowledge and one of finite, it is obvious that the former must speak sometimes according to the views of the latter, unless it be his pleasure to raise him almost to his own level. In short, unless revelation be universal; that is, unless it extend to the removal of all error, and the communication of all truth, there must be an accommodation in it to the opinions of mankind, on all points where those opinions are not meant to be specially corrected. When God chooses a being of finite knowledge to be the medium of his revelations, it is at once understood that the faculties of this being are left in their natural state, except so far as regards the especial message with which he is intrusted. But, perhaps, we do not enough consider how, in the very message itself, there must be a mixture of accommodation to our ignorance; for complete knowledge, on any one point, could not be given without extending itself to other points; nay, the very means by which we receive all our knowledge, that is, language, and the observations of our senses, are themselves so imperfect, that they could not probably convey to the mind other than imperfect notions of truth. This, again, is allowed for, at least professedly, in interpreting those expressions which the Scripture employs to describe the dealings of God with men: the 'wrath,' 'jealousy,' 'repentance,' etc., of the Divine Being; and, much more, his 'sitting on high in heaven,' his 'right hand,' 'eyes,' 'ears,' etc., are acknowledged to be accommodations; that is, to convey to us, not the very reality, but something as near the reality as God sees it expedient for us to know. But in the case of our Lord Jesus Christ, the necessity of this accommodation becomes more evident. When God dwelt among us, and vouchsafed to converse daily with us, it is manifest that infinity, thus communing with his finite creatures, must have adapted himself to their notions, or else he would have altered their nature to something far above humanity. He must have often spoken as a man who possessed no greater knowledge than the men of that time and country. We cannot, therefore, argue that all the opinions which Christ did not contradict he sanctioned with Divine authority; nay, he must have used himself the common language of men, if it were a point on which no revelation was intended to be made. And to say that this is to mislead mankind, is untrue, as well as irreverent, unless we are prepared to show how otherwise God could possibly have communed with mankind without making his revelation extend to every thing.

This, then, is accommodation, so far as regards our knowledge. Another sort of accommodation regards our practice. That God has not thought proper to raise mankind at once to its highest state of moral perfection, any more than individuals are born at once to their maturity, is a matter of actual experience. Why he has so willed it, is a question which it is vain to ask; and, because vain, presumptuous. The human species has gone through a state of less fulness of moral knowledge, of less enlightened conscience, as compared with its subsequent attainments, just as every individual has done. Now this less perfect state being a part of God's will, the training applied to it must have been suited to it; that is, it must have taken it as imperfect, and dealt with it as such; not anticipating the instructions of a more perfect state, but improving it in its imperfection; not changing spring into summer, but making of spring the best that could be made of it. At the same time the progress of mankind was to be provided for; perfection was to be prepared for, although not immediately made attainable. While, therefore, general principles of duty were given, all the conclusions which follow from them, with regard to our particular relations in life, were not at the same time developed; and men did not at once develope them for themselves.

Their notions, therefore, on many particular points of practice, were really irreconcilable with the principles which they acknowledged: but the inconsistency did not strike them; and revelation did not as yet interfere to make it palpable. This was an imperfection which belonged to their state of moral inexperience: and this imperfection God allowed, and treated individuals as good and just persons, notwithstanding their participation in it, if up to the extent of their knowledge they endeavoured to do what was right.

But, further, this imperfect moral knowledge on many particular points of practice being allowed, if an action, on any one of these points was capable of strengthening their moral principle generally, or tended to serve any other useful end, it would properly be commanded to *them*, however inconsistent it might be with more enlightened notions of particular duty. It might be commanded them, because it could do *them* no moral harm, but probably the contrary; and because, being a command in a particular case, and not a statement of a general principle, it could not justly interfere with the acquisition of purer views by future generations, when the dispensation of the fulness of time was come. And therefore not only would practices be tolerated by God in early times, but actions would positively be commanded, which, in a more advanced state of knowledge, men would be taught of God to shrink from as evil.

Now, from God's way of dealing with the childhood and youth of the human race, we may expect to derive a lesson for ourselves, in our treatment of the childhood and youth of an individual. We find exactly the same state of mind; that is to say, sound general principles acknowledged, but the application of them to particular cases of practice not yet made, and, therefore, the notions of right and wrong, in particular branches of conduct, confused and faulty. And our object being the formation of a perfect character in manhood, we must not mar this prospect by seeking to forestall it; we must not be too anxious to enlighten the conscience ere it be sufficiently strengthened; it being much more important to keep up the habit of obeying conscience implicitly, than to extend unseasonably its nominal dominion, at the risk of weakening its real hold upon the mind. Of course, the aids offered by Christianity enable us to enlighten the conscience earlier and more fully than we could dare to do without it, because they render obedience to conscience a matter of less hopeless difficulty. Still, while inculcating on a child's mind the principles of Christianity in all their purity, I should hesitate to press upon him all the deductions which follow from those principles, with regard to the various points of his own daily life. I should feel that he would not be able to bear them; that is to say, that his character would not have strength enough to conform to so pure a standard, and that it would be injurious to his future excellence, were I to familiarize him to the habit of acting constantly against his sense of duty.

A similar forbearance of instruction, amounting sometimes to an actual prohibition of what would be a duty in a more advanced state of moral proficiency, is practised also for another reason. When an action, right in itself, is almost sure to be performed from a wrong motive, we feel bound to prohibit it altogether; when an action, wrong in itself, is yet likely to be abstained from with a moral injury to the character, while its commission, owing to the unenlightened state of the conscience, would be attended with no harm at all, we should be afraid to see it forborne. Who dares do otherwise than forbid his children to inform him, unasked, of the faults of one another? Who would not be sorry to see a boy submitting passively to all sorts of ill usage from his companions, since, with a boy's notions of right and wrong, resistance would involve no breach of duty, while passiveness would imply and tend to encourage the habit of cowardice?

Undoubtedly the principle here spoken of is one of most difficult application; because as the standard of duty may not be too high for the strength of the character to bear, so, on the other hand, unless we are careful gradually to raise it, that excellence which is the object of education will never be attained at all. Still, however liable to be misapplied, it is a principle which God's dealings with the earlier ages of the human race strongly sanction, and which, though liable to abuse in our hands like every other rule of conduct, was employed by him with unmingled usefulness.

These two considerations then, That commandments given to persons differently circumstanced from ourselves, while they are not directly binding on us so far as this difference extends, are yet a most valuable guide indirectly and by analogy; and, That God's revelations to man, including in this term both communications of knowledge and directions for conduct, were adapted to his state at the several periods when they were successively made, so that actions may be even commanded at one period which, at another, men would have learnt to be evil, and which never, therefore, could be commanded to *them*; these two considerations will enable a young man, not only to read the Bible without perplexity, but to find in all of it, in the older dispensation no less than the new, a consistent and all-sufficient guide for his daily living.

To exemplify these two principles fully would be to write a

commentary on a large portion of the Old Testament. But, in order to illustrate my meaning, I will give one or two instances of the application of each, to which an attentive reader may easily add others in the course of his own study of the Scriptures.

1 The second commandment of the Decalogue forbids the making any representation whatever of the object of our worship. The principle of this commandment was to prevent us from forming unwarranted, and therefore necessarily unworthy, notions of God. (Compare Deuteronomy 4. 15–19.) 'Ye saw no similitude on the day that the Lord spake unto you in Horeb out of the midst of the fire:' no similitude therefore was warranted to them by God, and none might be lawfully imagined by them for themselves. The spirit of this commandment is eternal; man may never image to himself an object of worship, without the warrant of God. They then violate this commandment most flagrantly, who think of God otherwise than his revealed word authorizes; who imagine him to be less pure and holy, less severe against sin, less requiring perfect goodness in his creatures, than he himself declares himself to be. They also violate it, who dare to image, in any bodily form, the invisible and incomprehensible Father of all things.[a] And they too seem to violate it, who, not believing of God as he teaches us, would fain approach him through the mediation of his creatures, and go to him by another way than that only one which he has appointed, the mediation of his Son, Jesus Christ. But most assuredly they do not violate it, who represent him, who think of him, who worship him, under an image which he himself has sanctioned – the human form of the man Christ Jesus. For *this* similitude of God, we have God's warrant; he showed no likeness of himself when he spake in Horeb out of the midst of the fire; but he has shown one to the Christian Church, when 'the express Image of his Person' took upon him the nature of man, in order visibly to declare Him who, in his own essence is invisible. And therefore to object to this warranted similitude of God, and to deny ourselves the benefits which it was graciously intended to furnish, to turn from the image of Christ crucified[b] which God himself has given

[a] And though some of the best Christians have allowed themselves to do it, I cannot but think that to speak of the Holy Spirit as a dove, from a misapplication, and even a misinterpretation of a passage in Scripture, is a violation of the spirit of this commandment.
[b] I say the image of 'Christ crucified,' because representations of our Lord as a *child* do appear to me unwarranted, and only to have been introduced for the sake of the representation of the Virgin which always accompanies them. Nor do I deny that where the New Testament is kept out of the people's hands, and their knowledge of Christianity is corrupted with many superstitions, the crucifix may be often an object of superstitious worship; so that, very possibly, the English reformers were right at that time in doing away with the use of it. But I cannot conceive it otherwise than useful, where the Scriptures are generally circulated, and where Christianity is truly known; and as it may be most dangerous where men are most attached to it, so I think it is

us, because we may not make images of our own devices, seems to me an instance of the great mischief of applying to ourselves, directly, what was commanded to men under different circumstances, and with especial relation to that difference. While, on the other hand, to speak of the commandment as altogether obsolete, and to exclude it altogether from the Decalogue, as the Roman Catholics do in some of their popular catechisms, is an irreverent rejection of God's law, which must be eternal in its direct purport, so far as the circumstances are the same; and most useful indirectly, even where the circumstances are different.

2 God commanded Abraham to sacrifice his son Isaac; and Abraham's ready obedience is one of the most striking instances on record of self-devoting faith. A writer in the 'Morning Watch,'[5] while combating the view taken of the Old Testament by a writer in the 'Edinburgh Review,' speaks of this as 'God's approbation of an act of infanticide.' He chooses, I suppose, to use the offensive term *infanticide*, in order to express his belief that virtue and obedience are synonymous terms, and that what God commands, be it what it may, becomes instantly our duty to perform. A far more cautious and wiser writer, and one never to be named without respect, Bishop Butler, has made a wide distinction between principles and habits, and individual actions. 'God,' he says, 'could not command us to cultivate habits of deceit and cruelty; but he may command us to take away life in particular cases, because that is not in itself necessarily wrong.' This is perfectly true; but though all taking away life is not wrong, yet can it be otherwise than wrong, according to an enlightened view of our duty, for a father to take away the life of his innocent son, and to imagine himself, by such an act, offering an acceptable sacrifice to God? And the question is, whether our notions of God himself are not rather derived from those notions of goodness which he has implanted in us, than our notions of goodness derived from our idea of God: whether, therefore, it is not a contradiction to imagine God as commanding an act which, to our best reason, appears evil; and whether, in our ignorance of the unseen world, any vision, dream, or revelation whatsoever, so commanding us to evil, can bear with it an external attestation of its coming from God, sufficient to counterbalance the internal evidence that it does not come from him; whether, in short, a sane mind is not bound to consider such a suggestion or command as coming from an evil spirit, and permitted by God for the trial of his faith, rather than as

most wanted where the feeling against it would be the strongest, as in England at this moment, and still more in Scotland.[+]

the real will of God, for the guidance of his conduct. I confess that if we suppose the external and internal evidence, with respect to any message professing to come from God, to be thus opposed to one another, I see not how the human mind can escape from the agony of such a conflict but through insanity.

But now apply to the case of Abraham the principle which has been developed above; and not only does every difficulty vanish, but the story remains fraught with instruction for God's people in every age, let their advancement in moral knowledge be what it will. Human sacrifices, and particularly the sacrifice of children by their parents, were notoriously practised by the nations of Canaan (Deut. 12. 31). By the Moabites they were considered as the greatest possible mark of devotion, and performed, therefore, in circumstances of extraordinary peril, as the means of obtaining deliverance when every less precious offering was unavailing (compare Micah 6. 7, and II Kings 3. 27). So many years before God had declared his abhorrence of such sacrifices, in a time and country where they were practised as the most solemn rite of religion, and with the natural feeling so strongly prompting us to think that God will be propitiated by that which it costs us most to offer, what reason is there for thinking that the command to sacrifice his son Isaac was received by Abraham in any other light than as a command to a most painful duty, severely trying, indeed, to his feelings, but in no way startling to his conscience? And this is exactly the trial of faith which has been given to so many of Abraham's spiritual children; not that they have ever been commanded to do what they thought evil, but what they knew was severely painful, to part with what they loved most dearly for God's sake. The particular sort of sacrifice commanded to Abraham could not indeed be commanded to us, because *we* have learnt from God that such offerings are an abomination which he hateth: but analogously the trial is often repeated now, and fathers are still called upon, from time to time, to sacrifice their children's fairest earthly prospects, in order that they may obey the will of God.

I know there are some persons who cannot bear to suppose that Abraham was less aware than we are of the wickedness of human sacrifices in general, because they believe that he was, in all points of duty, no less enlightened than the most enlightened Christian. Do they think, then, that polygamy is a matter of indifference; or do they imagine that Abraham, judging of it as Christians do, yet lived habitually in known sin? Or what is the meaning of our Lord's declaration, that the least in the kingdom of God was greater than John the Baptist, than whom there had arisen, among all that were born of women, no greater prophet? Or how should the prophets and righteous men of old have desired, and desired in vain, to see and hear what Christ's apostles saw and heard, if they already had known as much as Christ, or his Spirit, could have taught them?

I proceed to another example of the same principle, the command given to Saul to destroy the Amalekites utterly, and his punishment for disobeying it. In this case, as in the command to extirpate the Canaanites, the precise point of difficulty is often misapprehended. Undoubtedly the destruction effected by an earthquake or a pestilence is just as unsparing and indiscriminate, without being thought to impeach the goodness of God. The difficulty relates not to the sufferers in this destruction, but to the agents of it; because to men, in an advanced state of moral knowledge and feeling, the command to perpetrate such general slaughter, to massacre women and infants, the sick and the decrepit, could not fail to be mischievous; or rather, it would be so revolting, that they could not, and ought not to think that God could possibly be the author of it. To men in the Christian stage of their moral progress, a command to trample the feelings of humanity under foot, and to acquire that brutality which is the inevitable result of such a conquest, could not but be injurious; at an earlier stage, or at a more advanced one, the case is different; half-civilized men, who have not risen to these feelings, or glorified saints, who need them not, because they are arrived at a state above the passions of humanity, may be the executioners of God's judgments; but the disciples of the Son of Man must, like their Master, not destroy men's lives, but save them. Now in Saul's time, and long afterwards, the laws of war, if so they may be called, were so thoroughly barbarous, that no amount of slaughter, committed against enemies, was likely to shock the feelings of any one. Every one knows the passage in Homer (Iliad VI. 55–62), in which the poet expresses his approbation of the advice given by Agamemnon to Menelaus, not to spare a single Trojan, young or old, even to the babe in its mother's womb. In such a state of feeling, when lives were spared, it was not from humanity, but from avarice or lust; and therefore, the command given to the Israelites under Joshua, and again to Saul, when attacking the Amalekites, to destroy every thing, and take none of the spoil to themselves, so far from hurting their notions of right and wrong, was in fact a trial of their self-denial; it called upon them to renounce the ordinary fruits of victory, the slaves, the female captives, the cattle, and the silver and gold, and to act merely as men who fought for God and not for themselves. This command Saul could not persuade himself to obey: he spared the best of the spoil, of the sheep and of the oxen, for the purpose of having a great sacrificial feast; he spared Agag, to have the glory of exhibiting a captive king eating bread under his table. He could not, certainly, plead humanity as his motive, inasmuch as the women and children had been destroyed, so far as it appears, without any scruple felt or pretended. In short, the command was no more shocking, from its requiring the Amalekites to be slaughtered rather than kept as slaves, than it would be now, if a general were ordered to destroy the cannon and baggage that he had taken, instead of keeping them as a source of prize-money. Such an order might be very disappointing, and might be a hard trial to his obedience; but certainly could not be objected to, as commanding what he could scruple, on conscientious grounds, to execute.

These instances will sufficiently explain my meaning, and will show, I think, how completely the principle which they illustrate will remove all the principal difficulties of the Old Testament. One more I will notice, because it was quoted by Carlile, some years ago, in his defence on a charge of blasphemy.[6] He read aloud, in court, the seventeenth and eighteenth verses of the thirty-first chapter of Numbers, containing the command of Moses to spare only the virgins among the women of Midian, and to destroy all the rest. And he then asked if it was possible to believe that a book, containing such atrocities, could ever have proceeded from God. Certainly God would never give such a command to any one whose moral feelings would be shocked by it; but they to whom it was addressed felt it only as a restraint on their self-indulgence; they were not allowed to plunge into those sensual excesses to which the grown up women of Midian were addicted, as part of their religious rites.

How little men, even at a much later period, were likely to scruple morally at the act of putting such a number of women to death, may be judged of from the sweeping execution of all the female slaves of their household, by Ulysses and Telemachus, in the Odyssey, and by the utterly indifferent, or rather almost exulting manner, in which the poet describes their sufferings.

7. Benjamin Jowett, 'On the Interpretation of Scripture' from 'Essays and Reviews' (1860), Section 3

The aftermath of *Essays and Reviews* is a famous story (well told by Owen Chadwick in his *The Victorian Church*, 1972, vol. II, pp. 75–90) of muddled persecution. All that it made clear was that biblical criticism was neither a safe nor an honoured pursuit for clergymen. But before the book came out its contributors were known and suspect to the orthodox. Publication exposed them as a target.

Jowett had been in hot water five years before. In his commentary on *Romans* he had included an essay on the doctrine of atonement. He attacked the version of it, as morally objectionable as it was fraught with psychological melodrama, in which Christ's death was seen as a substitutionary propitiation of God's anger against sinful humanity. He was denounced to the Vice-Chancellor of Oxford and summoned to his study to re-subscribe to the Thirty-nine Articles. It was a ludicrous episode. But the indignity of it hurt him – as a Christian believer and as an eminent don who had just missed the Mastership of his college, Balliol. Also, his appointment as Professor of Greek in the preceding year (1854) had set off a tangled and humiliating train of events. Pusey, mingling decency with vindictiveness, attempted to get Jowett paid a proper salary so long as this could be dissociated from any apparent endorsement by the authorities of Jowett's views. That conundrum was not solved until 1865. When the Bishop of Oxford, Samuel Wilberforce, read Jowett's contribution to *Essays and Reviews* he detected 'a certain sense of disappointment and bitterness' (*Quarterly Review*, January 1861). Jowett had cause for both, but they are not evident in his essay. Rather, it was motivated by a determination not to surrender the Church of England to dogmatic authoritarians. Already in 1849 he had written to Arthur Stanley 'we must act boldly and feel the world around us, as a swimmer feels the resisting stream' (*Letters of Dean Stanley*, pp. 134f.). Subsequent experience had hardened his resolve not to submit to terrorism in his efforts to preserve Christianity as the religion of free and cultivated people. It had also made him anti-clerical, and his essay is continuous with Deist attempts to wrest the Bible from the clergy – though it does it with a religious commitment and sensitivity which is Victorian.

Jowett's piety was deep and derived from many sources. The enlightenment was one. He believed in independent individual judgement. It was the mainspring of his celebrated achievements as a Tutor. 'His greatest skill consisted, like Socrates', said Warden Brodrick, 'in helping us to learn and think for ourselves' (*Jowett* by G. Faber, 1957, p. 167). The analogy with

Socrates was very apt. Jowett was an educator of young men and a Platonist to the core. Indeed, when the furore over *Essays and Reviews* had put him off speaking his theological mind again he turned to Plato, whose works he holds in his 1871 portrait by Laugée at Balliol. As an enlightened idealist, German philosophy was congenial to him. In 1844 he visited Germany with Stanley. They read Kant and began, but never finished, a translation of Hegel's *Logic*. It was Jowett who brought Hegel to Oxford and passed the torch to T. H. Green and Edward Caird. The Common Room at Balliol was a place where German was spoken, and German culture nurtured two leading characteristics of Jowett's thinking. There was the sense of moral imperative, of the 'Idea of Good' conforming the inner life to itself, so that the inner life was what mattered in religion. Then there was the historical aspect of this whereby the sense of history became the history of ideas. In 1847 he and Stanley began a study of the entire New Testament centred on 'the "subjective mind" of the Apostolic Age *historisch- psychologisch dargestellt*' (*Life and Letters of Benjamin Jowett*, Abbott and Campbell 1897, I, p. 100). The essay 'On the Interpretation of Scripture' is an *hors d'oeuvre* from this unrealised *magnum opus* – a fortuitous resemblance to Coleridge's *Confessions of an Inquiring Spirit*. There, it would have been an essay connected to St John's gospel – *mutatis mutandis*. So it had been a decade in the making and the thinking. The final version, designed for the collection of essays, was worked out while Jowett was staying with Tennyson on the Isle of Wight in 1859 (like Queen Victoria, he considered *In Memoriam* a foundation document of modern religion).

The third section of it is printed here (misnumbered '2' in the first edition, which is otherwise followed). Like the rest of the essay it is an effort, quiet but sustained, in bringing complex, precise and penetrating arguments into the service of liberating both text and reader from the pressures which beset them. The 'intelligent mind' must be free to 'ask its own questions', the text to say what it wants. Jowett has complete confidence in the value and possibility of both. The one thing needful for just interpretation is sincerity. It is the threshold to the historical path which leads to the 'one meaning' of a text – 'the meaning which it had to the mind of the Prophet or Evangelist who first uttered or wrote, to the hearers who first received it'. This was a programme to dominate theological faculties for a century, whatever the Church thought of it or Jowett. Like Coleridge, Jowett reads the Bible like any other book in order to find out how extraordinary it is. But unlike Coleridge he does not call in the Church to supplement the Bible. His own experience and protestantism forbad that. Like Arnold, he believed history to be the philosopher's best ally in the search for truth. It provided a corrective to doctrinal overlays and pressure, and restored pristine significances. In section 2 of the essay Jowett wished for a history of biblical interpretation. 'Nothing would be more likely to restore a natural feeling on the subject.' Jowett is at one with F. C. Baur, whom he rightly admired, in holding that the history of doctrines is their critique. German theology had developed dramatically since Arnold knew it, not least because of Baur and his pupil Strauss. There was now a more sophisticated and detailed method, indebted to Hegel, than Arnold's 'accommodation' by which to follow the passages of thoughts through time. Jowett wards off 'accommodation' lest it allow a clutter of ecclesiastical accumulation to bury the original and luminous 'one meaning' in a text. He did not want Pusey and his Church Fathers coming between him and the source of his religious life. So 'the true use of interpretation is to get rid of interpretation, and leave us alone in company with the author'. That is the voice of a master-exegete indicating the goal of all criticism. It is all the sadder that the ensuing terrorism (including Jowett's aborted trial by the Vice-Chancellor's court, which *The Times* called 'a rusty engine of intolerance' and Pusey 'the majesty of justice', in 1862) silenced him as a theologian.

On the Interpretation of Scripture

§ 3

It is probable that some of the preceding statements may be censured as a wanton exposure of the difficulties of Scripture.[1] It will be said that such inquiries are for the few, while the printed page lies open to the many, and that the obtrusion of them may offend some weaker brother, some half-educated or prejudiced soul, 'for whom,' nevertheless, in the touching language of St Paul, 'Christ died' [Romans 14. 15]. A confusion of the heart and head may lead sensitive minds into a desertion of the principles of the Christian life, which are their own witness, because they are in doubt about facts which are really external to them. Great evil to character may sometimes ensue from such causes. 'No man can serve two' opinions without a sensible harm to his nature [Matthew 6. 24]. The consciousness of this responsibility should be always present to writers on theology. But the responsibility is really two-fold; for there is a duty to speak the truth as well as a duty to withhold it. The voice of a majority of the clergy throughout the world, the half sceptical, half conservative instincts of many laymen, perhaps, also, individual interest, are in favour of the latter course; while a higher expediency pleads that 'honesty is the best policy,' and that truth alone 'makes free' [John 8. 32]. To this, it may be replied that truth is not truth to those who are unable to use it; no reasonable man would attempt to lay before the illiterate such a question as that concerning the origin of the Gospels. And yet it may be rejoined once more, the healthy tone of religion among the poor depends upon freedom of thought and inquiry among the educated. In this conflict of reasons, individual judgment must at last decide. That there has been no rude, or improper unveiling of the difficulties of Scripture in the preceding pages, is thought to be shown by the following considerations:

First, that the difficulties referred to are very well known; they force themselves on the attention, not only of the student, but of every intelligent reader of the New Testament, whether in Greek or English. The treatment of such difficulties in theological works is no measure of public opinion respecting them. Thoughtful persons, whose minds have turned towards theology, are continually discovering that the critical observations which they make themselves have been made also by others apparently without concert. The truth is that they have been led to them by the same causes, and these again lie deep in the tendencies of education and literature in the present age. But no one is willing to break through the reticence which is observed on these subjects; hence a sort of smouldering scepticism. It is probable that the distrust is greatest at the time when the greatest efforts are made to conceal it. Doubt comes in at the window, when Inquiry is denied at the door. The thoughts of able and highly educated young men almost always stray towards the first principles of things; it is a great injury to them, and tends to raise in their minds a sort of incurable suspicion, to find that there is one book of the fruit of the knowledge of which they are forbidden freely to taste, that is, the Bible [Genesis 2. 17]. The same spirit renders the Christian minister almost powerless in the hands of his opponents. He can give no true answer to the mechanic or artizan who has either discovered by his mother-wit or who retails at second-hand the objections of critics; for he is unable to look at things as they truly are.

Secondly, as the time has come when it is no longer possible to ignore the results of criticism, it is of importance that Christianity should be seen to be in harmony with them. That objections to some received views should be valid, and yet that they should be always held up as the objections of infidels, is a mischief to the Christian cause. It is a mischief that critical observations which any intelligent man can make for himself, should be ascribed to atheism or unbelief. It would be a strange and almost incredible thing that the Gospel, which at first made war only on the vices of mankind, should now be opposed to one of the highest and rarest of human virtues – the love of truth. And that in the present day the great object of Christianity should be, not to change the lives of men, but to prevent them from changing their opinions; that would be a singular inversion of the purposes for which Christ came into the world. The Christian religion is in a false position when all the tendencies of knowledge are opposed to it. Such a position cannot be long maintained, or can only end in the withdrawal of the educated classes from the influences of religion. It is a grave consideration whether we ourselves may not be in an earlier stage of the same religious dissolution, which seems to have gone further in Italy and France.[2] The reason for thinking so is not to be sought in the external circumstances of our own or any other religious communion, but in the progress of ideas with which Christian teachers seem to be ill at ease. Time was when the Gospel was before the age; when it breathed a new life into a decaying world – when the difficulties of Christianity were difficulties of the heart only, and the highest minds found in its truths not only the rule of their lives, but a well-spring of intellectual delight. Is it to be held a thing impossible that the Christian religion, instead of shrinking into itself, may again embrace the thoughts of men upon the earth? Or is it true that since the Reformation 'all intellect has gone the other way?' and that in Protestant countries reconciliation is as hopeless as Protestants commonly believe to be the case in Catholic.

Those who hold the possibility of such a reconcilement or restoration of belief, are anxious to disengage Christianity from all suspicion of disguise or unfairness. They wish to preserve the historical use of Scripture as the continuous witness in all ages of the higher things in the heart of man, as the inspired source of truth and the way to the better life. They are willing to take away some of the external supports, because they are not needed and do harm; also, because they interfere with the meaning. They have a faith, not that after a period of transition all things will remain just as they were before, but that they will all come round again to the use of man and to the glory of God. When interpreted like any other book, by the same rules of evidence and the same canons of criticism, the Bible will still remain unlike any other book; its beauty will be freshly seen, as of a picture which is restored after many ages to its original state; it will create a new interest and make for itself a new kind of authority by the life which is in it. It will be a spirit and not a letter; as it was in the beginning, having an influence like that of the spoken word, or the book newly found. The purer the light in the human heart, the more it will have an expression of itself in the mind of Christ; the greater the knowledge of the development of man, the truer will be the insight gained into the 'increasing purpose' of revelation. In which also the individual soul has a practical part, finding a sympathy with its own imperfect feelings, in the broken utterance of the Psalmist or the Prophet as well as in the fulness of Christ. The harmony between Scripture and the life of man, in all its stages, may be far greater than appears at present. No one can form any notion from what we see around us, of the power which Christianity might have if it were at one with the conscience of man, and not at variance with his intellectual convictions. There, a world weary of the heat and dust of controversy – of speculations about God and man – weary too of the rapidity of its own motion, would return home and find rest.

But for the faith that the Gospel might win again the minds of intellectual men, it would be better to leave religion to itself, instead of attempting to draw them together. Other walks in literature have peace and pleasure and profit; the path of the critical Interpreter of Scripture is almost always a thorny one in England. It is not worth while for any one to enter upon it who is not supported by a sense that he has a Christian and moral object. For although an Interpreter of Scripture in modern times will hardly say with the emphasis of the Apostle, 'Woe is me, if I speak not the truth without regard to consequences' [I Cor. 9. 16: 'Woe is me if I preach not the gospel'], yet he too may feel it a matter of duty not to conceal the things which he knows. He does not hide the discrepancies of Scripture, because the acknowledgment of them is the first step towards agreement among interpreters. He would restore the original meaning, because 'seven other' meanings take the place of it [Luke 11. 26]; the book is made the sport of opinion and the instrument of perversion of life. He would take the excuses of the head out of the way of the heart; there is hope too that by drawing Christians together on the ground of Scripture, he may also draw them nearer to one another. He is not afraid that inquiries, which have for their object the truth, can ever be displeasing to the God of truth; or that the Word of God is in any such sense a word as to be hurt by investigations into its human origin and conception.

It may be thought another ungracious aspect of the preceding remarks, that they cast a slight upon the interpreters of Scripture in former ages. The early Fathers, the Roman Catholic mystical writers, the Swiss and German Reformers, the Nonconformist divines, have qualities for which we look in vain among ourselves; they throw an intensity of light upon the page of Scripture which we nowhere find in modern commentaries. But it is not the light of interpretation. They have a faith which seems indeed to have grown dim now-a-days, but that faith is not drawn from the study of Scripture; it is the element in which their own mind moves which overflows on the meaning of the text. The words of Scripture suggest to them their own thoughts or feelings. They are preachers, or in the New Testament sense of the word, prophets rather than interpreters. There is nothing in such a view derogatory to the saints and doctors of former ages. That Aquinas or Bernard did not shake themselves free from the mystical method of the Patristic times, or the Scholastic one which was more peculiarly their own; that Luther and Calvin read the Scriptures in connexion with the ideas which were kindling in the mind of their age, and the events which were passing before their eyes, these and similar remarks are not to be construed as depreciatory of the genius or learning of famous men of old; they relate only to their interpretation of Scripture, in which it is no slight upon them to maintain that they were not before their day.

What remains may be comprised in a few precepts, or rather is the expansion of a single one. *Interpret the Scripture like any other book.* There are many respects in which Scripture is unlike any other book; these will appear in the results of such an interpretation. The first step is to know the meaning, and this can only be done in the same careful and impartial way that we ascertain the meaning of Sophocles or of Plato. The subordinate principles which flow out of this general one will also be gathered from the observation of Scripture. No other science of Hermeneutics is possible but an inductive one, that is to say, one based on the language and thoughts and narrations of the sacred writers. And it would be well to carry the theory of interpretation no further than in the case of other works. Excessive system tends to create an impression that the meaning of Scripture is out of our reach, or is to be attained in some other way than by the exercise of manly sense and industry. Who would write a bulky treatise about the method to be pursued in interpreting Plato or Sophocles? Let us not set out on our journey so heavily equipped that there is little chance of our arriving at the end of it. The method creates itself as we go on, beginning only with a few reflections directed against plain errors. Such reflections are the rules of common sense, which we acknowledge with respect to other works written in dead languages: without pretending to novelty they may help us to 'return to nature' in the study of the sacred writings.

First, it may be laid down that Scripture has one meaning – the meaning which it had to the mind of the prophet or evangelist who first uttered or wrote, to the hearers or readers who first received it. Another view may be easier or more familiar to us, seeming to receive a light and interest from the circumstances of our own age. But such accommodation of the text must be laid aside by the interpreter, whose business is to place himself as nearly as possible in the position of the sacred writer. That is no easy task – to call up the inner and outer life of the contemporaries of our Saviour; to follow the abrupt and involved utterance of St Paul or one of the old Prophets; to trace the meaning of words when language first became Christian. He will often have to choose the more difficult interpretation (Galatians 2. 20; Romans 3. 15, etc.), and to refuse one more in agreement with received opinions, because the latter is less true to the style and time of the author. He may incur the charge of singularity, or confusion of ideas, or ignorance of Greek, from a misunderstanding of the peculiarity of the subject in the person who makes the charge. For if it be said that the translation of some Greek words is contrary to the usages of grammar (Galatians 4. 13), that is not in every instance to be denied; the point is whether the usages of grammar are always observed. Or if it be objected to some interpretation of Scripture that it is difficult and perplexing, the answer is 'that may very well be – it is the fact,' arising out of differences in the modes of thought of other times, or irregularities in the use of language which no art of the interpreter can evade. One consideration should be borne in mind, that the Bible is the only book in the world written in different styles and at many different times, which is in the hands of persons of all degrees of knowledge and education. The benefit of this outweighs the evil, yet the evil should be admitted – namely, that it leads to a hasty and partial interpretation of Scripture, which often obscures the true one. A sort of conflict arises between scientific criticism and popular opinion. The indiscriminate use of Scripture has a further tendency to maintain erroneous readings or translations; some which are allowed to be such by scholars have been stereotyped in the mind of the English reader; and it becomes almost a political question how far we can venture to disturb them.

There are difficulties of another kind in many parts of Scripture, the depth and inwardness of which require a measure of the same qualities in the interpreter himself. There are notes struck in places, which like some discoveries of science have sounded before their time; and only after many days have been caught up and found a response on the earth. There are germs of truth which after thousands of years have never yet taken root in the world. There are lessons in the Prophets which, however simple, mankind have not yet learned even in theory; and which the complexity of society rather tends to hide; aspects of human life in Job and Ecclesiastes which have a truth of desolation about them which we faintly realize in ordinary circumstances. It is, perhaps, the greatest difficulty of all to enter into the meaning of the words of Christ – so gentle, so human, so divine, neither adding to them nor marring their simplicity. The attempt to illustrate or draw them out in detail, even to guard against their abuse, is apt to disturb the balance of truth. The interpreter needs nothing short of 'fashioning' in himself the image of the mind of Christ. He has to be born again into a new spiritual or intellectual world, from which the thoughts of this world are shut out. It is one of the highest tasks on which the labour of a life can be spent, to bring the words of Christ a little nearer the heart of man.

But while acknowledging this inexhaustible or infinite character of the sacred writings, it does not, therefore, follow that we are willing to admit of hidden or mysterious meanings in them (in the same way we recognise the wonders and complexity of the laws of nature to be far beyond what eye has seen or knowledge reached, yet it is not therefore to be supposed that we acknowledge the existence of some other laws different in kind from those we know which are incapable of philosophical analysis). In like manner we have no reason to attribute to the Prophet or Evangelist any second or hidden sense different from that which appears on the surface. All that the Prophet meant may not have been consciously present to his mind; there were depths which to himself also were but half revealed. He beheld the fortunes of Israel passing into the heavens; the temporal kingdom was fading into an eternal one. It is not to be supposed that what he saw at a distance only was clearly defined to him; or that the universal truth which was appearing and reappearing in the history of the surrounding world took a purely spiritual or abstract form in his mind. There is a sense in which we may still say with Lord Bacon, that the words of prophecy are to be interpreted as the words of one 'with whom a thousand years are as one day, and one day as a thousand years,' [II Peter 3. 8]. But that is no reason for turning days into years, or for interpreting the things 'that must shortly come to pass' in the book of Revelation, as the events of modern history, or for separating the day of judgment from the destruction of Jerusalem in the Gospels. The double meaning which is given to our Saviour's discourse respecting the last things is not that 'form of eternity' [Revelation 1. 1] of which Lord Bacon speaks; it resembles rather the doubling of an object when seen through glasses placed at different angles. It is true also that there are types in Scripture which were regarded as such by the Jews themselves, as for example, the scape-goat, or the paschal lamb. But that is no proof of all outward ceremonies being types when Scripture is silent; — (if we assume the New Testament as a tradition running parallel with the Old, may not the Roman Catholic assume with equal reason a tradition running parallel with the New?) Prophetic symbols, again, have often the same meaning in different places (e.g., the four beasts or living creatures [Ezekiel 1. 5; Revelation 4. 6], the colours white or red); the reason is that this meaning is derived from some natural association (as of fruitfulness, purity, or the like); or again, they are borrowed in some of the later prophecies from earlier ones; we are not, therefore, justified in supposing any hidden connexion in the prophecies where they occur. Neither is there any ground for assuming design of any other kind in Scripture any more than in Plato or Homer. Wherever there is beauty and order, there is design; but there is no proof of any artificial design, such as is often traced by the Fathers, in the relation of the several parts of a book, or of the several books to each other. That is one of those mischievous notions which enables us, under the disguise of reverence, to make Scripture mean what we please. Nothing that can be said of the greatness or sublimity, or truth, or depth, or tenderness, of many passages, is too much. But that greatness is of a simple kind; it is not increased by double senses, or systems of types, or elaborate structure, or design. If every sentence was a mystery, every word a riddle, every letter a symbol, that would not make the Scriptures more worthy of a Divine author; it is a heathenish or Rabbinical fancy which reads them in this way. Such complexity would not place them above but below human compositions in general; for it would deprive them of the ordinary intelligibleness of human language. It is not for a Christian theologian to say that words were given to mankind to conceal their thoughts, neither was revelation given them to conceal the Divine.

The second rule is an application of the general principle; 'interpret Scripture from itself' as in other respects, like any other book written in an age and country of which little or no other literature survives, and about which we know almost nothing except what is derived from its pages. Not that all the parts of Scripture are to be regarded as an indistinguishable mass. The Old Testament is not to be identified with the New, nor the Law with the Prophets, nor the Gospels with the Epistles, nor the Epistles of St Paul to be violently harmonized with the Epistle of St James. Each writer, each successive age, has characteristics of its own, as strongly marked, or more strongly, than those which are found in the authors or periods of classical literature. These differences are not to be lost in the idea of a Spirit from whom they proceed or by which they were overruled. And therefore, illustration of one part of Scripture by another should be confined to writings of the same age and the same authors, except where the writings of different ages or persons offer obvious similarities. It may be said further that illustration should be chiefly derived, not only from the same author, but from the same writing, or from one of the same period of his life. For example, the comparison of St John and the 'synoptic' Gospels, or of the Gospel of St John with the Revelation of St John, will tend rather to confuse than to elucidate the meaning of either; while, on the other hand, the comparison of the Prophets with one another, and with the Psalms, offers many valuable helps and lights to the interpreter. Again, the connexion between the Epistles written by the Apostle St Paul about the same time (e.g., Romans, I and II Corinthians, Galatians – Colossians, Philippians, Ephesians – compared with Romans, Colossians, Ephesians, Galatians, etc.), is far closer than of Epistles which are separated by an interval of only a few years.

But supposing all this to be understood, and that by the interpretation of Scripture from itself is meant a real interpretation of like by like, it may be asked, what is it that we gain from a minute comparison of a particular author or writing? The indiscriminate use of parallel passages taken from one end of Scripture and applied to the other (except so far as earlier compositions may have afforded the material or the form of later ones) is useless and uncritical. The uneducated, or imperfectly educated person who looks out the marginal references of the English Bible, imagining himself in this way to gain a clearer insight into the Divine meaning, is really following the religious associations of his own mind. Even the critical use of parallel passages is not without danger. For are we to conclude that an author meant in one place what he says in another? Shall we venture to mend a corrupt phrase on the model of some other phrase, which memory, prevailing over judgment, calls up and thrusts into the text? It is this fallacy which has filled the pages of classical writers with useless and unfounded emendations.

The meaning of the Canon '*Non nisi ex Scripturâ Scripturam potes interpretari,*' is only this, 'That we cannot understand Scripture without becoming familiar with it.' Scripture is a world by itself, from which we must exclude foreign influences, whether theological or classical. To get inside that world is an effort of thought and imagination, requiring the sense of a poet as well as a critic – demanding much more than learning a degree of original power and intensity of mind. Any one who, instead of burying himself in the pages of the commentators, would learn the sacred writings by heart, and paraphrase them in English, will probably make a nearer approach to their true meaning than he would gather from any commentary. The intelligent mind will ask its own questions, and find for the most part its own answers. The true use of interpretation is to get rid of interpretation, and leave us alone in company with the author. When the meaning of Greek words is once known, the young student has almost all the real materials which are possessed by the greatest Biblical scholar, in the book itself. For almost our whole knowledge of the history of the Jews is derived from the Old Testament and the Apocryphal books, and almost our whole knowledge of the life of Christ and of the Apostolical age is derived from the New; whatever is added to them is either conjecture, or very slight topographical or chronological illustration. For this reason the rule given above, which is applicable to all books, is applicable to the New Testament more than any other.

Yet in this consideration of the separate books of Scripture it is not to be forgotten that they have also a sort of continuity. We make a separate study of the subject, the mode of thought, in some degree also of the language of each book. And at length the idea arises in our minds of a common literature, a pervading life, an overruling law. It may be compared to the effect of some natural scene in which we suddenly perceive a harmony or picture, or to the imperfect appearance of design which suggests itself in looking at the surface of the globe. That is to say, there is nothing miraculous or artificial in the arrangement of the books of Scripture; it is the result, not the design, which appears in them when bound in the same volume. Or if we like so to say, there *is* design, but a natural design which is revealed to after ages. Such continuity or design is best expressed under some notion of progress or growth, not regular, however, but with broken and imperfect stages, which the want of knowledge prevents our minutely defining. The great truth of the unity of God was there from the first; slowly as the morning broke in the heavens, like some central light, it filled and afterwards dispersed the mists of human passion in which it was itself enveloped. A change passes over the Jewish religion from fear to love, from power to wisdom, from the justice of God to the mercy of God, from the nation to the individual, from this world to another; from the visitation of the sins of the fathers upon the children, to 'every soul shall bear its own iniquity' [Ezekiel 18]; from the fire, the earthquake, and the storm, to the still small voice [I Kings 19. 12]. There never was a time after the deliverance from Egypt, in which the Jewish people did not bear a kind of witness against the cruelty and licentiousness of the surrounding tribes. In the decline of the monarchy, as the kingdom itself was sinking under foreign conquerors; whether springing from contact with the outer world, or from some reaction within, the undergrowth of morality gathers strength; first, in the anticipation of prophecy, secondly, like a green plant in the hollow rind of Pharisaism, and individuals pray and commune with God each one for himself. At length the tree of life blossoms; the faith in immortality which had hitherto slumbered in the heart of man, intimated only in doubtful words (II Sam. 12. 23; Psalm 17. 15), or beaming for an instant in dark places (Job 19. 25), has become the prevailing belief.

There is an interval in the Jewish annals which we often exclude from our thoughts, because it has no record in the canonical writings – extending over about four hundred years, from the last of the prophets of the Old Testament to the forerunner of Christ in the New. This interval, about which we know so little, which is regarded by many as a portion of secular rather than of sacred history, was nevertheless as fruitful in religious changes as any similar period which preceded. The establishment of the Jewish sects, and the wars of the Maccabees, probably exercised as great an influence on Judaism as the captivity itself. A third influence was that of the Alexandrian literature, which was attracting the Jewish intellect, at the same time that the Galilæan zealot was tearing the nation in pieces with the doctrine that it was lawful to call 'no man master but God.' In contrast with that wild fanaticism as well as with the proud Pharisee, came One most unlike all that had been before, as the kings or rulers of mankind. In an age which was the victim of its own passions, the creature of its own circumstances, the slave of its own degenerate religion, our Saviour taught a lesson absolutely free from all the influences of a surrounding world. He made the last perfect revelation of God to man; a revelation not indeed immediately applicable to the state of society or the world, but in its truth and purity inexhaustible by the after generations of men. And of the first application of the truth which he taught as a counsel of perfection to the actual circumstances of mankind, we have the example in the epistles.

Such a general conception of growth or development in Scripture, beginning with the truth of the Unity of God in the earliest books and ending with the perfection of Christ, naturally springs up in our minds in the perusal of the sacred writings. It is a notion of value to the interpreter, for it enables him at the same time to grasp the whole and distinguish the parts. It saves him from the necessity of maintaining that the Old Testament is one and the same everywhere; that the books of Moses contain truths or precepts, such as the duty of prayer or the faith in immortality, or the spiritual interpretation of sacrifice, which no one has ever seen there. It leaves him room enough to admit all the facts of the case. No longer is he required to defend or to explain away David's imprecations against his enemies, or his injunctions to Solomon, any more than his sin in the matter of Uriah. Nor is he hampered with a theory of accommodation. Still the sense of 'the increasing purpose which through the ages ran' is present to him, nowhere else continuously discernible or ending in a divine perfection. Nowhere else is there found the same interpenetration of the political and religious element – a whole nation, 'though never good for much at any time,' possessed with the conviction that it was living in the face of God – in whom the Sun of righteousness shone upon the corruption of an Eastern nature – the 'fewest of all people' [Deuteronomy 7. 7] yet bearing the greatest part in the education of the world. Nowhere else among the teachers and benefactors of mankind is there any form like His, in whom the desire of the nation is fulfilled, and 'not of that nation only' [John 11. 52] but of all mankind, whom He restores to His Father and their Father, to His God and their God.

Such a growth or development may be regarded as a kind of progress from childhood to manhood. In the child there is an anticipation of truth; his reason is latent in the form of feeling; many words are used by him which he imperfectly understands; he is led by temporal promises, believing that to be good is to be happy always; he is pleased by marvels and has vague terrors. He is confined to a spot of earth, and lives in a sort of prison of sense, yet is bursting also with a fulness of childish life: he imagines God to be like a human father, only greater and more awful; he is easily impressed with solemn thoughts, but soon 'rises up to play' [Exodus 32. 6; I Corinthians 10. 7] with other children. It is observable that his ideas of right and wrong are very simple, hardly extending to another life; they consist chiefly in obedience to his parents, whose word is his law. As he grows older he mixes more and more with others; first with one or two who have a great influence in the direction of his mind. At length the world opens upon him; another work of education begins; and he learns to discern more truly the meaning of things and his relation to men in general. (You may complete the image, by supposing that there was a time in his early days when he was a helpless outcast 'in the land of Egypt and the house of bondage' [Joshua 24. 17].) And as he arrives at manhood he reflects on his former years, the progress of his education, the hardships of his infancy, the home of his youth (the thought of which is ineffaceable in after life), and he now understands that all this was but a preparation for another state of being, in which he is to play a part for himself. And once more in age you may imagine him like the patriarch looking back on the entire past [Genesis 45. 4–8], which he reads anew, perceiving that the events of life had a purpose or result which was not seen at the time; they seem to him bound 'each to each by natural piety.'

'Which things are an allegory,' [Galatians 4. 24] the particulars of which any one may interpret for himself. For the child born after the flesh is the symbol of the child born after the Spirit. 'The law was a schoolmaster to bring men to Christ' [Galatians 4. 24] and now 'we are under a schoolmaster' no longer [Galatians 3. 24f.]. The anticipation of truth which came from without to the childhood or youth of the human race is witnessed to within; the revelation of God is not lost but renewed in the heart and understanding of the man. Experience has taught us the application of the lesson in a wider sphere. And many influences have combined to form the 'after life' of the world. When at the close (shall we say) of a great period in the history of man, we cast our eyes back on the course of events, from the 'angel of his presence in the wilderness' to the multitude of peoples, nations, languages, who are being drawn together by His Providence – from the simplicity of the pastoral state in the dawn of the world's day, to all the elements of civilization and knowledge which are beginning to meet and mingle in a common life, we also understand that we are no longer in our early home, to which, nevertheless, we fondly look; and that the end is yet unseen, and the purposes of God towards the human race only half revealed. And to turn once more to the Interpreter of Scripture, he too feels that the continuous growth of revelation which he traces in the Old and New Testament, is a part of a larger whole extending over the earth and reaching to another world.

8. *Matthew Arnold, 'Literature and Dogma' (1873), Chapters IV–VI*

Literature and Dogma is Matthew Arnold's best work in the criticism of religion, which he believed to be the most important field in which he deployed his fine wit and penetration. For the next fifty years it exerted its influence, most notably on Anglican and Catholic modernists and on Leo Tolstoy. Its genesis, by coincidences which betray the often sudden nature of historical process, gathered around three consecutive days in the June of 1870. A review of them will serve to introduce the central part of the text which is printed here.

On June 21 the University of Oxford made Arnold Doctor of Civil Laws at its annual Commemoration. It already knew him as its Professor of Poetry, the office in which Lowth had delivered his lectures a century earlier. It was a great and very positive day for Arnold. The Chancellor, Lord Salisbury, was flattering to him. And the 'very loud acclamations' (*The Times*, 22 June 1870) which greeted him in the Sheldonian Theatre were the best possible boost to his confidence in himself as a liberal and reforming critic of society and religion. He had recently published in both fields. *Culture and Anarchy* came out in January 1869, *St Paul and Protestantism* in May 1870. Now he was a prophet honoured in his own university, the centre of so much crucial religious controversy. His mood was very different from that of the poetry of his youth. Belief in his ability to do public good had replaced despair contained by dandyism. But the temperamental change did not alter the agenda. In *Stanzas from the Grande Chartreuse* (c. 1852) he had faced the crucial problem of the mutability and mortality of religions and the pain of the modern soul

> Wandering between two worlds, one dead,
> The other powerless to be born.

In 1870 he still felt between worlds. But the wandering, that *leitmotiv* of his poetry, was now superseded by purpose and direction. The Arnold of 1870 was a public man, seasoned by a decade of work at the basic levels of education. He was also a devoted and bereaved father, had become what his father had been once – what he had not yet become when he remembered him in 'Rugby Chapel' (1857):

> But thou woulds't not *alone*
> Be saved, my father! *alone*
> Conquer and come to thy goal,
> Leaving the rest in the wild.

Now it was up to him to be 'cheerful, and helpful, and firm.' And in *Literature and Dogma* he is, in fact, all those things. Christianity had played a major part in the transition. He interiorised St Paul's teaching on death and resurrection, as Paul himself intended, as a death to self and a rising to new life, lived for others. In so doing he grasped a truth which became central to his thought. Resurrection as an external miracle was a liability for Christianity in the modern world. But resurrection as Paul had taught it, as an inward experience with public moral consequences, was the true ground of Christianity and its direct evidence, saving it from scientific discredit and concentrating its ethical force. Here was a triumphant example of what religious criticism should be: sensitive because sensed in the critic's own experience, uncovering the buried life of the past so as to vivify its relevance to the buried lives of the present and animate them. Arnold, briefly and modestly, called this critical tact.

On 22 June nothing much was happening in Oxford, but at Westminster the seeds of a public furore were sown. A. P. Stanley, the Dean and Matthew Arnold's friend as well as Thomas Arnold's disciple, ingenuously invited the revisers of the King James Bible to a celebration of Holy Communion in Henry VII's Chapel before their first meeting in the Jerusalem Chamber. They included Scottish Presbyterians, English Dissenters and a Unitarian called Vance Smith. The rage of High Churchmen soon fell upon Stanley. His excommunication was demanded. Fifteen hundred clergymen signed a protest. After a brief intermission in the autumn while people took notice of the Franco-Prussian War, Bishop Wilberforce swung into action in Convocation in February 1871. He focused on Vance Smith and moved 'that no person who denies the Godhead of Our Lord Jesus Christ' should be a reviser of the Bible. Dogma must dominate over literary work, marking out 'that infinite separation for time and for eternity which is involved in declaring the Eternal Son to be a mere creature' (*The Guardian*, 22 February 1871). The Bishop of Gloucester supported Wilberforce and, introducing a collection of essays on *Modern Scepticism* in 1871, enunciated 'the blessed truth that the God of the universe is a PERSON'. That phrase, and the episcopal efforts to 'do something for the honour of Our Lord's Godhead' by denouncing Stanley and upholding the Athanasian Creed (the status of which was controverted between 1870 and 1873), were used by Arnold in *Literature and Dogma* as the catch-phrases of the dogmatisers whom they exposed as his target.

On 23 June, back in Oxford, Arnold stood among Butterfield's startling new buildings for Keble College listening to a harangue from Lord Salisbury to raise funds for their completion. Keble was Arnold's godfather, but the 'twinkling intransigence' which he noticed in him prevented the veneration in which Keble was more generally held. All the same, he was there out of family piety. Salisbury, who had been so charming to him two days before, now appalled him with words which were to echo through *Literature and Dogma*:

I think this college exists to pledge us to a religion which shall not be the formless, shapeless creature of fable such as goes by the name of unsectarian religion – but shall be unsectarian in the higher sense because it is thoroughly Catholic; and that there shall be no more within these walls the idea of severing religion and dogma than there is the idea of severing the daylight from the sun. (*The Guardian*, 29 June 1870)

Within three days Arnold was writing to his mother about Salisbury in terms which laid out the programme for *Literature and Dogma*:

Religion he knows, and physical science he knows, but the immense work between the two, which is for literature to accomplish, he knows nothing of, and all his speeches at Oxford pointed this way. On the one hand, he was full of the great future for physical science, and begging the University to make up her mind to it, and to resign much of her literary studies; on the other hand, he was full, almost defiantly full, of counsels and resolves for retaining the old ecclesiastical and dogmatic forms of religion. From a juxtaposition of this kind nothing but shocks and collisions can come; and I know no one, indeed, more likely to provoke shocks and collisions than men like Lord Salisbury. All this pressed a good deal upon my mind at Oxford, and made me anxious, but I do hope that what influence I have may be of use in the troubled times which I see are before us as a healing and reconciling influence, and it is this which makes me glad to find – what I find more and more – that I *have* influence. (*Letters*, II, 35)

The note of active preparation in those last lines is clear. The confidence Arnold had got in the Sheldonian was to be used against the target which had been presented to him at Keble, and was to be presented again and again in the polemics which issued from what had happened at Westminster on the intervening day. Literature was to redeem biblical Christianity from its dogmatic enslavement and he was its prophet. *Literature and Dogma*, begun as articles for the *Cornhill Magazine* which Leslie Stephen as editor decided not to continue, was published in February 1873.

The first word of the following extract from it is the German *Aberglaube*. Arnold translates it as 'extra-belief' and elucidates it straight away in a manner which exemplifies his critical tact. It stands primarily for the myths and tales which objectify the truths of religious aspiration. Religion could not do without *Aberglaube* and it is not blameworthy. It goes wrong, however, when it is treated as certain. This is precisely the damage done by dogmatists. They commit the fatal category mistake of turning the Bible's poetry into pseudo-science. Having mistaken the Bible's nature, they then divert attention from its true end, which is not metaphysics but conduct, and put religion itself at the mercy of genuine science – which will prove very short indeed. At this critically dangerous point Arnold's critical vocation comes to the rescue. Who better to undo the muddle of science and anachronism generated by the dogmatic fallacy than the literary critic? He gets it right by apprehending the poetic character of biblical truth as

approximate language, thrown out, as it were, at certain great objects which the human mind augurs and feels after, but not language accurately defining them.

This is not the language of subjectivity but of approximate and relative response to objectivity which is ultimately Arnold's 'Eternal not-ourselves which makes for righteousness'. The relativity which is accepted here is, from another and historical angle, imposed in any case by the *Zeitgeist*, the historically-conditioned set of the mind which neither writers of texts in one age nor readers of them in another can escape. It is the job of criticism to be aware – or to be as aware as it can – of this spiritual time-of-day which most people take for granted and do not distinguish. Arnold does it brilliantly, but not infallibly. In sections 3 and 4 of 'The New Testament Record' his nineteenth-century liberal wishes can be seen spilling over onto the historical Jesus and relieving him of eschatological convictions which he may well, in fact, have held – as Schweitzer was to believe in the next generation. But then again, in England C. H. Dodd spent a lifetime following Arnold's line. So to end this anthology with Arnold is, in effect, to cover a good deal of the twentieth century, including even the literary study of the Bible in progress at the present as a testimony to Arnold's foresight.

Chapter IV
The Proof from Prophecy

'*Aberglaube* is the poetry of life.' That men should, by help of their imagination, take short cuts to what they ardently desire, whether the triumph of Israel or the triumph of Christianity, should tell themselves fairy-tales about it, should make these fairy-tales the basis for what is far more sure and solid than the fairy-tales, the desire itself – all this has in it, we repeat, nothing which is not natural, nothing blameable. Nay, the region of our hopes and presentiments extends, as we have also said, far beyond the region of what we can know with certainty. What we reach but by hope and presentiment may yet be true; and he would be a narrow reasoner who denied, for instance, all validity to the idea of immortality, because this idea rests on presentiment mainly, and does not admit of certain demonstration. In religion, above all, *extra-belief* is in itself no matter, assuredly, for blame. The object of religion is conduct; and if a man helps himself in his conduct by taking an object of hope and presentiment as if it were an object of certainty, he may even be said to gain thereby an advantage.

And yet there is always a drawback to a man's advantage in thus treating, when he deals with religion and conduct, what is extra-belief and not certain as if it were matter of certainty, and in making it his ground of action. *He pays for it.* The time comes when he discovers that it is *not* certain; and then the whole certainty of religion seems discredited, and the basis of conduct gone. This danger attends the reliance on prediction and miracle as evidences of Christianity.

They have been attacked as a part of the 'cheat' or 'imposture' of religion and of Christianity. For us, religion is the solidest of realities, and Christianity the greatest and happiest stroke ever yet made for human perfection. Prediction and miracle were attributed to it as its supports because of its grandeur, and because of the awe and admiration which it inspired. Generations of men have helped themselves to hold firmer to it, helped themselves in conduct, by the aid of these supports. 'Miracles *prove*,' men have said and thought, 'that the order of physical nature is not fate, nor a mere material constitution of things, but the subject of a free, omnipotent Master. Prophecy fulfilled *proves* that neither fate nor man are masters of the world.'[a]

And to take prophecy first. 'The conditions,' it is said, 'which form the true conclusive standard of a prophetic inspiration are these: That the prediction be known to have been promulgated before the event; that the event be such as could not have been foreseen, when it was predicted, by any effort of human reason; and that the event and the prediction correspond together in a clear accomplishment. There are prophecies in Scripture answering to the standard of an absolute proof. Their publication, their fulfilment, their supernatural prescience, are all fully ascertained.'[b] On this sort of ground men came to rest the proof of Christianity.

2

Now, it may be said, indeed, that a prediction fulfilled, an exhibition of supernatural prescience, proves nothing for or against the truth and necessity of conduct and righteousness. But it must be allowed, notwithstanding, that while human nature is what it is, the mass of men are likely to listen more to a teacher of righteousness, if he accompanies his teaching by an exhibition of supernatural prescience. And what were called the 'signal predictions' concerning the Christ of popular theology, as they stand in our Bibles, had and have undoubtedly a look of supernatural prescience. The employment of capital letters, and other aids, such as the constant use of the future tense, naturally and innocently adopted by interpreters who were profoundly convinced that Christianity needed these express predictions and that they *must* be in the Bible, enhanced, certainly, this look; but the look, even without these aids, was sufficiently striking.

Yes, that Jacob on his death-bed should two thousand years before Christ have 'been enabled,' as the phrase is, to foretell to his son Judah that 'the sceptre shall not depart from Judah until *Shiloh* (or the

[a] Davison's *Discourses on Prophecy*; Discourse ii, Part 2. [b] Discourses ix and xii.

Messiah) come, and unto him shall the gathering of the people be,'*a*
does seem, when the explanation is put with it that the Jewish
kingdom lasted till the Christian era and then perished, a miracle of
prediction in favour of our current Christian theology. That Jeremiah should during the captivity have 'been enabled' to foretell, in
Jehovah's name: 'The days come that I will raise unto David a
righteous Branch; in his days Judah shall be saved, and Israel shall
dwell safely; and this is his name whereby he shall be called, THE
LORD OUR RIGHTEOUSNESS!'*b* does seem a prodigy of prediction in
favour of that tenet of the Godhead of the Eternal Son, for which the
Bishops of Winchester and Gloucester are so anxious to do something. For unquestionably, in the prophecy here given, the Branch of
David, the future Saviour of Israel, who was Jesus Christ, appears to
be expressly identified with the Lord God, with Jehovah. Again, that
David should say: 'The Lord said unto my Lord, Sit thou on my
right hand until I make thine enemies thy footstool,'*c* does seem a
prodigy of prediction to the same effect. And so long as these
prophecies stand as they are here given, they no doubt bring to
Christianity all the support (and with the mass of mankind this is by
no means inconsiderable) which it can derive from the display of
supernatural prescience.

But who will dispute that it more and more becomes known, that
these prophecies*d* cannot stand as we have here given them?
Manifestly, it more and more becomes known, that the passage from
Genesis, with its mysterious *Shiloh* and the gathering of the people to
him, is rightly to be rendered as follows: 'The pre-eminence shall not
depart from Judah *so long as the people resort to Shiloh* (the national
sanctuary before Jerusalem was won); *and the nations* (the heathen
Canaanites) *shall obey him.*' We here purposely leave out of sight any
such consideration as that our actual books of the Old Testament
came first together through the instrumentality of the house of
Judah, and when the destiny of Judah was already traced; and that to
say roundly and confidently: '*Jacob was enabled to foretell*, The sceptre
shall not depart from Judah,' is wholly inadmissible. For this consideration is of force, indeed, but it is a consideration drawn from the
rules of literary history and criticism, and not likely to have weight
with the mass of mankind. Palpable error and mistranslation are what
will have weight with *them.*

---

a Gen. 49. 10.   *b* Jer. 23. 5, 6.   *c* Ps. 110. 1.
d A real *prediction* of Jesus Christ's Godhead, of the kind that popular religion desires, is to be
found in Benjamin's prophecy of the coming, in the last days, of the King of Heaven to judge
Israel, 'because when God came to them in the flesh they did not believe in him as their
deliverer.' But this *prediction* occurs in an apocryphal Christian writing of the end of the first

Matthew Arnold

And what, then, will they say as they come to know (and do not and must not more and more of them come to know it every day?) that Jeremiah's supposed signal identification of Jesus Christ with the Lord God of Israel: 'I will raise to David a righteous Branch, and this is the name whereby he shall be called, THE LORD OUR RIGHTEOUSNESS,' runs really: 'I will raise to David a righteous branch; in his days Judah shall be saved and Israel shall dwell safely; and this is the name whereby they shall call themselves: *The Eternal is our righteousness!*' The prophecy thus becomes simply one of the many promises of a successor to David under whom the Hebrew people should trust in the Eternal and follow righteousness; just as the prophecy from Genesis is one of the many prophecies of the enduring continuance of the greatness of Judah. 'The Lord said unto my Lord,' in like manner; will not people be startled when they find that it ought instead to run as follows: 'The Eternal said unto my lord the king,' a simple promise of victory to a royal leader of God's chosen people?

3

Leslie, in his once famous *Short and Easy Method with the Deists*, speaks of the impugners of the current evidences of Christianity as men who consider the Scripture histories and the Christian religion 'cheats and impositions of cunning and designing men upon the credulity of simple people.' Collins, and the whole array of writers at whom Leslie aims this, greatly need to be re-surveyed from the point of view of our own age. Nevertheless, we may grant that some of them, at any rate, conduct their attacks on the current evidences for Christianity in such a manner as to give the notion that in their opinion Christianity itself, and religion, is a cheat and an imposture. But how far more prone will be the mass of mankind to be hearken to this opinion, if they have been kept intent on predictions such as those of which we have just given specimens; if they have been kept full of the great importance of this line of mechanical evidence, and then suddenly find that this line of evidence gives way at all points? It can hardly be gainsaid, that, to a delicate and penetrating criticism, it has long been manifest that the chief *literal* fulfilment by Jesus Christ of things said by the prophets was the fulfilment such as would naturally be given by one who nourished his spirit on the prophets, and on living and acting their words. The great prophecies of Isaiah

century, the *Testaments of the Twelve Patriarchs*. See [J. A.] Fabricius, *Codex Pseudepigraphus Veteris Testamenti* [Hamburg, 1713], vol. i, p. 745.

and Jeremiah are, critics can easily see, not strictly *predictions* at all; and predictions which are strictly meant as such, like those in the Book of Daniel, are an embarrassment to the Bible rather than a main element of it. The 'Zeit-Geist,' and the mere spread of what is called *enlightenment*, superficial and barren as this often is, will inevitably, before long, make this conviction of criticism a popular opinion, held far and wide. And then, what will be *their* case, who have been so long and sedulously taught to rely on supernatural predictions as a mainstay?

The same must be said of miracles. The substitution of some other proof of Christianity for this accustomed proof is now to be desired most by those who most think Christianity of importance. That old friend of ours on whom we have formerly commented,[a] who insists upon it that Christianity is and shall be nothing else but this, 'that Christ promised Paradise to the saint and threatened the worldly man with hell-fire, *and proved his power to promise and to threaten by rising from the dead and ascending into heaven*,' is certainly not the guide whom lovers of Christianity, if they could discern what it is that he really expects and aims at, and what it is which they themselves really desire, would think it wise to follow.[1]

But the subject of miracles is a very great one; it includes within itself, indeed, the whole question about 'supernatural prescience,' which meets us when we deal with prophecy. And this great subject requires, in order that we may deal with it properly, some little recapitulation of our original design in this essay, and of the circumstances in which the cause of religion and of the Bible seems to be at this moment placed.

Chapter V
The Proof from Miracles

We have seen that some new treatment or other the religion of the Bible certainly seems to require, for it is attacked on all sides, and the theologians are not so successful as one might wish in defending it. One critic says, that if these islands had no religion at all it would not enter into his mind to introduce the religious and ethical idea by the agency of the Bible.[2] Another, that though certain commonplaces are common to all systems of morality, yet the Bible-way of enunciating

---

[a] See *St Paul and Protestantism*, p. 93.

these commonplaces no longer suits us. And we may rest assured, he adds, that by saying what we think in some other, more congenial, language, we shall really be taking the shortest road to discovering the new doctrines which will satisfy at once our reason and our imagination. Another critic goes farther still, and calls Bible-religion not only destitute of a modern and congenial way of stating its commonplaces of morality, but a defacer and disfigurer of moral treasures which were once in better keeping. The more one studies, the more, says he, one is convinced that the religion which calls itself revealed contains, in the way of what is good, nothing which is not the incoherent and ill-digested residue of the wisdom of the ancients. To the same effect the Duke of Somerset, who has been affording proof to the world that our aristocratic class are not, as has been said, inaccessible to ideas and merely polite, but that they are familiar, on the contrary, with modern criticism of the most advanced kind, the Duke of Somerset finds very much to condemn in the Bible and its teaching; although the soul, he says, has (outside the Bible, apparently) one unassailable fortress to which she may retire, faith in God.[3]

All this seems to threaten to push Bible-religion from the place it has long held in our affections. And even what the most modern criticism of all sometimes does to save it and to set it up again, can hardly be called very flattering to it. For whereas the Hebrew race imagined that to them were committed the oracles of God, and that their God, 'the Eternal who loveth righteousness,'[a] was the God to whom 'every knee shall bow and every tongue shall swear,'[b] there now comes M. Émile Burnouf, the accomplished kinsman of the gifted orientalist Eugène Burnouf, and will prove to us in a thick volume[c] that the oracles of God were not committed to a Semitic race at all, but to the Aryan; that the true God is not Israel's God at all, but is 'the idea of the absolute' which Israel could never properly master. This 'sacred theory of the Aryas,' it seems, passed into Palestine from Persia and India, and got possession of the founder of Christianity and of his greatest apostles St Paul and St John; becoming more perfect, and returning more and more to its true character of a 'transcendent metaphysic,' as the doctors of the Christian Church developed it. So that we Christians, who are Aryas, may have the satisfaction of thinking that 'the religion of Christ has not come to us from the Semites,' and that 'it is in the hymns of the Veda, and not in the Bible, that we are to look for the primordial source of our religion.' The theory of Christ is accordingly the theory of the Vedic

[a] Ps. ii. 7.   [b] Is. 45. 23.   [c] *La Science des Religions*; Paris, 1872.

Agni, or *fire*. The Incarnation represents the Vedic solemnity of the production of *fire*, symbol of force of every kind, of all movement, life, and thought. The Trinity of Father, Son, and Spirit is the Vedic Trinity of Sun, Fire, and Wind; and God, finally, is 'a cosmic unity.'

Such speculations almost take away the breath of a mere man of letters. What one is inclined to say of them is this. Undoubtedly these exploits of the Aryan genius are gratifying to us members of the Aryan race. The original God of the Hebrews, M. Burnouf says expressly, 'was *not* a cosmic unity;' the religion of the Hebrews 'had *not* that transcendent metaphysic which the genius of the Aryas requires;' and, 'in passing from the Aryan race to the inferior races, religion underwent a deterioration due to the physical and moral constitution of these races.' For religion, it must be remembered, is, in M. Burnouf's view, fundamentally a *science*; 'a metaphysical conception, a theory, a synthetic explanation of the universe.' Now, 'the perfect Arya is capable of a great deal of science; the Semite is inferior to him.' As Aryas or Aryans, then, we ought to be pleased at having vindicated the greatness of our race, and having not borrowed a Semitic religion as it stood, but transformed it by importing our own metaphysics into it.

And this seems to harmonise very well with what the Bishops of Winchester and Gloucester say about 'doing something for the honour of Our Lord's Godhead,' and about 'the infinite separation for time and for eternity which is involved in rejecting the Godhead of the Eternal Son, Very God of Very God, Light of Light;' and also with the Athanasian Creed generally, and with what the clergy write to the *Guardian* about 'eternal life being unquestionably annexed to a right knowledge of the Godhead.'[4] For all these have in view high science and metaphysics, worthy of the Aryas. But to Bible-religion, in the plain sense of the word, it is not flattering; for it throws overboard almost entirely the Old Testament, and makes the essence of the New to consist in an esoteric doctrine not very visible there, but more fully developed outside of it. The metaphysical element is made the fundamental element in religion. But, 'the Bible-books, especially the more ancient of them, are destitute of metaphysics, and consequently of method and classification in their ideas.' Israel, therefore, instead of being a light of the Gentiles and a salvation to the ends of the earth, falls to a place in the world's religious history behind the Arya. He is dismissed as ranking anthropologically between the Aryas and the yellow men; as having frizzled hair, thick lips, small calves, flat feet, and belonging, above all, to those 'occipital races' whose brain cannot grow above the age of sixteen; whereas the brain of a theological Arya, such as one of our bishops, may go on growing all his life.

But we, who think that the Old Testament leads surely up to the New, who believe that, indeed, 'salvation is of the Jews,'[a] and that, for what concerns conduct or righteousness (that is, for what concerns three-fourths of human life), they and their documents can no more be neglected by whoever would make proficiency in it, than Greece can be neglected by anyone who would make proficiency in art, or Newton's discoveries by whoever would comprehend the world's physical laws, *we* are naturally not satisfied with this treatment of Israel and the Bible. And admitting that Israel shows no talent for metaphysics, we say that his religious greatness is just this, that he does *not* found religion on metaphysics, but on moral experience, which is a much simpler matter; and that, ever since the apparition of Israel and the Bible, religion is no longer what, according to M. Burnouf, to our Aryan forefathers in the valley of the Oxus it was, and what perhaps it really was to *them*, metaphysical theory, but is what Israel has made it.

And what Israel made, and how he made it, we seek to show from the Bible itself. Thus we hope to win for the Bible and its religion, which seem to us so indispensable to the world, an access to many of those who now neglect them. For there is this to be said against M. Burnouf's metaphysics: no one can allege that the Bible has failed to win access for want of metaphysics being applied to it. Metaphysics are just what all our theology runs up into, and our bishops, as we know, are here particularly strong. But we see every day that the making religion into metaphysics is the weakening of religion; now, M. Burnouf makes religion into metaphysics more than ever. Yet evidently the metaphysical method lacks power for laying hold on people, and compelling them to receive the Bible from it; it is felt to be inconclusive as thus employed, and its inconclusiveness tells against the Bible. This is the case with the old metaphysics of our bishops, and it will be the case with M. Burnouf's new metaphysics also. They will be found, we fear, to have an inconclusiveness in their recommendation of Christianity. To very many persons, indeed to the great majority, such a method, in such a matter, *must* be inconclusive.

2

Therefore we would not allow ourselves to start with any metaphysical conception at all, not with the monotheistic idea, as it is styled, any more than with the pantheistic idea; and, indeed, we are

[a] John 4. 22.

quite sure that Israel himself began with nothing of the kind. The idea of *God*, as it is given us in the Bible, rests, we say, not on a metaphysical conception of the necessity of certain deductions from our ideas of cause, existence, identity, and the like; but on a moral perception of a rule of conduct not of our own making, into which we are born, and which exists whether we will or no; of awe at its grandeur and necessity and of gratitude at its beneficence. This is the great original revelation made to Israel, this is his 'Eternal.'

Man, however, as Goethe says, *never knows how anthropomorphic he is.*[5] Israel described his Eternal in the language of poetry and emotion, and could not thus describe him but with the characters of a man. Scientifically he never attempted to describe him at all. But still the Eternal was ever at last reducible, for Israel, to the reality of experience out of which the revelation sprang; he was 'the righteous Eternal who loveth righteousness.' They who 'seek the Eternal,' and they who 'follow after righteousness,' were identical; just as, conversely, they who 'fear the Eternal,' and they who 'depart from evil,' were identical.[a] Above all: *'Blessed* is the man that feareth the Eternal;' 'it is *joy* to the just to do judgment;' 'righteousness tendeth to *life*;' 'the righteous is *an everlasting foundation.*'[b]

But, as time went on, facts seemed, we saw, to contradict this fundamental belief, to refute this faith in the Eternal; material forces prevailed, and God appeared, as they say, to be on the side of the big battalions. The great unrighteous kingdoms of the world, kingdoms which cared far less than Israel for righteousness and for the Eternal who makes for righteousness, overpowered Israel. Prophecy assured him that the triumph of the Eternal's cause and people was certain: *Behold the Eternal's hand is not shortened, that it cannot save.*[c] The triumph was but adjourned through Israel's own sins: *Your iniquities have separated between you and your God.*[d] Prophecy directed its hearers to the future, and promised them a new, everlasting kingdom, under a heaven-sent leader. The characters of this kingdom and leader were more spiritualised by one prophet, more materialised by another. As time went on, in the last centuries before our era, they became increasingly turbid and phantasmagorical. In addition to his original experimental belief in the Almighty Eternal who makes for righteousness, Israel had now a vast *Aberglaube*, an after or extra-belief, not experimental, in an approaching kingdom of the saints, to be established by an Anointed, a Messiah, or by 'one like the Son of Man,' commissioned from the Ancient of Days and coming in the clouds of heaven.

[a] Is. 51. 1; Prov. 3. 7.   [b] Ps. 112. 1; Prov. 21. 15; 11. 19; 10. 25.   [c] Is. 59. 1.   [d] Is. 59. 2.

Jesus came, calling himself the Messiah, the Son of Man, the Son of God; and the question is, what is the true meaning of these assertions of his, and of all his teaching? It is the same question we had about the Old Testament. Is the language scientific, or is it, as we say, *literary*? that is, the language of poetry and emotion, approximative language, thrown out, as it were, at certain great objects which the human mind augurs and feels after, but not language accurately defining them? Popular religion says, we know, that the language is scientific; that the God of the Old Testament is a great Personal First Cause, who thinks and loves (for this too, it seems, we ought to have added), the moral and intelligent Governor of the universe. Learned religion, the metaphysical theology of our bishops, proves or confirms the existence of this personal God by abstruse reasoning from our ideas of cause, design, existence, identity, and so on. Popular religion rests it altogether on revelation and miracle. The God of Israel, for popular religion, is a magnified and non-natural man who has really worked stupendous miracles, whereas the Gods of the heathen were vainly imagined to be able to work them, but could not, and had therefore no real existence. Of this God, Jesus for popular religion is the Son. He came to appease God's wrath against sinful men by the sacrifice of himself; and he proved his Sonship by a course of stupendous miracles, and by the wonderful accomplishment in him of the supernatural Messianic predictions of prophecy. Here, again, learned religion elucidates and develops the relation of the Son to the Father by a copious exhibition of metaphysics; but for popular religion the relationship, and the authority of Jesus which derives from it, is altogether established by *miracle*.

Now, we have seen that our bishops and their metaphysics are so little convincing, that many people throw the Bible quite aside and will not attend to it, because they are given to understand that the metaphysics go necessarily along with it, and that one cannot be taken without the other. So far, then, the talents of the Bishops of Winchester and Gloucester, and their zeal to do something for the honour of the Eternal Son's Godhead, may be said to be actual obstacles to the receiving and studying of the Bible. But the same may now be also said of the popular theology which rests the Bible's authority and the Christian religion on miracle. To a great many persons this is tantamount to stopping their use of the Bible and of the Christian religion; for they have made up their minds that what is popularly called *miracle* never does really happen, and that the belief in it arises out of either ignorance or mistake. To these persons we restore the use of the Bible, if, while showing them that the Bible-language is not scientific, but the language of common speech or of poetry and eloquence, approximative language thrown out at certain great objects of consciousness which it does not pretend to define fully, we convince them at the same time that this language deals with facts of positive experience, most momentous and real.

We have sought to do this for the Old Testament first, and we now seek to do it for the New. But our attempt has in view those who are incredulous about the Bible and inclined to throw it aside, not those who at present receive it on the grounds supplied either by popular theology or by metaphysical theology. For persons of this kind, what we say neither will have, nor seeks to have, any constraining force at all; only it is rendered necessary by the want of constraining force, for others than themselves, in their own theology. How little constraining force metaphysical dogma has, we all see. And we have shown, too, how the proof from the fulfilment in Jesus Christ of a number of detailed predictions, supposed to have been made with supernatural prescience about him long beforehand, is losing, and seems likely more and more to lose, its constraining force. It is found that the predictions and their fulfilment are not what they are said to be.

Now we come to *miracles*, more specially so called. And we have to see whether the constraining force of this proof, too, must not be admitted to be far less than it used to be, and whether some other source of authority for the Bible is not much to be desired.

3

That miracles, when fully believed, are felt by men in general to be a source of authority, it is absurd to deny. One may say, indeed: Suppose I could change the pen with which I write this into a penwiper, I should not thus make what I write any the truer or more convincing. That may be so in reality, but the mass of mankind feel differently. In the judgment of the mass of mankind, could I visibly and undeniably change the pen with which I write this into a penwiper, not only would this which I write acquire a claim to be held perfectly true and convincing, but I should even be entitled to affirm, and to be believed in affirming, propositions the most palpably at war with common fact and experience. It is almost impossible to exaggerate the proneness of the human mind to take miracles as evidence, and to seek for miracles as evidence; or the extent to which religion, and religion of a true and admirable kind, has been, and is still, held in connexion with a reliance upon miracles. This reliance will long outlast the reliance on the supernatural prescience of prophecy, for it is not exposed to the same tests. To pick Scripture miracles one by one to pieces is an odious and repulsive task; it is also an unprofitable one, for whatever we may think of the affirmative demonstrations of them, a negative demonstration of them is, from the circumstances of the case, impossible. And yet the human mind is assuredly passing away, however slowly, from this hold of reliance also; and those who make it their stay will more and more find it fail them, will more and more feel themselves disturbed, shaken, distressed, and bewildered.

For it is what we call the *Time-Spirit* which is sapping the proof from miracles, it is the 'Zeit-Geist' itself. Whether we attack them, or whether we defend them, does not much matter. The human mind, as its experience widens, is turning away from them. And for this reason: *it sees, as its experience widens, how they arise*. It sees that, under certain circumstances, they always do arise; and that they have not more solidity in one case than another. Under certain circumstances, wherever men are found, there is, as Shakespeare says:

> No natural exhalation in the sky,
> No scape of nature, no distemper'd day,
> No common wind, no customed event,
> But they will pluck away his natural cause,
> And call them meteors, prodigies, and signs,
> Abortives, presages, and tongues of heaven.[6]

Imposture is so far from being the general rule in these cases, that it is the rare exception. Signs and wonders men's minds will have, and they create them honestly and naturally; yet not so but that we can see *how* they create them.

Roman Catholics fancy that Bible-miracles and the miracles of their Church form a class by themselves; Protestants fancy that Bible-miracles, alone, form a class by themselves. This was eminently the posture of mind of the late Archbishop Whately:[7] to hold that all other miracles would turn out to be impostures, or capable of a natural explanation, but that Bible-miracles would stand sifting by a London special jury or by a committee of scientific men. No acuteness can save such notions, as our knowledge widens, from being seen to be mere extravagances, and the Protestant notion is doomed to an earlier ruin than the Catholic. For the Catholic notion admits miracles, so far as Christianity, at least, is concerned, in the mass; the Protestant notion invites to a criticism by which it must before long itself perish. When Stephen was martyred, he looked up into heaven, and saw the glory of God and Jesus standing on the right hand of God. That, says the Protestant, is solid fact. At the martyrdom of St Fructuosus the Christian servants of the Roman governor, Babylas and Mygdone, saw the heavens open, and the saint and his deacon Eulogius carried up on high with crowns on their heads. That is, says the Protestant, imposture or else illusion. St Paul hears on his way to Damascus the voice of Jesus say to him: 'Saul, Saul, why persecutest thou me?' That is solid fact. The companion of St Thomas Aquinas hears a voice from the crucifix say to the praying saint: 'Thou hast written well of me, Thomas; what recompense dost thou desire?' That is imposture or else illusion. Why? It is impossible to find any criterion by which one of these incidents may establish its claim to a solidity which we refuse to the others.[8]

One of two things must be made out in order to place either the Bible-miracles alone, or the Bible-miracles and the miracles of the Catholic Church with them, in a class by themselves. Either they must be shown to have arisen in a time eminently unfavourable to such a process as Shakespeare describes, to amplification and the production of legend; or they must be shown to be recorded in documents of an eminently historical mode of birth and publication. But surely it is manifest that the Bible-miracles fulfil neither of these conditions. It was said that the waters of the Pamphylian Sea miraculously opened a passage for the army of Alexander the Great. Admiral Beaufort, however, tells us that, 'though there are no tides in this part of the Mediterranean, a considerable depression of the sea is caused by long-continued north winds, and Alexander, taking advantage of such a moment, may have dashed on without impediment.'[a] And we accept the explanation as a matter of course. But the waters of the Red Sea are said to have miraculously opened a passage for the children of Israel; and we insist on the literal truth of *this* story, and reject natural explanations as impious. Yet the time and circumstances of the flight from Egypt were a thousand times more favourable to the rise of some natural incident into a miracle, than the age of Alexander. They were a time and circumstances of less broad daylight. It was said, again, that during the battle of Leuctra the gates of the Heracleum at Thebes suddenly opened, and the armour of Hercules vanished from the temple, to enable the god to take part with the Thebans in the battle. Probably there was some real circumstance, however slight, which gave a foundation for the story. But this is the utmost we think of saying in its favour; the literal story it never even occurs to one of us to believe. But that the walls of Jericho literally fell down at the sound of the trumpets of Joshua, we are

---

[a] Beaufort's *Karamania*, p. 116.

asked to believe, told that it is impious to disbelieve it. Yet which place and time were most likely to generate a miraculous story with ease, Hellas and the days of Epaminondas, or Palestine and the days of Joshua? And of documentary records, which are the most historical in their way of being generated and propagated, which the most favourable for the admission of legend and miracle of all kinds, the Old Testament narratives with their incubation of centuries, and the New Testament narratives with their incubation of a century (and tradition active all the while), or the narratives, say, of Herodotus or Plutarch?

None of them are what we call critical. Experience of the history of the human mind, and of men's habits of seeing, sifting, and relating, convinces us that the miraculous stories of Herodotus or Plutarch do grow out of the process described by Shakespeare. But we shall find ourselves inevitably led, sooner or later, to extend the same rule to all miraculous stories; nay, the considerations which apply in other cases, apply, we shall most surely discover, with even greater force in the case of Bible-miracles.

4

This being so, there is nothing one would more desire for a person or document one greatly values, than to make them independent of miracles. And with regard to the Old Testament we have done this; for we have shown that the essential matter in the Old Testament is the revelation to Israel of the immeasurable grandeur, the eternal necessity, the priceless blessing of that with which not less than three-fourths of human life is indeed concerned, *righteousness*. And it makes no difference to the preciousness of this revelation, whether we believe that the Red Sea miraculously opened a passage to the Israelites, and the walls of Jericho miraculously fell down at the blast of Joshua's trumpet, or that these stories arose in the same way as other stories of the kind. But in the New Testament the essential thing is the revelation of Jesus Christ. For this too, then, if one values it, one's great wish must in like manner be to make it independent of miracle, if miracle is a stay which one perceives, as more and more we are all coming to perceive it, to be not solid.

Now, it may look at first sight a strange thing to say, but it is a truth which we will make abundantly clear as we go on, that one of the very best helps to prepare the way for valuing the Bible and believing in Jesus Christ, is to convince oneself of the liability to mistake in the Bible-writers. Our popular theology supposes that the

Old Testament writers were miraculously inspired, and could make no mistakes; that the New Testament writers were miraculously inspired, and could make no mistakes; and that there this miraculous inspiration stopped, and all writers on religion have been liable to make mistakes ever since. It is as if a hand had been put out of the sky presenting us with the Bible, and the rules of criticism which apply to other books did not apply to the Bible. Now, the fatal thing for this supposition is, that its owners stab it to the heart the moment they use any palliation or explaining away, however small, of the literal words of the Bible; and *some* they always use. For instance, it is said in the eighteenth Psalm, that a consuming fire went out of the mouth of God, so that coals were kindled at it. The veriest literalist will cry out: Everyone knows that this is not to be taken literally! The truth is, even *he* knows that *this* is not to be taken literally; but others know that a great deal more is not to be taken literally. He knows very little; but, as far as his little knowledge goes, he gives up his theory, which is, of course, palpably hollow. For indeed it is only by applying to the Bible a criticism, such as it is, that such a man makes out that criticism does not apply to the Bible.

There has grown up an irresistible sense that the belief in miracles was due to man's want of experience, to his ignorance, agitation, and helplessness. And it will not do to stake all truth and value of the Bible upon its having been put out of the sky, upon its being guaranteed by miracles, and upon their being true. If we present the Bible in this fashion, then the cry, *Imposture!* will more and more, in spite of all we can do, gather strength, and the book will be thrown aside more and more.

But when men come to see, that, both in the New Testament and in the Old, what is given us is words *thrown out* at an immense reality not fully or half fully grasped by the writers, but, even thus, able to affect us with indescribable force; when we convince ourselves that, as in the Old Testament we have Israel's inadequate yet inexhaustibly fruitful testimony to *the Eternal that makes for righteousness*, so we have in the New Testament a report inadequate, indeed, but the only report we have, and therefore priceless, by men, some more able and clear, others less able and clear, but *all* full of the influences of their time and condition, partakers of some of its simple or its learned ignorance, inevitably, in fine, expecting miracles and demanding them, a report, I say, by these men of that immense reality not fully or half fully grasped by them, *the mind of Christ*, then we shall be drawn to the Gospels with a new zest and as by a fresh spell. We shall throw ourselves upon their narratives with an ardour answering to the value of the pearl of great price they hold, and to the difficulty of reaching it.

So, to profit fully by the New Testament, the first thing to be done is to make it perfectly clear to oneself that its reporters both could err and did err. For a plain person, an incident in the report of St Paul's conversion, which comes into our minds the more naturally as this incident has been turned against something we have ourselves said,[a] would, one would think, be enough. We had spoken of the notion that St Paul's miraculous vision at his conversion proved the truth of his doctrine. We related a vision which converted Sampson Staniforth, one of the early Methodists;[9] and we said that just so much proving force, and no more, as Sampson Staniforth's vision had to confirm the truth of anything he might afterwards teach, St Paul's vision had to establish *his* subsequent doctrine. It was eagerly rejoined that Staniforth's vision was but a fancy of his own, whereas the reality of Paul's was proved by his companions hearing the voice that spoke to him. And so in one place of the Acts we are told they did; but in another place of the Acts we are told by Paul himself just the contrary: that his companions did *not* hear the voice that spoke to him. Need we say that the two statements have been 'reconciled'? They have, over and over again; but by one of those processes which are the opprobrium of our Bible-criticism, and by which, as Bishop Butler says, anything can be made to mean anything.[10] There is between the two statements a contradiction as clear as can be. The contradiction proves nothing against the good faith of the reporter, and St Paul undoubtedly had his vision; he had it as Sampson Staniforth had his. What the contradiction proves is the incurable looseness with which the circumstances of what is called and thought *a miracle* are related; and that this looseness the Bible-relaters of a miracle exhibit, just like other people. And the moral is: what an unsure stay, then, must miracles be!

But, after all, that there is here any contradiction or mistake, some do deny; so let us choose a case where the mistake is quite undeniably clear. Such a case we find in the confident expectation and assertion, on the part of the New Testament writers, of the approaching end of the world. Even this mistake people try to explain away; but it is so palpable that no words can cloud our perception of it. *The time is short. The Lord is at hand. The end of all things is at hand. Little children, it is the final time. The Lord's coming is at hand; behold, the*

[a] *St Paul and Protestantism*, pp. 34–5.

judge standeth before the door.[a] Nothing can really obscure the evidence furnished by such sayings as these. When Paul told the Thessalonians that they and he, at the approaching coming of Christ, should have their turn after, not before, the faithful dead: 'For the Lord himself shall descend from heaven with a shout, with the voice of the archangel and with the trump of God, and the dead in Christ shall rise first, then we which are alive and remain shall be caught up together with them in the clouds, to meet the Lord in the air,'[b] when he said this, St Paul was in truth simply mistaken in his notion of what was going to happen. This is as clear as anything can be.

And not only were the New Testament writers thus demonstrably liable to commit, like other men, mistakes in fact; they were also demonstrably liable to commit mistakes in argument. As before, let us take a case which will be manifest and palpable to everyone. St Paul, arguing to the Galatians that salvation was not by the Jewish law but by Jesus Christ, proves his point from the promise to Abraham having been made to him and his *seed*, not *seeds*. The words are not, he says, '*seeds*, as of many, but as of one; to thy *seed*, which is Christ.'[c] Now, as to the point to be proved, we all agree with St Paul; but his argument is that of a Jewish Rabbi, and is clearly both fanciful and false. The writer in Genesis never intended to draw any distinction between *one* of Abraham's seed, and Abraham's seed *in general*. And even if he had expressly meant, what Paul says he did *not* mean, Abraham's seed in general, he would still have said *seed*, and not *seeds*. This is a good instance to take, because the Apostle's substantial doctrine is here not at all concerned. As to the root of the matter in question, we are all at one with St Paul. But it is evident how he could, like the rest of us, bring forward a quite false argument in support of a quite true thesis.

And the use of prophecy by the writers of the New Testament furnishes really, almost at every turn, instances of false argument of the same kind. Habit makes us so lend ourselves to their way of speaking, that commonly nothing checks us; but, the moment we begin to attend, we perceive how much there is which ought to check us. Take the famous allegation of the parted clothes but lot-assigned coat of Christ, as fulfilment of the supposed prophecy in the Psalms: 'They parted my garments among them, and for my vesture did they cast lots.'[d] The words of the Psalm are taken to mean contrast, when they do in truth mean identity. According to the rules of Hebrew

[a] I Cor. 7. 29; Philipp. 4. 5; I Pet. 4. 7; I John 2. 18; James 5. 8, 9. We have here the express declarations of St Paul, St Peter, St John, and St James.
[b] I Thess. 4. 16, 17.　　[c] Gal. 3. 16.　　[d] Ps. 22. 18.

poetry, *for my vesture they did cast lots* is merely a repetition, in different words, of *they parted my garments among them*, not an antithesis to it. The alleged 'prophecy' is, therefore, due to a dealing with the Psalmist's words which is arbitrary and erroneous. So, again, to call the words, *a bone of him shall not be broken,*[a] a prophecy of Christ, fulfilled by his legs not being broken on the cross, is evidently, the moment one considers it, a playing with words which nowadays we should account childish. For what do the words, taken, as alone words can rationally be taken, along with their context, really prophesy? The entire *safety* of the righteous, not his death. *Many are the troubles of the righteous, but the Eternal delivereth him out of all; he keepeth all his bones, so that not one of them is broken.*[b] Worse words, therefore, could hardly have been chosen from the Old Testament to apply in that connexion where they come; for they are really contradicted by the death of Christ, not fulfilled by it.

It is true, this verbal and unintelligent use of Scripture is just what was to be expected from the circumstances of the New Testament writers. It was inevitable for them; it was the sort of trifling which then, in common Jewish theology, passed for grave argument and made a serious impression, as it has in common Christian theology ever since. But this does not make it the less really trifling; or hinder one nowadays from seeing it to be trifling, directly we examine it. The mistake made will strike some people more forcibly in one of the cases cited, some in another, but in one or other of the cases the mistake will be visible to everybody.

Now, this recognition of the liability of the New Testament writers to make mistakes, both of fact and of argument, will certainly, as we have said, more and more gain strength, and spread wider and wider. The futility of their mode of demonstration from prophecy, of which we have just given examples, will be more and more felt. The fallibility of that demonstration from miracles to which they and all about them attached such preponderating weight, which made the disciples of Jesus believe in him, which made the people believe in him, will be more and more recognised.

Reverence for all, who, in those first dubious days of Christianity, chose the better part, and resolutely cast in their lot with 'the despised and rejected of men'! Gratitude to all, who, while the tradition was yet fresh, helped by their writings to preserve and set clear the precious record of the words and life of Jesus! And honour, eternal honour, to the great and profound qualities of soul and mind which some of these writers display! But the writers are admirable for

[a] See John 19. 36.   [b] Ps. 34. 19, 20.

what they are, not for what, by the nature of things, they could not be. It was superiority enough in them to attach themselves firmly to Jesus; to feel to the bottom of their hearts that power of his *words*, which alone held permanently, held, when the miracles, in which the multitude believed as well as the disciples, failed to hold. The good faith of the Bible-writers is above all question, it speaks for itself; and the very same criticism, which shows us the defects of their exegesis and of their demonstrations from miracles, establishes their good faith. But this could not, and did not, prevent them from arguing in the methods by which everyone around them argued, and from expecting miracles where everybody else expected them.

In one respect alone have the miracles recorded by them a more real ground than the mass of miracles of which we have the relation. Medical science has never gauged, never, perhaps, enough set itself to gauge, the intimate connexion between moral fault and disease. To what extent, or in how many cases, what is called *illness* is due to moral springs having been used amiss, whether by being over-used or by not being used sufficiently, we hardly at all know, and we far too little inquire. Certainly it is due to this very much more than we commonly think; and the more it is due to this, the more do moral therapeutics rise in possibility and importance.[a] The bringer of light and happiness, the calmer and pacifier, or invigorator and stimulator, is one of the chiefest of doctors. Such a doctor was Jesus; such an operator, by an efficacious and real, though little observed and little employed agency, upon what we, in the language of popular superstition, call the *unclean spirits*, but which are to be designated more literally and more correctly as the *uncleared, unpurified spirits*, which came raging and madding before him. This his own language shows, if we know how to read it. '*What does it matter whether I say, Thy sins are forgiven thee! or whether I say, Arise and walk!*'[b] And again: '*Thou art made whole; sin no more, lest a worse thing befall thee.*'[c] His reporters, we must remember, are men who saw thaumaturgy in all that Jesus did, and who saw in all sickness and disaster visitations from God, and they bend his language accordingly. But indications enough remain to show the line of the Master, his perception of the large part of moral cause in many kinds of disease, and his method of addressing to this part his cure.

It would never had done, indeed, to have men pronouncing right and left that this and that was a judgment, and how, and for what,

[a] Consult the *Charmides* of Plato (cap. v.) for a remarkable account of the theory of such a treatment, attributed by Socrates to Zamolxis, the god-king of the Thracians.
[b] Matth. 9. 5.   [c] John 5. 14.

and on whom. And so, when the disciples, seeing an afflicted person, asked whether this man had done sin or his parents, Jesus checked them and said: 'Neither the one nor the other, but that the works of God might be made manifest in him.'[1] Not the less clear is his own belief in the moral root of much physical disease, and in moral therapeutics; and it is important to note well the instances of miracles where this belief comes in. For the action of Jesus in these instances, however it may be amplified in the reports, was real; but it is not, therefore, as popular religion fancies, thaumaturgy, it is not what people are fond of calling the *supernatural*, but what is better called the *non-natural*. It is, on the contrary, like the grace of Raphael, or the grand style of Phidias, eminently natural; but it is above common, low-pitched nature. It is a line of nature not yet mastered or followed out.

Its significance as a guarantee of the authenticity of Christ's mission is trivial, however, compared with the guarantee furnished by his sayings. Its importance is in its necessary effect upon the beholders and reporters. This element of what was really wonderful, unprecedented, and unaccountable, they had actually before them; and we may estimate how it must have helped and seemed to sanction that tendency which in any case would have carried them, circumstanced as they were, to find all the performances and career of Jesus miraculous.

But, except for this, the miracles related in the Gospels will appear to us more and more, the more our experience and knowledge increases, to have but the same ground which is common to all miracles, the ground indicated by Shakespeare; to have been generated under the same kind of conditions as other miracles, and to follow the same laws. When once the 'Zeit-Geist' has made us entertain the notion of this, a thousand things in the manner of relating will strike us which never struck us before, and will make us wonder how we could ever have thought differently. Discrepancies which we now labour with such honest pains and by such astonishing methods to explain away, the voice at Paul's conversion, heard by the bystanders according to one account, not heard by them according to another; the Holy Dove at Christ's baptism, visible to John the Baptist in one narrative, in two others to Jesus himself, in another, finally, to all the people as well; the single blind man in one relation, growing into two blind men in another; the speaking with tongues, according to St Paul a sound without meaning, according to the Acts an intelligent and intelligible utterance, all this will be felt

[a] John 9. 3.

to require really no explanation at all, to explain itself, to be natural to the whole class of incidents to which these miracles belong, and the inevitable result of the looseness with which the stories of them arise and are propagated.

And the more the miraculousness of the story deepens, as after the death of Jesus, the more does the texture of the incidents become loose and floating, the more does the very air and aspect of things seem to tell us we are in wonderland. Jesus after his resurrection not known by Mary Magdalene, taken by her for the gardener; appearing *in another form*, and not known by the two disciples going with him to Emmaus and at supper with him there; not known by his most intimate apostles on the borders of the Sea of Galilee; and presently, out of these vague beginnings, the recognitions getting asserted, then the ocular demonstrations, the final commissions, the ascension; one hardly knows which of the two to call the most evident here, the perfect simplicity and good faith of the narrators or the plainness with which they themselves really say to us: *Behold a legend growing under your eyes!*

And suggestions of this sort, with respect to the whole miraculous side of the New Testament, will meet us at every turn; we here but give a sample of them. It is neither our wish nor our design to accumulate them, to marshal them, to insist upon them, to make their force felt. Let those who desire to keep them at arm's length continue to do so, if they can, and go on placing the sanction of the Christian religion in its miracles. Our point is, that the objections to miracles do, and more and more will, without insistence, without attack, without controversy, make their own force felt; and that the sanction of Christianity, if Christianity is not to be lost along with its miracles, must be found elsewhere.

Chapter VI
The New Testament Record

Now, then, will be perceived the bearing and gravity of what I some little way back said, that the more we convince ourselves of the liability of the New Testament writers to mistake, the more we really bring out the greatness and worth of the New Testament. For the more the reporters were fallible and prone to delusion, the more does Jesus become independent of the mistakes they made, and unaffected by them. We have plain proof that here was a very great spirit; and the greater he was, the more certain were his disciples to misunderstand him. The depth of their misunderstanding of him is really a kind of measure of the height of his superiority. And this superiority is what interests us in the records of the New Testament; for the New Testament exists to reveal Jesus Christ, not to establish the immunity of its writers from error.

Jesus himself is not a New Testament writer; he is the object of description and comment to the New Testament writers. As the Old Testament speaks about the Eternal and bears an invaluable witness to him, without yet ever adequately in words defining and expressing him; so, and even yet more, do the New Testament writers speak about Jesus and give a priceless record of him, without adequately and accurately comprehending him. They are altogether on another plane from Jesus, and their mistakes are not his. It is not Jesus himself who relates his own miracles to us; who tells us of his own apparitions after his death; who alleges his crucifixion and sufferings as a fulfilment of the prophecy: *The Eternal keepeth all the bones of the righteous, so that not one of them is broken;*[a] who proves salvation to be by Christ alone, from the promise to Abraham being made to *seed* in the singular number, not the plural. If, therefore, the human mind is now drawing away from reliance on miracles, coming to perceive the community of character which pervades them all, to understand their natural laws, so to speak, their loose mode of origination and their untrustworthiness, and is inclined rather to distrust the dealer in them than to pin its faith upon him; then it is good for the authority of Jesus, that his reporters are evidently liable to ignorance and error. He is reported to deal in miracles, to be above all a thaumaturgist. But the more his reporters were intellectually men of their nation and time, and of its current beliefs, the more, that is, they were open to mistakes, the more certain they were to impute miracles to a wonderful and half-understood personage like Jesus, whether he would or no. He himself may, at the same time, have had quite other notions as to what he was doing and intending.

Again, the mistake of imagining that the world was to end, as St Paul announces, within the lifetime of the first Christian generation, is palpable. But the reporters of Jesus make him announcing just the same thing: 'This generation shall not pass away till they shall see the Son of Man coming in the clouds with great power and glory, and then shall he send his angels and gather his elect from the four winds.'[b] Popular theology can put a plain satisfactory sense upon

^a Ps. 34. 20.   ^b Matth. 29. 30, 31, 34.

this, but, as usual, through that process described by Butler by which anything can be made to mean anything; and from this sort of process the human mind is beginning to shrink. A more plausible theology will say that the words are an accommodation; that the speaker lends himself to the fancies and expectations of his hearers. A good deal of such accommodation there is in this and other sayings of Jesus; but accommodation to the *full extent* here supposed would surely have been impossible. To suppose it, is most violent and unsatisfactory. Either, then, the words were, like St Paul's announcement, a mistake, or they are not really the very words Jesus said, just as he said them. That is, the reporters have given them a turn, however slight, a tone and a colour, a connexion, to make them comply with a fixed idea in their own minds, which they unfeignedly believed was a fixed idea with Jesus also. Now, the more we regard the reporters of Jesus as men liable to err, full of the turbid Jewish fancies about 'the grand consummation' which were then current, the easier we can understand these men inevitably putting their own eschatology into the mouth of Jesus, when they had to report his discourse about the kingdom of God and the troubles in store for the Jewish nation, and the less need have we to make Jesus a co-partner in their eschatology.

Again, the futility of such demonstrations from prophecy as those of which I have quoted examples, and generally of all that Jewish exegesis, based on a mere unintelligent catching at the letter of the Old Testament, isolated from its context and real meaning, of which the New Testament writers give us so much, begins to disconcert attentive readers of the Bible more and more, and to be felt by them as an embarrassment to the cause of Jesus, not a support. Well, then, it is good for the authority of Jesus, that those who establish it by arguments of this sort should be clearly men of their race and time, not above its futile methods of reasoning and demonstration. The more they were this, and the more they were sure to mix up much futile logic and exegesis with their presentation of Jesus, the less is Jesus himself responsible for such logic and exegesis, or at all dependent upon it. He may himself have rated such argumentation at precisely its true value, and have based his mission and authority upon no grounds but solid ones. Whether he did so or not, his hearers and reporters were sure to base it on their own fantastic grounds also, and to credit Jesus with doing the same.

In short, the more we conceive Jesus as almost as much over the heads of the disciples and reporters then, as he is over the heads of the mass of so-called Christians now, and the more we see his disciples to have been, as they were, men raised by a truer moral susceptiveness above their countrymen, but in intellectual conceptions and habits much on a par with them, all the more do we make room, so to speak, for Jesus to be a personage immensely great and wonderful; as wonderful as anything his reporters imagined him to be, though in a different manner.

2

We make room for him to be this, and through the inadequate reporting of his followers there breaks and shines, and will more and more break and shine the more the matter is examined, abundant evidence that he *was* this. It is most remarkable, and the best proof of the simplicity, seriousness, and good faith, which intercourse with Jesus Christ inspired, that witnesses with a fixed prepossession, and having no doubt at all as to the interpretation to be put on his acts and career, should yet admit so much of what makes against themselves and their own power of interpreting. For them, it was a thing beyond all doubt, that by miracles Jesus manifested forth his glory, and induced the faithful to believe in him. Yet what checks to this paramount and all-governing belief of theirs do they report from Jesus himself! Everybody will be able to recall such checks, although he may never yet have been accustomed to consider their full significance. *Except ye see signs and wonders, ye will not Believe!*[a] as much as to say: 'Believe on right grounds you cannot, and you must needs believe on wrong!' And again: 'Believe me that I am in the Father and the Father in me; *or else believe for the very works' sake!*'[b] as much as to say: 'Acknowledge me on the ground of my healing and restoring acts being miraculous, if you must; but it is not the right ground.' No, not the right ground; and when Nicodemus came and would put conversion on this ground ('We know that thou art a teacher come from God, *for no one can do the miracles that thou doest except God be with him*'), Jesus rejoined: 'Verily, verily, I say unto thee, *except a man be born from above*, he cannot see the kingdom of God!' thus tacitly changing his disciple's ground and correcting him.[c] Even distress and impatience at this false ground being taken is visible sometimes: 'Jesus *groaned in his spirit* and said, Why doth this generation ask for a sign? Verily I say unto you, there shall no sign be given to this generation!'[d] Who does not see what double and treble importance these checks from Jesus to the reliance on miracles gain, through their being reported by those who relied on miracles devoutly? Who

[a] John 4. 48.   [b] John 14. 11.   [c] John 3. 2, 3.   [d] Mark 8. 12.

Literature and Dogma

does not see what a clue they offer as to the real mind of Jesus? To convey at all to such hearers of him that there was any objection to miracles, his own sense of the objection must have been profound; and to get them, who neither shared nor understood it, to repeat it a few times, he must have repeated it many times.

Take, again, the eschatology of the disciples, their notion of final things, of the approaching great judgment and end of the world. This consisted mainly in a literal appropriation of the apocalyptic pictures of the book of Daniel and the book of Enoch, and a transference of them to Jesus Christ and his kingdom. It is not surprising, certainly, that men with the mental range of their time, and with so little flexibility of thought, that, when Jesus told them to beware of 'the leaven of the Pharisees,'[a] or when he called himself 'the bread of life' and said, *He that eateth me shall live by me*,[b] they stuck hopelessly fast in the literal meaning of the words, and were accordingly puzzled or else offended by them, it is not surprising that these men should have been incapable of dealing in a large spirit with prophecies like those of Daniel, that they should have applied them to Jesus narrowly and literally, and should therefore have conceived his kingdom unintelligently. This is not remarkable; what *is* remarkable is, that they should themselves supply us with their Master's blame of their too literal criticism, his famous sentence: 'The kingdom of God is *within* you!'[c] Such an account of the kingdom of God has more right, even if recorded only once, to pass with us for Jesus Christ's own account, than the common materialising accounts, if repeated twenty times; for it was manifestly quite foreign to the disciples' own notions, and they could never have invented it. Evidence of the same kind, again, evidence borne by the reporters themselves against their own power of rightly understanding what their Master, on this topic of the kingdom of God and its coming, meant to say, is Christ's warning to his apostles, that the subject of final things was one where they were all out of their depth: '*It is not for you to know* the times and the seasons which the Father hath put in his own power.'[d]

So, too, with the use of prophecy and of the Old Testament generally. A very small experience of Jewish exegesis will convince us that, in the disciples, their catching at the letter of the Scriptures, and mistaking this play with words for serious argument, was nothing extraordinary. The extraordinary thing is that Jesus, even in the report of these critics, uses Scripture in a totally different manner; he wields it as an instrument of which he truly possesses the use. Either he puts prophecy into act, and by the startling point thus made he

[a] Matth. 16. 6–12.   [b] John 6. 48, 57.   [c] Luke 17. 21.   [d] Acts 1. 7.

engages the popular imagination on his side, makes the popular familiarity with prophecy serve him; as when he rides into Jerusalem on an ass, or clears the Temple of buyers and sellers. Or else he applies Scripture in what is called 'a superior spirit,' to make it yield to narrow-minded hearers a lesson of wisdom; as, for instance, to rebuke a superstitious observance of the Sabbath he employs the incident of David's taking the shewbread. His reporters, in short, are the servants of the Scripture-letter, Jesus is its master; and it is from the very men who were servants to it themselves, that we learn that he was master of it. How signal, therefore, must this mastery have been! how eminently and strikingly different from the treatment known and practised by the disciples themselves!

Finally, for the reporters of Jesus the rule was, undoubtedly, that men 'believed on Jesus when they saw the miracles which he did.'[a] Miracles were in these reporters' eyes, beyond question, the evidence of the Christian religion. And yet these same reporters indicate another and a totally different evidence offered for the Christian religion by Jesus Christ himself. *Every one that heareth and learneth from the Father, cometh unto me.*[b] *As the Father hath taught me, so I speak;*[c] *he that is of God heareth the words of God;*[d] *if God was your Father, ye would have loved me!*[e] This is inward evidence, direct evidence. From that previous knowledge of God, as 'the Eternal that loveth righteousness,' which Israel possessed, the hearers of Jesus could and should have concluded irresistibly, when they heard his words, that he came from God. Now, miracles are outward evidence, indirect evidence, not conclusive in this fashion. To walk on the sea cannot really prove a man to proceed from the Eternal that loveth righteousness; although undoubtedly, as we have said, a man who walks on the sea will be able to make the mass of mankind believe about him almost anything he chooses to say. But there is, after all, no necessary connexion between walking on the sea and proceeding from the Eternal that loveth righteousness. Jesus propounds, on the other hand, an evidence of which the whole force lies in the necessary connexion between the proving matter and the power that makes for righteousness. This is *his* evidence for the Christian religion.

His disciples felt the force of the evidence, indeed. Peter's answer to the question, 'Will ye also go away?' – '*To whom should we go? thou hast the words of eternal life?*'[f] proves it. But feeling the force of a thing is very different from understanding and possessing it. The evidence, which the disciples were *conscious* of understanding and possessing,

[a] John 2. 23.   [b] John 6. 45.   [c] John 8. 28.   [d] John 8. 47.   [e] John 8. 42.
[f] John 6. 68.

was the evidence from miracles. And yet, in their report, Jesus is plainly shown to us insisting on a different evidence, an internal one. The character of the reporters gives to this indication a paramount importance. That they should indicate this internal evidence once, as the evidence on which Jesus insisted, is more significant, we say, than their indicating, twenty times, the evidence from miracles as the evidence naturally convincing to mankind, and recommended, as they thought, by Jesus. The notion of the one evidence they would have of themselves; the notion of the other they could only get from a superior mind. This mind must have been full of it to induce them to feel it at all; and their exhibition of it, even then, must of necessity be inadequate and broken.

But is it possible to overrate the value of the ground thus gained for showing the riches of the New Testament to those who, sick of the popular arguments from prophecy, sick of the popular arguments from miracles, are for casting the New Testament aside altogether? The book contains all that we know of a wonderful spirit, far above the heads of his reporters, still farther above the head of our popular theology, which has added its own misunderstanding of the reporters to the reporters' misunderstanding of Jesus. And it was quite inevitable that anything so superior and so profound should be imperfectly understood by those amongst whom it first appeared, and for a very long time afterwards; and that it should come at last gradually to stand out clearer only by time, *Time*, as the Greek maxim says, *the wisest of all things, for he is the unfailing discoverer.*[11]

Yet, however much is discovered, the object of our scrutiny must still be beyond us, must still transcend our adequate knowledge, if for no other reason, because of the character of the first and only records of him. But in the view now taken we have, even at the point to which we have already come, at least a wonderful figure transcending his time, transcending his disciples, attaching them but transcending them; in very much that he uttered going far above their heads, treating Scripture and prophecy like a master while they treated it like children, resting his doctrine on internal evidence while they rested it on miracles; and yet, by his incomparable lucidity and penetrativeness, planting his profound veins of thought in their memory along with their own notions and prepossessions, to come out all mixed up together, but still distinguishable one day and separable; and leaving his word thus to bear fruit for the future.

Surely to follow and extract these veins of true ore is a wise man's business; not to let them lie neglected and unused, because the beds where they are found are not all of the same quality with them. The beds are invaluable because they contain the ore; and though the search for it in them is undoubtedly a grave and difficult quest, yet it is not a quest of the elaborate and endless kind that it will at first, perhaps, be fancied to be. It is a quest with this for its governing idea: *Jesus was over the heads of his reporters; what, therefore, in their report of him, is Jesus, and what is the reporters?*

Now, this excludes as unessential much of the criticism which is bestowed on the New Testament, and gives a sure point of view for the remainder. And what it excludes are those questions as to the exact date, the real authorship, the first publication, the rank of priority, of the Gospels; questions which have a great attraction for critics, which are perhaps in themselves good to be entertained, which lead to much close and fruitful observation of the texts, and in which very high ingenuity may be shown and very great plausibility reached, but not more; they cannot be really settled, the data are insufficient. And for our purpose they are not essential. Neither is it essential for our purpose to get at the very primitive text of the New Testament writers, deeply interesting and deeply important as this is. The changes that have befallen the text show, no doubt, the constant tendency of popular Christianity to add to the element of theurgy and thaumaturgy, to increase and develop it. To clear the text of these changes, will show the New Testament writers to have been less preoccupied with this tendency, and is, so far, very instructive. But it will not, by re-establishing the real words of the writers, necessarily give the real truth as to Jesus Christ's religion; because to the writers themselves this religion was, in a considerable degree certainly, a theurgy and a thaumaturgy, although not quite in the mechanical and extravagant way that it is in our present popular theology.

For instance, the famous text of the three heavenly witnesses[a] is an imposture, and an extravagant one. It shows us, no doubt, theologians like our bishops already at work, men with more metaphysics than literary tact, full of the Aryan genius, of the notion that religion is a metaphysical conception; anxious to do something for the thesis of 'the Godhead of the Eternal Son,' or of 'the blessed truth that the God of the universe is a person,' or, as the Bishop of Gloucester writes it, 'PERSON,' and so on. But *something* of the same intention is

[a] I John 5. 7.

unquestionably visible, never, indeed, in Jesus, but in the author of
the Fourth Gospel. Much of the conversation with Nicodemus is a
proof of it; the forty-sixth verse of the sixth chapter is a signal proof
of it. One can there almost see the author, after recording Christ's
words: *Every one that heareth and learneth of the father cometh unto me*,
take alarm at the notion that this looks too downright and natural,
and, sincerely persuaded that he 'did something' for the honour of
Jesus by making him more abstract, bring in and put into the mouth
of Jesus the 46th verse: *Not that any one hath seen the father, except he
that is from God, he hath seen the father*. This verse has neither rhyme
nor reason where it stands in Christ's discourse, it jars with the words
which precede and follow, and is in quite another vein from them.
Yet it is the author's own, it is no interpolation.

Again, Unitarians lay much stress on the probability that in the
first words of St Mark's Gospel: 'The beginning of the gospel of
Jesus Christ, the Son of God,' *the Son of God* is an interpolation. And,
no doubt, if the words are an interpolation, this shows that the desire
to prove the dogma of Christ's Godhead was not so painfully ever-
present to the writer of the Second Gospel as it became to later
theologians. But it shows no more; it does not show that he had the
least doubt about Jesus being the Son of God. Ten verses later, in an
undisputed passage, he calls him so.

Again, in the last chapter of the same Gospel, all which follows the
eighth verse, all the account of Christ's resurrection and ascension, is
probably an addition by a later hand. But the resurrection is plainly
indicated in the first eight verses; and that the writer of the Second
Gospel stops after the eighth verse, proves rather that he was writing
briefly than that he did not believe in the resurrection and ascension
as much as, for instance, the writer of the Third Gospel; unless,
indeed, there are other signs (for example, in his way of relating such
an incident as the Transfiguration) to show that he was suspicious of
the preternatural. But there are none; and he plainly was not, and
could not have been.

Again; it seems impossible that the very primitive original of the
First Gospel should have made Jesus say, that 'the sign of Jonas'
consisted in his being three days and three nights in the whale's belly
as the Son of Man was to be a like time in the heart of the earth.[a] It
spoils the argument, and in the next verse the argument is given
simply and rightly. Jonas was a sign to the Jews, because the Nine-
vites repented at his preaching and a greater than Jonas stood now
preaching to the Jews. But whether the words are genuine (and there

[a] Matthew 12. 40.

seems no evidence to the contrary) in that particular place or not, to get rid of them brings us really but a very little way, when it is plain that their argument is exactly one which the Evangelists would be disposed to use, and to think that Jesus meant to use. For so they make him to have said, for instance: *Destroy this temple, and in three days I will raise it up!ᵃ* in prediction of his own death and resurrection.

In short, to know accurately the history of our documents is impossible, and even if it were possible, we should yet not know accurately what Jesus said and did; *for his reporters were incapable of rendering it, he was so much above them.* This is the important thing to get firmly fixed in our minds. And the more it becomes established to us, the more we shall see the futility of what is called *rationalism*, *rationalism* proper, and the *rationalistic* treatment of the New Testament; of the endeavour, that is, to reduce all the supernatural in it to real events, much resembling what is related, which have got a little magnified and coloured by being seen through the eyes of men having certain prepossessions, but may easily be brought back to their true proportions and made historical and reasonable. A famous specimen of this kind of treatment is Schleiermacher's fancy of the death on the cross having been a swoon, and the resurrection of Jesus a recovery from this swoon. Victorious indeed, whatever may be in other ways his own shortcomings, is Strauss's demolition of this fancy of Schleiermacher's! Like the rationalistic treatment of Scripture throughout, it makes far more difficulties than it solves, and rests on too narrow a conception of the history of the human mind, and of its diversities of operation and production. It puts us ourselves in the original disciples' place, imagines the original disciples to have been men rational in our sense and way, and then explains their record as it might be made explicable if it were ours. And it may safely be said that in this fashion it is *not* explicable. Imaginations so little creative, and with so substantial a framework of fact for each of their wonderful stories as this theory assumes, would never have created so much as they did; at least, they could not have done so and retained their manifest simplicity and good faith. They must have fallen, we in like case should fall, into arrangement and artifice.

But the original disciples were *not* men rational in our sense and way. The real wonderfulness of Jesus, and their belief in him, being given, they needed no such full and parallel body of fact for each miracle as we suppose. Some hint and help of fact, undoubtedly, there almost always was, and we naturally seek to explore it. Sometimes our guesses may be right, sometimes wrong, but we can never

ᵃ John 2. 19.

be *sure*, the range of possibility is so wide; and we may easily make them too elaborate. Shakespeare's explanation is far the soundest:

> No natural exhalation in the sky,
> No scape of nature, no distemper'd day,
> No common wind, no customed event,
> But they will pluck away his natural cause,
> And call them meteors, prodigies, and signs,
> Abortives, presages, and tongues of heaven.

And it must be remembered, moreover, that of none of these record-ers have we, probably, the very original record. The whole record, when we first get it, has passed through at least half a century, or more, of oral tradition, and through more than one written account. Miraculous incidents swell and grow apace; they are just the elements of a tradition that swell and grow most. These incidents, therefore, in the history of Jesus, the preternatural things he did, the preternatural things that befell him, are just the parts of the record which are least solid. Beyond the historic outlines of the life of Jesus, his Galilean origin, his preaching in Galilee, his preaching in Jerusalem, his crucifixion, much the firmest element in the record is his *words*. Happily it is of these that he himself said: 'The *words* that I speak unto you, they are spirit and they are life.'[a] But in reading them, we have still to bear in mind our governing idea, that they are words of one *inadequately comprehended by his hearers*, men though these be of pureness of heart, discernment to know and love the good, perfect uprightness of intention, faithful simplicity.

What they will have reported best, probably, is discourse where there was the framework of a story and its application to guide them, discourse such as the parables. Instructive and beautiful as the para-bles are, however, they have not the importance of the direct teaching of Jesus. But in his direct teaching we are on the surest ground in single sentences, which have their ineffaceable and unforgettable stamp: *My yoke is kindly and my burden light; Many are called, few chosen; They that are whole need not a physician, but they that are sick; No man having put his hand to the plough, and looking back, is fit for the kingdom of God.*[b] The longer trains of discourse, and many sayings in immediate connexion with miracles, present much more difficulty. Probably there are very few sayings attributed to Jesus which do not contain what he on some occasion actually said, or much of what he actually said. But the connexion, the juncture, is plainly often missed; things are put out of their true place and order. Failure of memory

[a] John 6. 63.   [b] Matthew 6. 30; 22. 14; 9. 12; Luke 9. 62.

would occasionally cause this with any reporters; failure of comprehension would with the reporters of Jesus frequently cause it. The surrounding tradition insensibly biases them, their love of miracles biases them, their eschatology biases them. All these three exercise an attraction on words of Jesus, and draw them into occasions, placings, and turns, which are not exactly theirs. The one safe guide to the extrication and right reception of what comes from Jesus is the internal evidence. And wherever we find what enforces this evidence or builds upon it, there we may be especially sure that we are on the trace of Jesus; because turn or bias in this direction the disciples were more likely to omit from his discourse than to import into it, they were themselves so wholly preoccupied with the evidence from miracles.

[4]

This is what gives such eminency and value to the Fourth Gospel.*a* The confident certainty with which Ewald settles the authorship of this gospel, and assigns it to St John, is an exhibition of that learned man's weakness. To settle the authorship is impossible, the data are insufficient; but from what data we have, to believe that the Gospel is St John's is extremely difficult. But, on the other hand, the stress which Ewald, following Luther, lays on this Gospel, the value which he attributes to it, is an exhibition of his power, of his deep, sure feeling, and true insight, in the essential matters of religious history; and of his superiority, here, to the best of his rivals, Baur, Strauss, and even M. Renan.[12] 'The true evangelical bread,' says Strauss, 'Christians have always gone to the three first Gospels for!'[13] But what, then, means this sentence of Luther, who stands as such a good, though favourable, representative of ordinary Christianity: 'John's Gospel is the one proper Head-Gospel, and far to be preferred to the three others'?[14] Again, M. Renan, often so ingenious as well as eloquent, says that the narrative and incidents in the Fourth Gospel are probably in the main historical, the discourses invented.[15] Reverse the proposition, and it would be more plausible! The narrative, so meagre, and skipping so unaccountably backwards and for-

---

a Some critics object that the Fourth Gospel has been proved by Baur to be entirely unhistorical, and to give for sayings of Jesus, wherever it does not follow the synoptics, the free inventions of some Christian dogmatist of late date. So little do I think Baur to have *proved* this, that I hold adherence to his thesis to be a conclusive sign of the adherent's want of real critical insight. To discuss controversially in the text the date, mode of composition, and character of the Fourth Gospel would be quite unsuitable to the design of the present work. But I have noticed objections, and amongst them this as to my use of the Fourth Gospel, elsewhere. See *God and the Bible: A Review of Objections to Literature and Dogma*. [*Prose Works*, ed. Super, VII].

wards between Galilee and Jerusalem, might well be thought, not indeed invented, but a matter of infinitely little care and attention to the writer of the Gospel, a mere slight framework in which to set the doctrine and discourses of Jesus. The doctrine and discourses of Jesus, on the other hand, *cannot* in the main be the writer's, because in the main they are clearly out of his reach.

The Fourth Gospel delights the heart of M.Burnouf. For its writer shows, M. Burnouf thinks, signal traces of the Aryan genius, has much to favour the notion that religion is a metaphysical conception, and was perhaps even capable, with time, of reaching the grand truth that God is a cosmic unity! And undoubtedly the writer of the Fourth Gospel seems to have come in contact, in Asia or Egypt, with Aryan metaphysics whether from India or Greece; and to have had this advantage, whatever it amounts to, in writing his Gospel. But who, that has eyes to read, cannot see the difference between the places in his Gospel, such as the introduction, where the writer speaks in his own person, and the places where Jesus himself speaks? The moment Jesus speaks, the metaphysical apparatus falls away, the simple intuition takes its place; and wherever in the discourse of Jesus the metaphysical apparatus is intruded, it jars with the context, breaks the unity of the discourse, impairs the thought, and comes evidently from the writer, not Jesus. It may seem strange and incredible to M. Burnouf that metaphysics should not always confer the superiority upon their possessor; but such is the case.

Who, again, cannot understand that the philosophical acquirements of the author of the Fourth Gospel, like the rabbinical training and intellectual activity of Paul, though they may have sometimes led each of them astray, must yet have given each of them a range of thought, and an enlarged mental horizon, enabling them to perceive and follow ideas of Jesus which escaped the ken of the more scantily endowed authors of the synoptical Gospels? Plato sophisticates somewhat the genuine Socrates; but it is very doubtful whether the culture and mental energy of Plato did not give him a more adequate vision of this true Socrates than Xenophon had. It proves nothing for the superiority of the first three Gospels that their authors are without the logic of Paul and the metaphysics of John (by this commonly received name let us for shortness' sake call the author of the Fourth Gospel), and that Jesus also was without them. Jesus was without them because he was above them; the authors of the synoptical Gospels because they were (we say it without any disrespect) below them. Therefore, the author of the Fourth Gospel, by the very characters which make him inferior to Jesus, was made superior to the three synoptics, and better able than they to seize and reproduce the higher teaching of Jesus.

Does it follow, then, that his picture of Christ's teaching can have been his own invention? By no means; since Christ's teaching is as plainly over his head (at that time of day it could not have been otherwise) as it is over theirs. He deals in miracles as confidingly as they do, while unconsciously indicating, far more than they do, that the evidence of miracles is superseded. In those two great chapters, the fifth and sixth, where Jesus deals with the topics of life, death, and judgement, and with his thesis: *He that eateth me shall live by me!*[a] invaluable and full of light as is what is given, the eschatology and the materialising conceptions of the writer do yet evidently intervene, as they did with all the disciples, as they did with the Jews in general, to hinder a perfectly faithful mirroring of the thought of Jesus. We have already remarked how his metaphysical acquirements intervene in like manner. In the discourse with Nicodemus in the third chapter, from the thirteenth verse to the end, phrases and expressions of Jesus of the highest worth are scattered; but they are manifestly set in a short theological lecture interposed by the writer himself, a lecture which is, as a whole, without vital connexion with the genuine discourse of Jesus, and needing only to be carefully studied side by side with this for its disparateness to become apparent.

But a failure of right understanding, which will be visible to every one, occurs with this writer in his seventh chapter. Jesus, with a reference to words of the second Isaiah,[b] says here: 'He that believeth on me, as the Scripture saith, out of his belly shall flow rivers of living water.'[c] The thought is plain; it belongs to the same order as the thought of the saying: 'If any thirst, let him come unto me and drink;' or of the words to the woman of Samaria: 'If thou hadst known the gift of God, and who it is that talketh with thee, thou wouldst have asked of him and he would have given thee living water.' It means that a man, receiving Jesus, obtains a source of refreshment for himself and becomes a source of refreshment for others; and it means this generally, without any limitation to a special time. But the reporter explains: 'Now this he said concerning the Spirit (*Pneuma*) which they who believed on him should receive, for *Pneuma* was not yet, because Jesus was not yet glorified.'[d] A clearer instance of a narrow and mechanical interpretation of a great and free

---

[a] John 6. 57.
[b] Chap. 58. 11; where it is promised to the righteous: 'Thou shalt be like a watered garden, and like a spring of water, whose waters fail not.'
[c] John 7. 38.   [d] John 7. 39.

thought can hardly be imagined; and the words of Jesus himself enable us here to control the inadequacy of the interpretation, and to make it palpable.

So that the superior point of view in the Fourth Gospel, the more spiritual treatment of things, the insistence on internal evidence, not external, cannot, we say, be the writer's, for they are above him; and while his gifts and acquirements are such as to make him report them, they are not such as to enable him to originate them. The great evidential line of this Gospel: 'You are always talking about God, and about your founder Abraham, the father of God's faithful people; here is a man who says nothing of his own head, who tells you the truth, as he has learnt it of God; if you were really of God you would hear the words of God! if you were really Abraham's children you would follow the truth like Abraham!' this simple but profound line, sending Israel back to amend its conventional, barren notions of God, of righteousness, and of the founders of its religion, sending it to explore them afresh, to sound them deeper, to gather from them a new revelation and a new life, was, we say, at once too simple and too profound for the author of the Fourth Gospel to have invented. Our endless gratitude is due to him, however, for having caught and preserved so much of it. And our business is to keep hold of the clue he has thus given to us, and to use it as profitably as possible.

3 [5]

Truly, then, some one will exclaim, we may say with the 'Imitation:' *Magna ars est scire conversari cum Jesu!*[16] And so it is. To extract from his reporters the true Jesus entire, is even impossible; to extract him in considerable part is one of the highest conceivable tasks of criticism. And it is vain to use that favourite argument of popular theology that man could never have been left by Providence in difficulty and obscurity about a matter of so much importance to him. For the cardinal rule of our present inquiry is that rule of Newton's: *Hypotheses non fingo*;[17] and this argument of popular theology rests on the eternal hypothesis of a magnified and non-natural man at the head of mankind's and the world's affairs. And a further answer is, that, as to the argument itself, even if we allowed the hypothesis, yet the course of things, so far as we can see, is *not* so; things do *not* proceed in this fashion. Because a man has frequently to make sea-passages, he is *not* gifted with an immunity from sea-sickness; because a thing is of the highest interest and importance to know, it is *not*, therefore, easy to know; on the contrary, in general, in proportion to its magnitude it is difficult, and requires time.

But the right commentary on the sentence of the 'Imitation' is given by the 'Imitation' itself in the sentence following: *Esto humilis et pacificus, et erit tecum Jesus!* What men could take at the hands of Jesus, what they could use, what could save them, he made as clear as light; and Christians have never been able, even if they would, to miss seeing it. No, never; but still they have superadded to it a vast *Aberglaube*, an after or extra-belief of their own; and the *Aberglaube* has pushed on one side, for very many, the saving doctrine of Jesus, has hindered attention from being riveted on this and on its line of growth and working, has nearly effaced it, has developed all sorts of faults contrary to it. This *Aberglaube* has sprung out of a false criticism of the literary records in which the doctrine is conveyed; what is called 'orthodox divinity' is, in fact, an immense literary misapprehension. Having caused the saving doctrines enshrined in these records to be neglected, and having credited the records with existing for the sake of its own *Aberglaube*, this blunder now threatens to cause the records themselves to be neglected by all those (and their numbers are fast increasing) whom its own *Aberglaube* fills with impatience and aversion. Therefore it is needful to show the line of growth of this *Aberglaube*, and its delusiveness; to show, and with more detail than we have admitted hitherto, the line of growth of Jesus Christ's doctrine, and the far-reaching sanctions, the inexhaustible attractiveness, the grace and truth, with which he invested it. The doctrine itself is essentially simple; and what *is* difficult, the literary criticism of the documents containing the doctrine, is not the doctrine.

This literary criticism, however, *is* extremely difficult. It calls into play the highest requisites for the study of letters; great and wide acquaintance with the history of the human mind, knowledge of the manner in which men have thought, of their way of using words and of what they mean by them, delicacy of perception and quick tact, and besides all these, a favourable moment and the 'Zeit-Geist.' And yet everyone among us criticises the Bible, and thinks it is of the essence of the Bible that it can be thus criticised with success! And the Four Gospels, the part of the Bible to which this sort of criticism is most applied and most confidently, are just the part which for literary criticism is infinitely the hardest, however simple they may look, and however simple the saving doctrine they contain really is. For Prophets and Epistlers speak for themselves: but in the Four Gospels reporters are speaking for Jesus, who is far above them.

Now, we all know what the literary criticism of the mass of mankind is. To be worth anything, literary and scientific criticism require, both of them, the finest heads and the most sure tact; and they require, besides, that the world and the world's experience shall have come some considerable way. But, ever since this last condition has been fulfilled, the finest heads for letters and science, the surest tact for these, have turned themselves in general to other departments of work than criticism of the Bible, this department being occupied already in such force of numbers and hands, if not of heads, and there being so many annoyances and even dangers in freely approaching it. As our Reformers were to Shakespeare and Bacon in tact for letters and science, or as Luther, even, was to Goethe in this respect, such almost has on the whole been, since the Renascence, the general proportion in rate of power for criticism between those who have given themselves to secular letters and science, and those who have given themselves to interpreting the Bible, and who, in conjunction with the popular interpretation of it both traditional and contemporary, have made what is called 'orthodox theology.' It is as if some simple and saving doctrines, essential for men to know, were enshrined in Shakespeare's *Hamlet* or in Newton's *Principia* (though the Gospels are really a far more complex and difficult object of criticism than either); and a host of second-rate critics, and official critics, and what is called 'the popular mind' as well, threw themselves upon *Hamlet* and the *Principia*, with the notion that they could and should extract from these documents, and impose on us for our belief, not only the saving doctrines enshrined there, but also the right literary and scientific criticism of the entire documents. A pretty mess they would make of it! and just this sort of mess is our so-called orthodox theology. And its professors are nevertheless bold, over-weening, and even abusive, in maintaining their criticism against all questioners; although really, if one thinks seriously of it, it was a kind of impertinence in such professors to attempt any such criticism at all.

Happily, the faith that saves is attached to the saving doctrines in the Bible, which are very simple; not to its literary and scientific criticism, which is very hard. And no man is to be called 'infidel!' for his bad literary and scientific criticism of the Bible; but if he were, how dreadful would the state of our orthodox theologians be! They themselves freely fling about this word *infidel* at all those who reject their literary and scientific criticism, which turns out to be quite false. It would be but just to mete to them with their own measure, and to condemn them by their own rule; and, when they air their unsound criticism in public, to cry indignantly: *The Bishop of So-and-so, the Dean of So-and-so, and other infidel lecturers of the present day!* or: *That rampant infidel, the Archdeacon of So-and-so, in his recent letter on the Athanasian Creed!* or: 'The Rock,' 'The Church Times,'[18] *and the rest of the infidel press!* or: *The torrent of infidelity which pours every Sunday from our pulpits!* Just would this be, and by no means inurbane; but hardly, perhaps, Christian. Therefore we will not permit ourselves to say it; but it is only kind to point out, in passing, to these loud and rash people, to what they expose themselves at the hands of adversaries less scrupulous than we are.

Notes

I ANTHONY COLLINS

1 The main argument of John Locke's *The Reasonableness of Christianity as Delivered in the Scriptures*, London, 1695. But Collins is about to overturn Locke's faith expressed at the outset of his book that the Bible is 'in general and necessary points to be understood in the plain direct meaning of the words and phrases, such as they may be supposed to have had in the mouths of speakers, who used them according to the language of that time and country wherin they lived, without such learned, artificial and forced senses of them as one sought out, and put upon them in most systems of Divinity'. Collins was close to Locke in the eighteen months before Locke's death in 1704. See J. O'Higgins, *Anthony Collins, the Man and his Works*, The Hague, 1970, pp. 1–24.

2 The theory that elements of Jewish religion derived from Egyptian is highly plausible as well as very old. For a recent instance of it concerning the scribes who wrote the biblical books see E. W. Heaton, *Solomon's New Men*, London, 1974.

3 Johnson (*Dictionary*, 1755) explains banter as 'ridicule, raillery'; it also had a connotation of nonsense (see Oxford English Dictionary).

4 A collection of Greek, Roman, Jewish and Christian prophecies. Their authenticity was much debated among Collins's contemporaries (Whiston defended them) but the immense complexities of the text prevented any real advance in criticism. See Emil Schurer, *A History of the Jewish People in the Age of Jesus Christ*, vol. III, Edinburgh, 1986, for a recent assessment.

5 On Surenhusius see the introductory note on Collins here and J. O'Higgins, *Anthony Collins*, pp. 166–8. He was Professor of Hebrew at Amsterdam at the beginning of the eighteenth century, expert in the rabbinic interpretation of scripture and editor and translator of the Mishnah – the great rabbinic law code.

6 Talmud is the rabbinic elaboration of Mishnah (see above). There is a Babylonian and a Palestinian Talmud. Cabala denotes the mystical and symbolic interpretation of scripture.

7 The numbers of theses are Collins's own addition to the text of de la Roche's resumé which he is using here (see his footnote (c) above).

8 Gemara denotes Mishnaic lore and so, generally and particularly, the Talmud.

9 Collins is doing just that – quoting de la Roche's resumé of Surenhusius – with the 'ten ways' enumerated below. The scriptural references are all to

imprecise quotations of the Old Testament by New Testament writers (except for Acts 3.3, which is an error). The explanations of the methods of change given here are not in favour nowadays, but the fact that the Christian writers altered the Old Testament quotations to suit themselves is unassailable – unless like Collins's opponent Whiston, one can believe that these Christian writers had the original text which the rabbis, and not they, altered. And no one at all believes that now.

10 This is a well-attested practice which sometimes arguably restored the original reading. By 'organ', the root is presumably meant.

11 Luther's conversations with the devil, told with realism, are in his *Table Talk*, Works, vol. 54, Philadelphia, 1967, ed. and trans. Tappert. A recent treatment is chapter 5 of H. G. Haile, *Luther*, London, 1980.

12 The scriptural references for these Old Testament 'types' (prefigurations) are: Genesis 21. 2, Genesis 22. 9, Genesis 22. 6, Numbers 21. 9.

13 Collins is right. The derivation of this text is still very uncertain, and the guesses by Surenhusius which follow are as good as any. See R. H. Gundry, *The Use of the Old Testament in Matthew's Gospel*, Leiden, 1967, pp. 97 ff.

14 William Wotton's *Miscellaneous Discourses of the Scribes and Pharisees*, 1718, treats the Mishnah as a very early book and a source for Jewish customs and exegetical methods at the time of Jesus. Simon Ockley was the prodigiously learned Professor of Arabic at Cambridge and pioneer of Oriental Studies to whom Wotton sent his work for approval – and got it in the lettter to which he refers. Both are important predecessors of Collins.

15 Unlike the Sadducees and Pharisees, the Essenes do not figure in the New Testament text, but are described by the Jewish historian Josephus and other ancient writers as an ascetic and learned Jewish sect. They are now commonly agreed to be the same as the community at Qumran which produced the Dead Sea Scrolls: a consensus which has settled previous centuries of more exotic speculation about them. But the discovery of the Scrolls, which are full of enigmatic apocalyptic allegory, vindicates Collins's point that this is an instance of 'allegorical method in the time of Jesus and the Apostles'. (See G. Vermes, *The Dead Sea Scrolls*, Harmondsworth, 1986, and subsequent editions.)

16 'If anyone knows how to speak obscurely, let him speak: if not, let him be quiet.'

17 'Heaven is a complete fable.'

18 See J. Pepin, *Mythe et Allegorie*, Paris, 1958, and R. P. C. Hanson, *Allegory and Event*, London, 1959.

2 THOMAS SHERLOCK

1 II Peter 1. 19.

2 John Toland, *Christianity not Mysterious*, 1696, taught that revelation, or manifestation, abolished mystery and achieved utter clarity.

3 An obvious reference to Collins.

4 II Peter 1. 19.

5 Sherlock's 'ancient prophecies' is an unusual interpretation of 'parables',

stemming from his previous argument. The parables within Mark's gospel are probably meant. But Sherlock's idea is possible as well.

6 Sherlock is agreeing with Collins here, who says on pp. 31f. of *Grounds and Reasons* that 'miracles can never render a foundation valid, which is in itself invalid; can never make a false inference true; can never make a Prophesy fulfill'd, which is not fulfill'd'.

7 Hebrews 5. 12 and 6. 1.

8 A favourite argument of Benjamin Whichcote who insisted that the incarnation of Christ was not meant by God 'to beget a notion, or to raise a talk ... God doth nothing for so light an end', *Select Sermons*, ed. Shaftesbury, 1698, pp. 331–60.

9 St Paul's Epistle to the Romans, particularly chapters 1–8, is the dominant influence on this whole paragraph.

10 Genesis has only two such communications: at 1. 29–30 giving man dominion over the earth, and at 2. 16–17 forbidding him to eat the fruit of the tree of knowledge. 'Frequent' is Sherlock's gloss. He is right, though, to put prophecy after the fall with none before.

11 Sherlock has Collins in mind, among others. See his mockery of Taylor ('an eminent divine') in chapter IV of *Grounds and Reasons*.

12 This is Zoroastrian theology, older than Jewish and influential on it chiefly in its apocalyptic phase which is later than the writing of Genesis, which is free of it as Sherlock says.

13 Sanchoniathon's history is preserved in Eusebius, *Preparatio Evangelica* I, 9–10 and IV, 16. Its cosmogony and genealogical narratives, as well as its very early date (middle of the second millennium BC) and provenance (Palestine) make comparison with Genesis irresistible. An edition of it, consisting of translation, commentary and notes, by R. Cumberland, was published in 1720, as *Sanchoniathon's Phoenician History*. Sherlock refers to this work, which treats Sanchoniathon with the historical fairness which Sherlock wants for Genesis. This plea to treat a biblical text as one would any other venerable literature appears here nearly a century before Coleridge's famous use of it in *Confessions of an Inquiring Spirit*.

14 Genesis 4.

15 Hebrews 9. 22.

16 Sherlock's version of Hebrews 11. 4.

17 Imprecise quotation of I Peter 2. 9.

3 ROBERT LOWTH

1 Pairs of lines of verse which make units of sense: couplets.

2 Pointed, pithy: packed into short spaces or sentences.

3 Ben Sirach is putting forward a reciprocal view of the structure of reality, indicating the deep roots and wide scope of the poetic form which Lowth is anatomising.

4 Lowth's eloquent plea for empathy with remote cultures was taken up by Herder.

5 Lowth's hierarchy of images is derived from Locke (*Essay concerning Human Understanding*).

6 Hebrew for 'parable': but in a much wider sense than we are used to, and including striking sayings and oracles. Lowth's learning and tact are evident in his not translating it.

7 This difference, here first noticed by Lowth, remains a problem of the text of Job.

8 Contrast with Collins's attitude to enthusiasm shows the enormous difference made to exegesis by Lowth's sympathy with his material.

9 'By real ideas, I mean such as have a Foundation in Nature; such as have a conformity ... with their Archetypes.' Locke, *Essay Concerning Human Understanding* (1695) II, XXX, 205.

10 'Catharsis'.

11 A 'proasm' was an introductory verse, an 'epode' the part of a lyric song which follows the strophe and antistrophe as a kind of refrain.

12 Versicle belongs to form and denotes either half of the verse of a psalm. Parallelism belongs to content and denotes the symmetry or similarity of subject between one verse or half and the other. See Lowth's own Preliminary Discourse to his *Isaiah* p. 10: 'the correspondence of one verse, or line, with another, I call *parallelism*. When a proposition is delivered and another subjoined to it or drawn under it, equivalent or contrasted with it, in sense; or similar to it in reforms of grammatical construction, these I call parallel lines; and the words and phrases answering one another in the corresponding lines, parallel terms.'

13 By Palnemon in Virgil, *Eclogue*, 3. 59.

14 The 'Masorites' were the editors or preservers of the ancient Hebrew scriptural texts which became authoritative around AD 100.

5 SAMUEL TAYLOR COLERIDGE

1 Newton and Herschel (1738–1822) are here used by Coleridge as great modern astronomers with modern instruments, in contrast to the shepherd with his staff and astrolabe.

2 Genesis 32. 24.

3 'by that name'.

4 Presumably 'sensualist' because the Sadducees disbelieved the Pharisaic doctrines of resurrection and angels.

5 John 9. 1–12 and John 1. 43–51.

6 The Talmud is the body of Jewish Law, including Mishnah and Gamara, derived from the Pentateuch, or first five biblical books. Hence a Talmudist is an author or exponent of Talmud.

7 The received text of the Old Testament, worked out by Jewish grammarians in the sixth to tenth centuries AD but questioned by the greatest English Old Testament scholar of Coleridge's time, Alexander Geddes.

8 See R. H. Charles, *The Apocrypha and Pseudepigrapha of the Old Testament*, II, pp. 83–112. The Septuagint is the Greek translation of the Old Testament, and Aristeas's legend a fiction about its origin, written in the last two centuries BC, which strenuously protests its own veracity.

9 Eighteenth-century critics of the text of the Bible.

10 Genesis 37. 7. Joseph's dream of his superiority to his brothers.

11 Shakespeare, *King Lear*, IV, iv, 3–6.
12 'Order of tradition which the Apostles handed on to those to whom they entrusted the churches' . . . 'if certain Apostles had not left us scriptures'. Unaeus, *Adversus Haereses*, III, iv, 1.
13 'Rule of faith' . . . 'Sacrament ordained as a token of remembrance' . . . 'you know this to be the foundation of the Catholic faith upon which the edifice of the church was raised'. Augustine, *De Symbolo ad catechumenos sermo alius*, Migue, *Patrologia Latina*, XL, 651.
14 'pattern (or "norm") of the catholic and ecclesiastical mind', Canon 7 of the third Council of Constantinople (AD 680–1).
15 Daniel Waterland in his admired anti-Deist book, *The Importance of the Doctrine of the Holy Trinity*, 1734, especially chapter VI. Coleridge's annotated copy is in the British Museum/Library.
16 'Church tradition to which . . . many nations of those who believe in Christ assent without paper and ink, having salvation written in their hearts by the spirit, and keeping the old tradition diligently', *Adversus Haereses*, III, iv, 1.
17 A quotation of Article 6 of the Thirty-nine Articles of the Church of England (printed in its Book of Common Prayer).
18 The Old Testament Books other than 'the Law and the Prophets' and later than them to become canonical.
19 Chillingworth's phrase which, in its popular (ab)use, Coleridge disliked.
20 Exodus 16.
21 Quotation untraced. Thomas Fuller (1608–61) was a church historian and prolific writer of practical spirituality.
22 In the sense of fanatical claim to inspiration.
23 Numbers 24.
24 'work done' or *fait accompli* (the French phrase is better).
25 Romans 8, 15 and 16.
26 II Timothy 4. 13.
27 The reference seems to be to *The Genuine Works of R. Leighton D.D.* 1820, I, 202. But 'extensive' and 'intensive' are Coleridge's words, not Leighton's. See William West's edition of Leighton (1870–5), VII, 428.

6 THOMAS ARNOLD

1 In contrast to the thousand and more years in which the various biblical books were written (by various writers and for various audiences), the Koran is densely unified. It comprises, on the traditional view, divine revelations to Muhammad between AD 610–632, through the archangel Gabriel.
2 The Nicolaitans are anathematised at Revelation 2. 6 and 15. They are associated with 'the teaching of Balaam, who taught Balak to put a stumbling block before the sons of Israel, that they might eat food sacrificed to idols and practice immorality' (Revelation 2. 14, interpreting Numbers 31. 16 with the aid of Numbers 25. 12). In subsequent Christian tradition this liberal attitude to pagan customs, also condemned by St Paul in I Corinthians 8 and 10 for the damage it did to the cohesive

identity of a church, made the Nicolaitans a byword for laxity – doctrinal or moral. This is of course, the occupational disease of accommodation in orthodox eyes. Arnold believes the Nicolaitans to have been gnostics of some sort ('riper knowledge'), probably by associating them with the followers of Jezebel at Revelation 2. 19–24, who ate food sacrificed to idols and knew 'the deep things of Satan'. So their laxity was the product of moral superiority.

3 Arnold is suggesting, tactfully, that God has to adjust his plans to the reality of evil: the reality which opponents of accommodation forget.

4 Arnold is ahead of his time here. Crucifixes were extremely rare on Anglican altars in his day. As a result they lacked the high church, post-Tractarian, association which would have put him off them. This recommendation of them is firmly and characteristically educational, in the teeth of rigid Protestantism.

5 *The Morning Watch or Quarterly Journal on Prophecy* began publication in 1829. Its base was the conferences for the study of unfulfilled prophecy at Albury, the home of Henry Drummond, which were dominated by the famous Edward Irving. Irving was then still a presbyterian preacher, his enthusiasm and energy concentrated on apocalyptic exegesis. *The Morning Watch* was a dense, learned and intransigent magazine. Arnold's attention may have been drawn to it by a furiously adverse review of his *The Duty of Granting the Claims of Roman Catholics* in 1, 496–508. The *Edinburgh Review*, by contrast, was the organ of intellectual liberalism.

6 Richard Carlile, radical publisher, was tried in 1819. His speech in his own defence was prolix, but the trial was a celebrated landmark in the history of the free press, though Carlile was convicted and imprisoned. See Joel H. Weiner, *Radicalism and Freethought in Nineteenth-Century Britain: The Life of Richard Carlile* (Contributions in Labor History, 13), Westpoint and London, 1983.

7 BENJAMIN JOWETT

1 In the first two sections of his essay, Jowett has argued for the exegetical authority of scholars, as against that of ecclesiastics, as leading to the true (i.e. original) meaning of the texts which is the reward of historical enquiry. Holding the view of Sherlock and, more ardently, Coleridge, that the Bible should be read like other books, but being more dismissive of post-biblical theology than they, Jowett puts more weight than ever on history. The 'difficulties' to which he refers are therefore the intricacies of historical research and reconstruction.

2 Jowett may be thinking of intellectual secularism in France, with Comte in the Academie Francaise; and of the secular government's encroachment on papal lands in Italy from 1859.

8 MATTHEW ARNOLD

1 The 'old friend' is James Fitzjames Stephen and the reference to his article 'The Present State of Religious Controversy' in *Fraser's Magazine*,

November 1869. 'What he really expects and aims at' there is negation of the factual basis of Christianity.

2 T. H. Huxley in a speech to the London School Board on 22 February 1871, reported in *The Times* next day.

3 In 1872 the Duke of Somerset published *Christian Theology and Modern Scepticism*, a book marked by very optimistic progressivism.

4 The Reverend Malcolm MacColl in *The Guardian* of 7 September 1870.

5 In *Maximen und Reflexionen*.

6 *King John*, III, iv, 153–8.

7 Whately was a fellow of Oriel with Thomas Arnold and godfather to Matthew's son Richard. The reference may be to his *Essays on Some of the Difficulties in the Writings of St Paul* (1828) or his *Introductory Lectures on Morals, and Christian Evidences* (1857). See R. H. Super, *Complete Prose Works of Matthew Arnold*, VI, 481.

8 Arnold got the martyrdom of St Fructuosus from Alban Butler's *The Lives of the Fathers, Martyrs and other Principal Saints*, Paul on the way to Damascus from Acts 9. 4, and Aquinas from the Bollandist *Acra Sanctorum* under March 7.

9 Staniforth had a vision of Jesus on the cross and heard him say 'Thy sins are forgiven thee' while on sentry duty in France in 1745 (Southey, *Life of Wesley*, 1846, II, 48). Arnold's own footnote gives the reference to his retailing of it in *St Paul and Protestantism*. The rejoinder which he rebuts here was in *The Guardian*, 9 November 1870.

10 *Works*, ed. Gladstone 1896, II, 44–5: 'they are in truth merely the occasions, as any thing may be of any thing, upon which our nature carries us on according to its own previous bent and bias' – the tendency which Arnold sees in any *Zeitgeist*.

11 Attributed to Thales by Digenus Laertes, I, 35 and used by Arnold as an epigraph to *Empedocles on Etna and Other Poems*, 1852.

12 Ewald, *History of Israel*, tr. J. F. Smith 1883, VI, 144–5.

13 *Das Leben Jesu fur das Deutsche Volk bearbeitet: Gesammelte Schriften* 1877, III, 180 (a popular and mollified version of his notorious *Leben Jesu* of 1835).

14 In his *Preface to the New Testament*.

15 See Renan's *Vie de Jesus* (numerous editions), Introduction.

16 'It is a great art to know how to converse with Jesus', Thomas a Kempis, *Invitation of Christ*, II, viii, 3.

17 'I do not form hypotheses', *Principia Mathematica*, end of Book III.

18 *The Rock* was a low-church weekly, *The Church Times* high-church.

Select booklist

(A guide to further reading, not a full bibliography of the subject)

PRIMARY SOURCES

(Bibliographical details of the main texts can be found in the headnotes)

Coleridge, Samuel Taylor, 'Marginalia on Eichhorn' in *Marginalia II, The Collected works of Samuel Taylor Coleridge*, Bollingen Series, LXXV.

Michael de la Roche, *Memoirs of Literature* (1717 and 1722).

Eichhorn, J. D., *Einleitung in das Neue Testament* (1810).

Geddes, Alexander, *Prospectus of a New Translation of the Holy Bible from corrected Texts of the Originals* (1786).

Critical Remarks on the Hebrew Scriptures (1800).

Goethe, Johann Wolfgang, *Wilhelm Meister*, trans. Carlyle (1824).

Hobbes, Thomas, *Leviathan* (1651, ed. C. B. MacPherson, Harmondsworth, 1968).

Jenkin, Robert, *The Reasonableness and Certainty of the Christian Religion* (1700).

LeClerc, Jean, *Sentiments de Quelques Theologiens de Hollande sur l'Histoire Critique du Vieux Testament de M. Richard Simon* (1685).

Locke, John, *An Essay Concerning Human Understanding* (1700, ed. P. H. Nidditch, Oxford, 1975).

Lettres inedites de John Locke a ses amis Nicholas Thoynard, Philippe van Limborch et Edward Clarke, ed. H. Ollion and T. J. de Boer (1912).

A Paraphrase and Notes on the Epistles of St Paul (1707, ed. A. W. Wainwright, Oxford, 1987).

The Reasonableness of Christianity as Delivered in the Scriptures (1695).

Lowth, Robert, *Isaiah* (1778).

Marsh, Herbert, and Michaelis J. D., *Introduction to the New Testament by J. D. Michaelis; Translated from the 4th Edition of the German, and considerably enlarged with notes and a dissertation on the Origin and Composition of the Three First Gospels by H. Marsh* (1802).

Newman, John Henry, *The Theological Papers of John Henry Newman on Biblical Inspiration and Authority*, ed. J. D. Holmes, Oxford, 1979.

Reimarus, H. S., *Fragments*, ed. C. H. Talbert (1971).

Sherlock, Thomas, *The Tryal of the Witnesses* (1729).

Works, ed. Hughes (1830).

Simon, Richard, *A Critical History of the Old Testament* (1682).

Smith, Robertson, 'The Bible' in *Encyclopedia Britannica IX*, vol III (1875).

Select booklist

Spinoza, Benedict de, *A Theologico-Political Treatise*, ed. R. H. M. Elwes (New York, 1951).

Tindal, Matthew, *Christianity as Old as the Creation* (1730).

Strauss, David Friedrich, *The Life of Jesus Critically Examined* (1835, translated by George Eliot and ed. P. C. Hodgson, London, 1973).

Thoynard, Nicholas, *Evangeliorum Harmonia* (1707).

Toland, John, *Christianity not Mysterious* (1696).

Whiston, William, *An Essay Towards Restoring the True Text of the New Testament* (1722).

SECONDARY MATERIAL

General studies

Henning Graf von Reventlow's massive book *The Authority of the Bible and the Rise of the Modern World* (1984) treats seventeenth-century biblical criticism in its political and philosophical contexts. Its notes are as rich a resource as the text itself. Unfortunately it lacks a bibliography. Mark Pattison's essay 'Tendencies of Religious Thought in England' in *Essays and Reviews* (1860) is more quickly digestible and still a good introduction. Hans Frei's *The Eclipse of Biblical Narrative* (1974) combines erudition with philosophical and literary enquiry into the fundamental question of why modern biblical criticism, in forsaking figural exegesis, lost sight of the fundamentally narrative nature of the biblical material. It is the most interesting of recent books on the subject. The literary approach was pioneered in England by Elinor Shaffer in *Kubla Khan and the Fall of Jerusalem: the Mythological School in Biblical Criticism and Secular Literature 1770–1880* (1975). It contains pregnant chapters on Coleridge, Browning and George Eliot in the context of biblical criticism. Stephen Prickett's *Words and the Word: Language, Poetics and Biblical Interpretation* (1986) is full of allusions, references and sprightly observations on the inter-relations of biblical studies with secular thought and literature. Like Shaffer's book it is suggestive and picturesque, but hard to read for long stretches. Beginners in this subject would do best to start with an old but clear book, J. E. Carpenter's *The Bible in the Nineteenth Century* (1903) or Mark Pattison's essay. John Rogerson's *Old Testament Criticism in the Nineteenth Century* (1984) is not confined to England. Nor is Werner Kuemmel's *The New Testament: an Introduction to the History of the Investigation of its Problems* (1973). But together they give lucid introductions to the wider and continental history of the subject. Then the reader could move on to Reventlow, Prickett and, most interestingly, Frei for more detail of the English scene.

On the individual writers

Collins

J. O'Higgins's *Anthony Collins, the Man and his Works* (1970) is an excellent study, full and judicious, with plenty of leads towards further reading about its subject. Collins being Locke's disciple, two fine books about Locke

Select booklist

should be consulted: John Dunn's *Locke* (1984) and Maurice Cranston's *John Locke, a Biography* (1957). On the highly important topic of Locke's Dutch exile, R. L. Colie has written a seminal essay, 'John Locke in the Republic of Letters' in *Britain and the Netherlands* (1960) edited by J. S. Bromley and E. H. Kossmann. For the wider background to Collins, see Gerard Reedy, *The Bible and Reason* (1985) which deals mainly with the Restoration divines of the Church of England, and Philip Harth, *Contexts of Dryden's Thought* (1968) which makes the cultural setting vivid and is good on Richard Simon. Collins's fellow-radical-Lockean, John Toland, has been well treated in *John Toland: His Method, Manners and Mind* (1984) by S. H. Daniel. Leslie Stephen's *History of English Thought in the Eighteenth Century* (1876) is still a monumentally useful guide to the period despite its sarcasm and complacency. The lively portrait of Whiston in Force's *William Whiston, Honest Newtonian* (1985) gives a clear view of the theology of prophecy which Collins opposed.

Sherlock

There is a biography of him by E. F. Carpenter, *Thomas Sherlock* (1936), which gives the necessary background in the complex politics of his time but is rather elementary about his thought.

Lowth

His son's *Memoirs of the Life and Writings of the Late Right Reverend Robert Lowth DD* (1787) are biographically intimate and useful. Brian Hepworth deals with him fully in *Robert Lowth* (1978) and in his romantic context in *The Rise of Romanticism* (1978). Murray Royston's *Poet and Prophet* (1965) is more searching than Hepworth in the literary field, and M. H. Abrams, *Natural Supernaturalism* (1971) puts Lowth in a majestic frame of intellectual history.

Blake

His *Complete Poems* edited by W. H. Stevenson and D. V. Erdman is indispensable because its notes are elucidatory to the point of revelation. Jacob Bronowski's *William Blake and the Age of Revolution* (1972) is a general introduction. Kathleen Raine's *Blake and Tradition* (1968), and D. V. Erdman's *Blake: A Prophet Against Empire: A Poet's Interpretation of the History of His Own Times* are selected from a vast recent secondary literature for their relevance to Blake's absorption and exploitation of the Bible.

Coleridge

Walter Jackson Bate's *Coleridge* is the best brief overview of his life and thought on account of its acute psychological sympathy. A. J. Harding's *Coleridge and the Inspired Word* (1985) is the most recent treatment of his biblical criticism. Until *Confessions of an Inquiring Spirit* comes out in the

Select booklist

Bollingen collected edition of his works (which may be soon), H. StJ. Hart's 1956 edition is important for its inclusion of J. H. Green's 'Introduction' with its treatment of Coleridge's debt to Lessing. J. D. Boulger's *Coleridge as a Religious Thinker* (1961) goes wider and deeper than Harding.

Thomas Arnold

Duncan Forbes's *The Liberal Anglican Idea of History* (1952) is a brilliant introduction to his intellectual context. His pupil A. P. Stanley, Jowett's colleague in the study of St Paul, wrote his *Life* in 1846. Lytton Strachey's hostile treatment in *Eminent Victorians* has been superseded by the biographies of N. G. Wyner (1953) and T. W. Bamford (1960). Meriol Trevor's *The Arnolds: Thomas Arnold and his Family* includes Matthew's childhood and youth.

Jowett

There is a civilised, sympathetic and enjoyable biography of him by Geoffrey Faber: *Jowett* (1957). I. Ellis's *Seven Against Christ* deals with all the contributors to *Essays and Reviews* and their various fates. But Peter Hinchcliffe's *Benjamin Jowett and the Christian Religion* (1987) treats Jowett's whole religion with empathetic historical and intellectual criticism which makes it the best book about him as a believer and a critic.

Matthew Arnold

The text to use is *The Complete Prose Works of Matthew Arnold* edited by R. H. Super, Volume VI having the text of *Literature and Dogma* which has been used here and the notes on which the notes here gratefully depend. Arnold's *Poems* have been as splendidly edited by Kenneth and Miriam Allott (1979) and are as important as his prose as sources for his thought and feelings about Christianity. The background to *Literature and Dogma* was elucidated by William Blackburn in an article with that title in *Modern Philology*, November 1945. The wider background to his thought is explored in William Robbins's *The Ethical Idealism of Matthew Arnold: A study of the Nature and Sources of his Moral and Religious Ideas* (1959). There are two good recent studies of his Christianity: Ruth Roberts's *Arnold and God* (1983) and J. C. Livingston's *Matthew Arnold and Christianity: His Religious Prose Writings* (1986).